JOURNAL FOR THE STUDY OF THE NEW TESTAMENT SUPPLEMENT SERIES

167

Sheffield Academic Press

John the Baptist in Life and Death

Audience-Oriented Criticism of Matthew's Narrative

Gary Yamasaki

Journal for the Study of the New Testament
Supplement Series 167

Published by Sheffield Academic Press Ltd
Mansion House
19 Kingfield Road
Sheffield S11 9AS
England

Printed on acid-free paper in Great Britain
by Bookcraft Ltd
Midsomer Norton, Bath

British Library Cataloguing in Publication Data

A catalogue record for this book is available
from the British Library

ISBN 1-85075-916-2

CONTENTS

ACKNOWLEDGMENTS

This book is a revision of my doctoral dissertation presented to Union Theological Seminary in Virginia in 1995. Both the original dissertation and this revision have not been solitary endeavours; many have helped to make the completion of these projects possible. I wish to express my gratitude especially to the following:

Dr Jack Dean Kingsbury, who provided invaluable guidance as my advisor for the original dissertation;

Dr Stanley Porter, for his editorial counsel in the transformation of the dissertation into the present study;

Dr Dorothy Jean Weaver, for introducing me to the field of biblical literary criticism and for the encouragement that she has provided in the years since;

The administration of Columbia Bible College, for granting me study leaves to pursue the research and writing needed for both the original dissertation and this revision;

The members of the Matthew Group of the Society of Biblical Literature, for lively debate on Matthean issues which has helped me to formulate many of the ideas presented in this work;

My wife, April, who has been a constant source of editorial advice, encouragement and support; without her, neither the original dissertation nor this revision would have been possible.

ABBREVIATIONS

AbrN	*Abr-Nahrain*
ANRW	Hildegard Temporini and Wolfgang Haase (eds.), *Aufstieg und Niedergang der römischen Welt: Geschichte und Kultur Roms im Spiegel der neuren Forschung* (Berlin: W. de Gruyter, 1972–)
ATR	*Anglican Theological Review*
AUSS	*Andrews University Seminary Studies*
BA	*Biblical Archaeologist*
BAGD	Walter Bauer, William F. Arndt, F. William Gingrich and Frederick W. Danker, *A Greek–English Lexicon of the New Testament and Other Early Christian Literature* (Chicago: University of Chicago Press, 2nd edn, 1979)
BDF	Friedrich Blass, A. Debrunner and Robert W. Funk, *A Greek Grammar of the New Testament and Other Early Christian Literature* (Cambridge: Cambridge University Press, 1961)
Bib	*Biblica*
BibRes	*Biblical Research*
BTB	*Biblical Theology Bulletin*
BT	*The Bible Translator*
BZ	*Biblische Zeitschrift*
CBQ	*Catholic Biblical Quarterly*
CurTM	*Currents in Theology and Mission*
EDNT	Horst Balz and Gerhard Schneider (eds.), *Exegetical Dictionary of the New Testament* (trans. Virgil P. Howard, James W. Thompson, John W. Medendorp and Douglas W. Stott; 3 vols.; Grand Rapids: Eerdmans, 1990–93).
ETR	*Etudes théologique et religieuses*
EvQ	*Evangelical Quarterly*
EvT	*Evangelische Theologie*
ExpTim	*Expository Times*
GTJ	*Grace Theological Journal*
HTR	*Harvard Theological Review*
IDB	George Arthur Buttrick (ed.), *The Interpreter's Dictionary of the Bible* (4 vols.; Nashville: Abingdon Press, 1962)
IDBSup	*IDB*, Supplementary Volume
Int	*Interpretation*

ISBE	Geoffrey Bromiley (ed.), *The International Standard Bible Encyclopedia* (4 vols.; Grand Rapids: Eerdmans, rev. edn, 1979–88)
JAAR	*Journal of the American Academy of Religion*
JB	*Jerusalem Bible*
JBL	*Journal of Biblical Literature*
JES	*Journal of Ecumenical Studies*
JETS	*Journal of the Evangelical Theological Society*
JJS	*Journal of Jewish Studies*
JR	*Journal of Religion*
JSNT	*Journal for the Study of the New Testament*
JTS	*Journal of Theological Studies*
NAB	*New American Bible*
NASB	*New American Standard Bible*
NEB	*New English Bible*
Neot	*Neotestamentica*
NIV	New International Version
NJB	*New Jerusalem Bible*
NovT	*Novum Testamentum*
NRSV	New Revised Standard Version
NTS	*New Testament Studies*
OrChr	*Oriens christianus*
RB	*Revue biblique*
ResQ	*Restoration Quarterly*
RevQ	*Revue de Qumran*
RevScRel	*Revue des sciences religieuses*
RHPR	*Revue d'histoire et de philosophie religieuses*
RSV	Revised Standard Version
RTR	*Reformed Theological Review*
TD	*Theology Digest*
TDNT	Gerhard Kittel and Gerhard Friedrich (eds.), *Theological Dictionary of the New Testament* (trans. Geoffrey W. Bromiley; 10 vols.; Grand Rapids: Eerdmans, 1964–76)
TynBul	*Tyndale Bulletin*
VC	*Vigiliae christianae*
ZNW	*Zeitschrift für die neutestamentliche Wissenschaft*

Part I

A New Approach to the Study of John the Baptist

While the Gospel of Matthew is a story about Jesus, other characters also play important roles in the narrative. These include such notable figures as Peter, the disciples as a group, and the religious leaders, all of whom have drawn considerable scrutiny from biblical scholars. One character who has received relatively little attention, however, is John the Baptist. At first glance, this neglect may appear to be justified; after all, John's role in baptizing Jesus is but one small component in the vast array of details making up the story of Jesus. However, a closer look at Matthew's Gospel reveals that, apart from the baptismal scene, John is referred to no less than seven times in the story-line.

Why does Matthew keep coming back to John? What role does Matthew have for him in this Gospel? To address these questions, this study adopts a literary-critical approach. Part I acts as a prelude to the exegetical work of this study: Chapter 1 surveys the past 200 years of historical studies on John and also the redaction-critical studies on John in Matthew's Gospel, Chapter 2 sets out the particular literary-critical methodology to be used, and Chapter 3 discusses the issue of what constitutes an appropriate structure for the exegetical work following in Part II.

Chapter 1

HISTORY OF RESEARCH ON JOHN THE BAPTIST

To a large extent, the history of research on John the Baptist has run on a parallel track to the development of research on Jesus. For this reason, this survey of the history of research on John follows the contours of the research on Jesus.

Historical Studies on John the Baptist

Just over two centuries ago, Gospel studies were on the brink of a new era with the work of Herman Samuel Reimarus. Up to that time, the Gospels were regarded as reliable historical sources of the words and deeds of Jesus. However, the influence of seventeenth- and eighteenth-century deism served to undermine this view of the Gospels. Deism rejected both the supernatural components of the Gospels and the prevailing dogmatic views on Jesus; thus, it prompted a rethinking of the traditional picture of Jesus as portrayed in the Gospels. In this way, the age of critical scholarship on Jesus was born. Critical scholarship attempted to get behind the Jesus of the Gospels to the Jesus of history in what has come to be known as the 'Quest of the Historical Jesus'. While this quest has held a prominent place in the annals of New Testament research, another less prominent quest developed alongside it, namely, the 'Quest of the Historical John the Baptist'.

Both of these quests were inaugurated by Reimarus's 'Von dem Zwecke Jesu und seiner Jünger', published posthumously in the late 1770s.[1] In this section of his unpublished manuscript, Reimarus probes

1. English translation: Hermann Samuel Reimarus, 'Concerning the Intention of Jesus and his Teaching', in Charles H. Talbert (ed.), *Reimarus: Fragments* (trans. Ralph S. Fraser; Philadelphia: Fortress Press, 1970), pp. 59-269, which constitutes one section of *Apologie oder Schutzschrift für die vernünftigen Verehrer Gottes* which Reimarus left unpublished during his lifetime.

behind the Jesus and John of the Gospels and finds a pair of revolutionaries trying to bring about a political kingdom on earth with Jesus as its messianic ruler. In order that Jesus might be established as Messiah, the two attempt to incite the Jewish people to rebel against the existing authorities.

According to Reimarus, John's role in this ploy is to plant in the people's minds the idea that Jesus is the long-awaited Messiah. To this end, John pretends not to know Jesus when he comes for baptism, feigns reception of heavenly revelations immediately after Jesus is baptized, and speaks of Jesus as the Christ, the Son of God.[2] As Reimarus put it, John engages in 'pre-arranged trickery and deception'.[3] Therefore, the quest of the historical John the Baptist begins with a picture of John as a conniving revolutionary.

Reimarus's work is significant because it anticipates the direction that Gospel studies would take over a century later. Reimarus had no influence, however, on scholarship of his own time. Instead, the direction of Gospel studies was set by a rationalistic perspective born of the Enlightenment. With its emphasis on reason, rationalism could not accept the supernatural phenomena portrayed in the Gospels. As a result, scholars of this era tended to be preoccupied with providing natural explanations for the supernatural phenomena in the Gospel accounts.[4]

In this era dominated by a rationalistic perspective, David Friedrich Strauss's *The Life of Jesus Critically Examined*[5] stands out as an anomaly. Like Reimarus's essay of six decades earlier, it was far ahead of its time. Based on his analysis of the Gospel accounts, Strauss asserts that the vast majority of the stories are predominantly myth,[6]

2. Reimarus, 'Concerning the Intention', pp. 139-41.

3. Reimarus, 'Concerning the Intention', p. 140.

4. See, for example, Friedrich Schleiermacher, *The Life of Jesus* (trans. S. MacLean Gilman; Philadelphia: Fortress Press, 1975), especially his general discussions on miracles (pp. 25-29, 193-94, 197-98) and his treatments of Jesus' virgin birth (pp. 56-62), his temptation in the wilderness (pp. 153-55), his healing miracles (pp. 202-206), his exorcisms (pp. 211-12) and his bringing dead people back to life (pp. 217-18).

5. David Friedrich Strauss, *The Life of Jesus Critically Examined* (ed. Peter C. Hodgson; trans. George Eliot; Philadelphia: Fortress Press, 1972); originally published in 1835.

6. By 'myth', Strauss means narrative detail that is the product of an idea of

and thus unhistorical. While he does find isolated pieces of historical fact, he makes no attempt to gather them together into a portrait of the historical Jesus. Therefore, it is not surprising that he also does not construct a portrait of the historical John. Such a portrait, however, may be gleaned from his work.

According to Strauss, the historical John engaged in a ministry of baptism that was most likely derived from Judaic religious lustrations.[7] While Strauss maintains that John did in fact baptize Jesus, he also claims that, at the time of the baptism, John did not actually believe that Jesus was the Messiah.[8] In fact, Strauss asserts that John had counted Jesus as one of his followers. In this way, John was able to influence Jesus with his beliefs in the approaching messianic kingdom. Only after John's imprisonment did Jesus start his own ministry, thus carrying on the work started by John, although with some modifications.[9]

Although Strauss's analysis represented a major advancement in the quest of the historical Jesus, it had no influence on the course of Gospel studies in his day; the rationalistic studies that dominated scholarship at that time simply continued unabated for decades.

During the first hundred years of critical scholarship on the Gospels, the figure of John did not enjoy independent standing. Reimarus and Strauss are representative of the way John was treated: attention accorded him did not amount to much more than ancillary analyses in works devoted to the life of Jesus. The final decades of the nineteenth century were to witness an end to such neglect of John. Numerous books appeared that focused exclusively on John, thus granting him an identity of his own.[10] These books, however, are almost entirely noncritical;[11] in analyzing the life of John, they unreservedly accept the

the early Christians, as opposed to an expression of an actual fact (*Life of Jesus*, pp. 86-87).

7. Strauss, *Life of Jesus*, p. 215.

8. Strauss, *Life of Jesus*, pp. 219-29.

9. Strauss, *Life of Jesus*, p. 233.

10. Examples include Archibald McCullagh, *The Peerless Prophet; or, The Life and Times of John the Baptist* (New York: Anson D.F. Randolph, 1888); Ross C. Houghton, *John the Baptist, the Forerunner of our Lord: His Life and Work* (New York: Hunt & Eaton, 1889); J. Feather, *The Last of the Prophets: A Study of the Life, Teaching, and Character of John the Baptist* (Edinburgh: T. & T. Clark, 1894); F.B. Meyer, *John the Baptist* (New York: Revell, 1900).

11. Both Houghton, *John the Baptist*, p. 99, and Feather, *Last of the Prophets*, pp. 94-95 and 98-99, appear to be familiar with Strauss's work, although neither

Gospel accounts as accurate historical records.

By the 1860s, the impact of rationalism on Gospel studies was in decline. In its place, theological liberalism was on the ascent as the dominant influence on the study of Jesus. As a result of theological liberalism's focus on the ethical and spiritual elements of the Gospels, the quest of the historical Jesus throughout the late nineteenth century produced portraits of Jesus primarily as an ethical teacher.[12]

These portraits are severely criticized in Albert Schweitzer's *The Quest of the Historical Jesus*.[13] Schweitzer accuses them of transforming the first-century Jesus into a nineteenth-century figure. Schweitzer contends that it is necessary for Jesus to be viewed within the context of Jewish apocalypticism, for this movement reached its apex during the first century and culminated in Jesus as well as John the Baptist and Paul.[14] So, according to Schweitzer, the portraits of Jesus that had emerged from the perspective of theological liberalism are flawed because of their failure to include the key element of 'eschatology'.

Schweitzer describes the early first century as a time when expectations of imminent judgment and subsequent glory were running high. According to Schweitzer, these expectations gave rise to a desire among the Jewish people to find some way to guarantee that they would survive the judgment and thus achieve the subsequent glory. In response to this concern, John set forth his baptism as a means to ensure certainty of this glory.[15] Schweitzer believes that Jewish apocalypticism expected the final judgment to be preceded by both the outpouring of the Spirit spoken of by Joel and the coming of Elijah spoken of by Malachi. John combined these two expectations by announcing the coming of the one who was greater than himself (Elijah), who

make any attempt to refute it. Further, Feather presents a source-critical discussion of the Two-Source Hypothesis, but finds against the existence of Q (pp. 147-53).

12. Adolf von Harnack, *What Is Christianity?* (trans. Thomas Bailey Saunders; Philadelphia: Fortress Press, 1986), demonstrates a portrait of Jesus that reflects the perspective of theological liberalism. For Harnack, Jesus was a morality preacher (p. 46). Further, the gospel Jesus preached was an ethical message (p. 70), and the entirety of his teaching concerned 'the higher righteousness' and 'the new commandment of love' (p. 77).

13. Albert Schweitzer, *The Quest of the Historical Jesus: A Critical Study of its Progress From Reimarus to Wrede* (trans. W. Montgomery; New York: Macmillan, 1948); originally published in 1906.

14. Schweitzer, *The Quest of the Historical Jesus*, p. 367.

15. Schweitzer, *The Quest of the Historical Jesus*, pp. 377-78.

would baptize with the Spirit (the outpouring of the Spirit). Therefore, John saw himself as the forerunner of Elijah. Jesus, on the other hand, felt compelled to identify John as Elijah himself because he believed that the appearance of Elijah had to occur before his own manifestation as the Son of Man.[16]

Scholars often assert that, with this study, Schweitzer brought an end to the 'first quest' of the historical Jesus and moved scholarship into a period of 'no quest', that is, a period in which scholars no longer sought to reconstruct the life of the historical Jesus. It should be pointed out, however, that Schweitzer did not bring an end to the 'first quest'; as noted above, he himself offered a contribution to it. Instead, the period of 'no quest' came about as the result of a growing awareness that the Gospels do not constitute reliable sources of historical data on the life of Jesus. Through the work of such authors as William Wrede,[17] scholarship began to appreciate the extent to which these documents are theologically motivated. As a result, the Gospels came to be seen as sources of historical facts about the lives of the communities producing them rather than sources of historical facts about the life of Jesus. With form criticism's shift of focus to the communities behind the Gospels, no focus remained on the historical Jesus.

If scholars no longer accepted the Gospels as reliable historical sources on the life of Jesus, it would seem to follow that they would not accept them as reliable historical sources on the life of John. The same views that brought an end to the quest of the historical Jesus might well have brought an end to the quest of the historical John. However, the quest of John did not end. Indeed, the form-critical methodology that totally ignored the question of the historical Jesus was the methodology of choice during the first half of the twentieth century as scholars continued to search for details on the historical John.

During this half-century period, form criticism produced four major studies on John the Baptist.[18] The first is Martin Dibelius's *Die*

16. Schweitzer, *The Quest of the Historical Jesus*, pp. 373-76.

17. William Wrede, *The Messianic Secret* (trans. J.C.G. Greig; Cambridge: James Clarke, 1971); originally published in 1901.

18. In the midst of these four major studies is one other that did not use this methodology: Robert Eisler, *The Messiah Jesus and John the Baptist: According to Flavius Josephus' Recently Rediscovered 'Capture of Jerusalem' and the Other Jewish and Christian Sources* (trans. Alexander Haggerty Knappe; New York: Dial Press, 1931). Eisler asserts that an Old Russian version of Josephus's *Jewish War* preserves the author's intentions much more accurately than does the extant Greek

urchristliche Überlieferung von Johannes dem Täufer.[19] Dibelius begins his study by attempting to ascertain the most reliable sources of historical data on John. He argues that the Christian community had a strong interest in preserving the words of Jesus; therefore, this part of the tradition would have solidified the earliest. Because of this, Dibelius concludes that, within the Gospels, the words of Jesus constitute the best sources of historical data. Thus, he holds that the words of Jesus pertaining to John represent the most reliable sources of historical data on John.[20] Based on this conclusion, Dibelius first analyzes Jesus' sayings on John, and then moves on to examine the narrative sections on John in light of his analysis of Jesus' words.

According to Dibelius, John appeared as a prophet in the southern part of the Jordan Valley.[21] Although the topic of his preaching was repentance, John did not come across as the morality preacher Josephus depicted him to be. Instead, he came across as an eschatological preacher who proclaimed the coming Messiah as a judge who would punish the unrighteous.[22] However, Dibelius asserts that, at the time John baptized Jesus, John did not recognize Jesus as this Messiah. Indeed, it was only after the imprisoned John heard about Jesus that he started to wonder whether Jesus might be the Messiah.[23]

Dibelius's study represents a kind of prolegomenon to twentieth-century form-critical work on the life of John the Baptist. Although it does not constitute a 'Life of John' with separate chapters on such topics as prophecies pertaining to John, his birth, his food and clothing, his baptism, his preaching and his death, it does establish the groundwork for subsequent form-critical work on John. One such study is

version, because the latter is the end-product of censorship by the Church. The Old Russian version speaks of a certain unnamed 'wild man', whom Eisler identifies as John the Baptist (pp. 223-26). This wild man was a high-priest—akin to an army chaplain—who prayed over Jewish rebels engaging in battle against Rome (pp. 265-66). He also administered a baptism that was a proselyte baptism for those who had committed apostasy by submitting to Rome, and who now wanted to be reinstated as Jews (pp. 268-69).

19. Martin Dibelius, *Die urchristliche Überlieferung von Johannes dem Täufer* (Göttingen: Vandenhoeck & Ruprecht, 1911).

20. Dibelius, *Die urchristliche Überlieferung*, p. 2.

21. Dibelius, *Die urchristliche Überlieferung*, pp. 132-33.

22. Dibelius, *Die urchristliche Überlieferung*, pp. 133-34.

23. Dibelius, *Die urchristliche Überlieferung*, p. 140.

Maurice Goguel's *Au seuil de l'Evangile: Jean-Baptiste.*[24] Goguel asserts that, while Christian tradition has seen John's whole identity as tied up in the term 'precursor',[25] this view does not reflect the historical reality concerning John. According to Goguel, the witnesses of the New Testament to John tend to adapt him into this role of precursor, thus leaving his true thoughts and work hidden. Nevertheless, Goguel is convinced that in these witnesses it is possible to detect the traditions on which the evangelists worked, and from these traditions it is possible to derive a picture of the historical John the Baptist.[26]

According to Goguel, John was a preacher whose message consisted of high moral teachings and a call to repentance.[27] John presented both the necessity of repentance and his baptism as its seal. In addition, his baptism acted as a rite of purification and a rite of admission into the group organized around John.[28] Goguel argues that Jesus did receive baptism from John, and for a time was even a disciple of John.[29] However, based on his reading of the Gospel of John, Goguel asserts, '...Jesus, after working on lines similar to those of the Baptist, separated from him as a result of a dispute or a discussion, due to a difference of opinion about purification or the question of baptism'.[30] Goguel suggests that after this separation, John viewed Jesus as 'an unfaithful disciple and almost a renegade'.[31]

Ernst Lohmeyer is the third scholar to conduct a major form-critical exploration of John.[32] Lohmeyer believes that John holds a decisive significance in the historical development of early Christianity. For Lohmeyer, the essence of the Church's message was the imminent end that God had set for all people and things. While Lohmeyer admits that Jesus was an early proclaimer of this eschatological message, he argues that, since Jesus had been John's disciple, John's eschatological

24. Maurice Goguel, *Au seuil de l'Evangile: Jean-Baptiste* (Paris: Payot, 1928); Goguel's findings on John the Baptist are found in a condensed form in his later book, *The Life of Jesus* (trans. Olive Wyon; New York: Macmillan, 1933).

25. Goguel, *Au seuil de l'Evangile*, p. 9.

26. Goguel, *Au seuil de l'Evangile*, p. 12.

27. Goguel, *Life of Jesus*, pp. 266-67.

28. Goguel, *Life of Jesus*, p. 268.

29. Goguel, *Life of Jesus*, p. 269.

30. Goguel, *Life of Jesus*, p. 275.

31. Goguel, *Life of Jesus*, p. 279.

32. Ernst Lohmeyer, *Das Urchristentum. 1. Buch: Johannes der Täufer* (Göttingen: Vandenhoeck & Ruprecht, 1932).

proclamation preceded that of Jesus. Therefore, John holds the distinction of being the first proclaimer of this essential component of the Church's message.[33]

In painting his portrait of John, Lohmeyer focuses on John's relationship to his Jewish background. He argues that John's message offered the Jewish people liberation from the cultus.[34] According to Lohmeyer, John was a high-priestly figure[35] who acted as a mediator, dispensing knowledge of salvation and offering baptism as a means of unifying the Jewish people.[36]

Lohmeyer also sees John in the role of forerunner for the one who was to bring about the eschatological completion of all things; therefore, Lohmeyer recognizes John as part of the dawning age.[37] Yet Lohmeyer views John as a person caught in the middle of the two ages, separated from his own people, yet working for them, and separated from the decisive day and the bringer of the eschatological completion, yet announcing them both.[38]

The last of the four major form-critical works that dominated the quest of the historical John during the first half of the twentieth century is Carl Kraeling's *John the Baptist*.[39] Kraeling sees significance in John's presence in the wilderness;[40] he argues that this separation from society was the result of John's relationship with the priesthood. Kraeling points out that John himself was from priestly circles, albeit rural ones.[41] Further, Kraeling suggests that John may have become disenchanted by the secularization of the urban Jerusalem priesthood and may even have been brushed aside in his attempts to be ordained because of his rural background.[42] Kraeling concludes that such experiences could have been responsible for driving John into the wilderness where contact with the supernatural was more immediate.[43]

33. Lohmeyer, *Das Urchristentum*, pp. 3-5.
34. Lohmeyer, *Das Urchristentum*, pp. 172-73.
35. Lohmeyer, *Das Urchristentum*, p. 183.
36. Lohmeyer, *Das Urchristentum*, p. 187.
37. Lohmeyer, *Das Urchristentum*, p. 187.
38. Lohmeyer, *Das Urchristentum*, p. 187.
39. Carl H. Kraeling, *John the Baptist* (New York: Charles Scribner's Sons, 1951).
40. Kraeling, *John the Baptist*, pp. 15-16.
41. Kraeling, *John the Baptist*, pp. 20-23.
42. Kraeling, *John the Baptist*, pp. 24-27.
43. Kraeling, *John the Baptist*, p. 28.

Kraeling characterizes the John who emerged from the wilderness as a prophet. In support of this picture, Kraeling points to two pieces of evidence: (1) John's own words, which place him in the prophetic tradition,[44] and (2) Jesus' words about John, which depict John as a prophet, but further as the one sent to prepare the way for the events of the last days.[45]

Kraeling agrees with Goguel that Jesus had been a disciple of John and that Jesus had subsequently broken with him.[46] However, while Goguel posits a break based on principle, Kraeling holds that the break occurred as a result of Jesus' experience of the presence of the Kingdom. Kraeling argues that Jesus saw events advancing toward the fulfillment of the purpose of history, and thus Jesus believed that the time for John's fasting and withdrawal was gone. Kraeling concludes that Jesus still respected John, but found his program inappropriate for the presence of the Kingdom.[47]

The works of Dibelius, Goguel, Lohmeyer and Kraeling demonstrate vastly superior historical analysis in comparison to the studies of the second half of the nineteenth century produced from the perspective of theological liberalism. However, each of these form-critical studies of John exhibits the same methodological weakness: the tendency to use details from the Gospel accounts without first determining their reliability as historical data. Therefore, by the middle of the twentieth century, the quest of the historical John still awaited a definitive historical study on John.

A turning point in Gospel studies came in 1953 when Ernst Käsemann gave an address entitled 'The Problem of the Historical Jesus'.[48] This address brought to an end the period of 'no quest' in the study of the historical Jesus. In its place emerged a new movement of research that probed the Gospel accounts for historical details on Jesus. This movement has come to be known as 'The New Quest of the Historical Jesus'. This new quest focused on the sayings of Jesus, applying the

44. Kraeling saw John's use of images involving a threshing floor and trees being cut down as placing John in the prophetic tradition (*John the Baptist*, pp. 44-45).

45. Kraeling, *John the Baptist*, pp. 137-45.

46. Kraeling, *John the Baptist*, pp. 151-52.

47. Kraeling, *John the Baptist*, pp. 152-53.

48. Ernst Käsemann, 'The Problem of the Historical Jesus', in *Essays on New Testament Themes* (trans. W.J. Montague; Naperville, IL: Allenson, 1964), pp. 15-47.

principles of dissimilarity[49] and multiple attestation in an attempt to separate the authentic sayings from the inauthentic ones.

The quest of the historical John the Baptist was not affected by this new methodological development. Instead, scholars were preoccupied with a different development in the biblical studies of that time: the discovery of the Dead Sea Scrolls. Noting similarities between the theologies of John and the Dead Sea Scrolls, scholars speculated whether John had been a member of the Qumran community.

The first scholar to write on a possible connection between John and Qumran was William Brownlee. In 1950, Brownlee discussed this issue in the last few pages of an article entitled 'A Comparison of the Covenanters of the Dead Sea Scrolls with Pre-Christian Jewish Sects'.[50] On the basis of this brief analysis, Brownlee offers a tentative suggestion that John's life and teachings are rooted in the Qumran community. A few years later, Brownlee wrote an article to explore this possibility in more detail.[51] As a result of this more thorough study, he concludes that it was 'not at all improbable' that John had spent his childhood at Qumran.[52] In coming to this conclusion, Brownlee extracts the content of John's teachings from a survey of the Gospels and compares each component of these teachings to the corresponding views expressed in the Qumran literature. Brownlee finds that almost every detail of John's teaching has a point of contact with Essene belief.[53] It should be noted, however, that for the most part Brownlee does not address the preliminary issue of whether the Gospel accounts can be considered reliable historical sources.[54]

John A.T. Robinson[55] approaches the issue of a possible connection

49. According to this principle, a saying of Jesus may be adjudged authentic if it is dissimilar to both contemporary Judaism and the interests of the early Church.

50. William Brownlee, 'A Comparison of the Covenanters of the Dead Sea Scrolls with Pre-Christian Jewish Sects', *BA* 13 (1950), pp. 49-72.

51. W.H. Brownlee, 'John the Baptist in the New Light of Ancient Scrolls', in Krister Stendahl (ed.), *The Scrolls and the New Testament* (New York: Harper & Brothers, 1957), pp. 33-53.

52. Brownlee, 'John the Baptist', p. 35.

53. Brownlee, 'John the Baptist', p. 52.

54. One notable exception is evident in Brownlee's handling of passages found in the Gospel of John. Brownlee expends considerable effort in arguing against the prevailing view that dismissed the fourth Gospel's portrait of the Baptist as nothing more than an anti-Baptist polemic ('John the Baptist', pp. 45-51).

55. John A.T. Robinson, 'The Baptism of John and the Qumran Community', in

between John and Qumran in much the same way as Brownlee. Robinson also compares the data on John in the Gospels with the details on the Qumran community in the Dead Sea Scrolls. Like Brownlee, Robinson also fails to demonstrate a full appreciation of the problems related to using the Gospels as sources of information on the historical John.[56] His discussion of the parallels between John and Qumran suggests a conviction that John had indeed been associated with the Qumran community. In the end, however, Robinson is not willing to say that an association between John and Qumran is anything more than a hypothesis.[57]

A.S. Geyser explores a possible connection between John and Qumran by noting the striking parallel between the treatments of John and Jesus in the Infancy Narrative of Luke. Geyser suggests that this narrative has its source in a Christian community that had originally descended from the followers of John.[58] Geyser also points out that the account of Jesus as a twelve-year-old is not matched by a parallel account of John. This leads Geyser to speculate that such a parallel account had existed in the source but had been suppressed by Luke.[59] In his effort to reconstruct this suppressed account, Geyser writes:

> Let us repeat briefly the salient points of the relative history of Jesus; it contains: 1) an illustration of Jesus' exceptional progress in knowledge of the Law; 2) his conference with the teachers; 3) his attitude towards his parents; 4) his consciousness of his calling by his Father; 5) the fact that He went back to the house of his parents; 6) that He obeyed them, and 7) the statement that Jesus waxed in wisdom and stature and in favour with God and man. I suggest that the parallel history of John, which is no longer extant because it was suppressed deliberately by Luke, contained mutatis mutandis a narrative in the same order. It would have told us an episode from the life of John as bar-mizwa, it would have supplied an illustration of his exceptional knowledge of the law as revealed in an examination by the Essene teachers. It would further have

Twelve New Testament Studies (London: SCM Press, 1962).

56. Robinson does make short arguments in favour of the historicity of the Infancy Narrative of Luke ('Baptism', p. 11) and the Johannine accounts about John the Baptist (pp. 25-26). However, on the whole, his treatment of the Gospel materials suggests that he does not fully appreciate the issues involved.

57. Robinson, 'Baptism', p. 27.

58. A.S. Geyser, 'The Youth of John the Baptist: A Deduction from the Break in the Parallel Account of the Lucan Infancy Story', *NovT* 1 (1956), pp. 70-75 (72-73).

59. Geyser, 'The Youth of John the Baptist', pp. 73-74.

> told us something in relation to his parents, perhaps the fact that, owing to their advanced age, John was already orphaned by this time, that he was nevertheless conscious of the fact that he belonged to his heavenly Father. He went with his adoptive parents to the Judean desert and obeyed them. This account must have ended with a verbal parallel of ii 52 in relation to John, just as i 80a is a verbal parallel of ii 40.[60]

Among the studies exploring a possible connection between John and Qumran, Geyser's analysis is rather unique in that it demonstrates at least some critical consideration of this issue. Unfortunately, this critical consideration is limited to only the source-critical issue outlined above. Geyser shows himself to have no more appreciation than Brownlee or Robinson for the issue of whether the Gospel accounts can be used as sources of historical data on John. For example, Geyser speaks favourably of Brownlee's efforts outlined above: 'W.H. Brownlee has *convincingly* brought [the discoveries from Qumran] into focus with what we know about John the Baptist from the New Testament and Josephus.'[61] Further, at the beginning of his article, Geyser poses a number of questions on John which clearly reveal that he considers the details of the Gospel accounts to be historical fact; however, Geyser makes no effort to establish them as such.[62]

While much of the research on John was preoccupied with this issue of a possible connection between John and Qumran, some scholars continued the form-critical work of Dibelius, Goguel, Lohmeyer and Kraeling. One such scholar was Charles H.H. Scobie.[63] According to Scobie, John should be analyzed against the background of the sectarian baptist movement of the first century. Scobie even goes so far as to call 'attractive' the suggestion that John had been adopted as a child by a baptist group that was part of this movement.[64] In Scobie's view, both

60. Geyser, 'The Youth of John the Baptist', p. 74.

61. Geyser, 'The Youth of John the Baptist', pp. 70-71 (emphasis added).

62. Geyser, 'The Youth of John the Baptist', p. 70. For example, 'Why did [John] wear clothes which, while resembling those of Elijah, were nevertheless wholly unpriestly?' This question presupposes that John did indeed wear a garment of camel's hair and a leather belt, but Geyser makes no attempt to verify that these details from the Gospel accounts represent historical fact.

63. Charles H.H. Scobie, *John the Baptist* (London: SCM Press, 1964).

64. Scobie, *John the Baptist*, p. 59; Scobie includes the Qumran community within this sectarian baptist movement. Further, although he discusses the views of authors who assert that John had been adopted by this community (pp. 58-59), he himself is not willing to be that specific.

John[65] and Jesus[66] considered John to be the eschatological prophet who was to prepare the way of the Messiah. Like Goguel, Scobie suggests that Jesus may have been a disciple of John who later separated from him. Unlike Goguel, however, Scobie believes that the separation had not necessarily involved ill-feeling.[67]

The most significant contribution of Scobie's book to the historical reconstruction of John the Baptist is its discussion of a possible Samaritan ministry by John. Scobie notes similarities between Samaritanism, especially sectarian Samaritanism, and the Jewish baptist movements from which John's ministry had originated.[68] Based on these similarities, Scobie suggests that perhaps some Samaritans had come to John for baptism and had persuaded him to return to Samaria with them in order to minister there.[69] In support of this reconstruction, Scobie points to Jn 3.22-23 which states that John was baptizing in 'Aenon near Salim',[70] a site that Scobie claims should be located in Samaria.[71]

The subtitle to Scobie's book reads, 'A New Quest of the Historical John'. An examination of Scobie's approach, however, reveals that he did not make use of the principles developed in the 'New Quest' in his analysis of John. Instead, he follows an approach similar to that of Dibelius, Goguel, Lohmeyer and Kraeling. Therefore, he also fails to take seriously the problem of extracting historical data from the Gospel accounts.

During the late 1970s, historical research on Jesus experienced a shift in focus; scholars began to adopt a social-historical approach to the study of Jesus and so examined Jesus' social, cultural and political environment as a crucial component in understanding Jesus as an historical figure.[72] Tom Wright designates this new impetus in Gospel

65. Scobie, *John the Baptist*, p. 123.

66. Scobie, *John the Baptist*, p. 126.

67. Scobie, *John the Baptist*, pp. 154-56.

68. Scobie, *John the Baptist*, p. 170.

69. Scobie, *John the Baptist*, p. 173.

70. Scobie, *John the Baptist*, pp. 173-74.

71. Scobie, *John the Baptist*, p. 164.

72. Major works employing this new methodology include Ben F. Meyer, *The Aims of Jesus* (London: SCM Press, 1979); A.E. Harvey, *Jesus and the Constraints of History* (Philadelphia: Westminster Press, 1982); Marcus J. Borg, *Conflict, Holiness and Politics in the Teachings of Jesus* (Lewiston, NY: Edwin Mellen Press, 1984); E.P. Sanders, *Jesus and Judaism* (Philadelphia: Fortress Press, 1985); Marcus J. Borg, *Jesus: A New Vision* (San Francisco: Harper & Row, 1987);

research the 'Third Quest' of the historical Jesus.[73]

This focus on the social, cultural and political environment of first-century Palestine also became evident in the quest of the historical John the Baptist. For example, Paul Hollenbach's analysis of John concentrates on the social and political context of John's preaching.[74] Hollenbach points out that the period between the death of Herod the Great and the Jewish Revolts was a time of relative prosperity for the privileged of society but a time of impoverishment for the masses. Against this backdrop, John appeared as a social revolutionary who attempted to rectify this imbalance by calling the relatively small middle class to exercise justice.[75] John also exhorted tax collectors to end their oppression of the poor by collecting no more than that for which they had contracted (Lk. 3.13). According to Hollenbach, John would have posed a major threat to the tax system, and this may have been the major reason why Herod Antipas took notice of him.[76] John spoke also with soldiers. Through their service to the ruling authorities, these soldiers were agents of oppression. John's exhortation to rob no one and to be content with their wages (Lk. 3.14) constituted a challenge aimed at the foundation of the social order.[77] It is Hollenbach's contention that, through such entreaties, John was instigating a social revolution and, in the eyes of Herod Antipas, perhaps even a political revolution.[78]

Hollenbach's focus on the social, cultural and political environment of first-century Palestine provides some interesting insights into the historical John. Hollenbach's execution of this new methodology, however, is marred by a failure to pay sufficient attention to the issue of the Gospels as reliable historical sources. He does recognize that the

Richard A. Horsley, *Jesus and the Spiral of Violence* (San Francisco: Harper & Row, 1987); James H. Charlesworth, *Jesus within Judaism* (New York: Doubleday, 1988).

73. Stephen Neill and Tom Wright, *Interpretation of the New Testament, 1861–1986* (Oxford: Oxford University Press, 2nd edn, 1988), p. 379; another recent spokesperson for this movement, James H. Charlesworth (*Jesus within Judaism*, p. 1), prefers the terminology 'Jesus Research' to any reference to 'quest' or 'search'.

74. Paul Hollenbach, 'Social Aspects of John the Baptizer's Preaching Mission in the Context of Palestinian Judaism', in *ANRW*, II.19.1, pp. 850-75.

75. Hollenbach, 'Social Aspects', p. 874.

76. Hollenbach, 'Social Aspects', pp. 871-72.

77. Hollenbach, 'Social Aspects', p. 873.

78. Hollenbach, 'Social Aspects', p. 874.

Gospel accounts do not necessarily provide accurate historical data; for example, he asserts that the birth story of John in the Gospel of Luke is legendary.[79] On the other hand, Hollenbach also displays a tendency to draw on details without giving any consideration to their reliability. For example, to support his assertion that John's alienation was indicated by the nature of his food and clothing, Hollenbach quotes Mk 1.6;[80] however, he makes no attempt to verify that the details of this verse are indeed factual. Because Hollenbach does not give consistent consideration to the reliability of the source material that he uses to develop his thesis, his findings are compromised.

By far the most significant work in this stream of social-historical research on John is *John the Baptizer and Prophet* by Robert Webb.[81] In this study, Webb limits himself to John's two public roles: baptizer and prophet. Regarding John's role as baptizer, Webb examines ablutions in the literature of the Old Testament, the Judaism of the Second Temple period, and the Qumran community. Against this backdrop, he analyzes the baptism of John. In his comparison of the functions of John's baptism[82] and the functions of the ablutions found in the Jewish sources, Webb finds both similarities and differences; nevertheless, he concludes that all the functions of John's baptism are understandable within the Jewish milieu.[83] Regarding John's role as prophet, Webb studies the prophetic activity in late Second Temple Judaism. He identifies three different types of prophet: clerical prophets, sapiential prophets and popular prophets. Webb places John in the category of popular prophet[84] and, more specifically, in the category of leadership popular prophet,[85] that is, one who leads a prophetic movement.

Unlike all the preceding offerings in the quest of the historical John, Webb's work does pay serious attention to the issue of whether the

79. Hollenbach, 'Social Aspects', p. 852.

80. Hollenbach, 'Social Aspects', p. 853.

81. Robert L. Webb, *John the Baptizer and Prophet* (Sheffield: JSOT Press, 1991).

82. Webb identifies six such functions: (1) an expression of conversionary repentance; (2) a mediation of divine forgiveness; (3) a purification from uncleanness; (4) a foreshadowing of the expected figure's ministry; (5) an initiation into the 'true Israel'; and (6) a protest against the temple establishment (*John the Baptizer*, pp. 184-205).

83. Webb, *John the Baptizer*, p. 216.

84. Webb, *John the Baptizer*, p. 351.

85. Webb, *John the Baptizer*, p. 354.

Gospels can be used as sources of reliable historical data. In a chapter surveying the traditions on John in early Christian gospels,[86] Webb undertakes a careful analysis of the issue. On the basis of his analysis, he concludes 'that the synoptic accounts are generally reliable sources for information concerning John the Baptist',[87] but that the fourth evangelist's portrayal of John is 'problematic from a historical point of view...'.[88] In addition to this general analysis, Webb also carefully examines various individual details of the Gospels' portrayals of John to determine the historical reliability of each detail.[89] Because of its rigorous attention to this issue, this book represents a landmark in the quest of the historical John.

One recent historical study on John the Baptist that does not share the same social-historical focus as the works of Hollenbach and Webb is W. Barnes Tatum's *John the Baptist and Jesus: A Report of the Jesus Seminar*.[90] While this study does examine the social world of John in its attempt to reconstruct his life and teachings, discussions of social, cultural and political details do not dominate the analysis in the way that they do in the offerings of the 'Third Quest'. Rather, this book is better categorized as a late entry in the 'New Quest' begun in the 1950s,[91] for its methodology is more akin to that developed by the 'New Questers'.

Tatum's book is the product of the Jesus Seminar's research into John the Baptist.[92] It is clearly intended for a popular, as opposed to a scholarly, audience; it lacks extensive documentation, and it includes

86. Webb covers not only the four canonical Gospels, but also the *Gospel of Thomas*, the *Gospel of the Ebionites*, the *Gospel of the Nazareans*, and the *Protoevangelium of James* (pp. 47-91).

87. Webb, *John the Baptizer*, p. 88; he presents five arguments to support this position (pp. 85-88).

88. Webb, *John the Baptizer*, p. 89.

89. See, for example, Webb's substantiation of the claim that John did perform a water rite called 'baptism' (*John the Baptizer*, pp. 163-64).

90. W. Barnes Tatum, *John the Baptist and Jesus: A Report of the Jesus Seminar* (Sonoma, CA: Polebridge, 1994).

91. See p. 20, above.

92. Tatum notes that, as the members of the Jesus Seminar were about to shift their focus from Jesus' words to his deeds, they decided to devote two of its semiannual sessions (24–27 October 1991 and 27 February–1 March, 1992) to the study of John the Baptist (Tatum, *John the Baptist and Jesus*, p. 8).

explanations of basic concepts such as the 'Two-Source Hypothesis'.[93] However, the research underlying the findings reported in this volume is rigorous. The material in the Gospels on John the Baptist is broken down into 'narrative statements',[94] and each is placed under the scrutiny of a number of 'rules of evidence'[95] to determine its historical veracity.

This rigorous consideration of the reliability of the historical data on John the Baptist in the Gospels serves as a corrective to the methodological shortcomings of the historical studies on John prior to Webb. However, Tatum's work is not without its own shortcomings, albeit minor ones. Tatum is consistent in subjecting each narrative statement to a thoroughgoing analysis as to its historical veracity. Occasionally, however, in his analysis of certain narrative statements, he draws in data from other passages without subjecting them to the same type of scrutiny. For example, in discussing the issue of whether John practised immersion, he asserts, 'The baptism of Jesus...is described in language that suggests immersion: "...he got up out of the water..." (Mk 1.9-11 par)'.[96] However, he makes no attempt to verify that this description of Jesus' actions is historically accurate. Further, in sketching a composite profile of John's disciples, Tatum attributes a number of traits to them—for example, their lives were marked by holy practices, they seemed to engage in debate with contemporaries on religious practices, their activity was not halted by John's imprisonment, they engaged in discussions on eschatological speculation, they took care of John's body after he was executed[97]—but, again, he makes these assertions without any consideration of whether they are historically accurate or not. Nevertheless, in the scope of the entire work, these slips are relatively insignificant.

One final significant offering in the social-historical research on John the Baptist is Joan E. Taylor's study entitled *The Immerser: John the Baptist within Second Temple Judaism*.[98] Taylor states her principal

93. Tatum, *John the Baptist and Jesus*, p. 35.

94. That is, statements descriptive of the contents of the Gospel narratives, as opposed to direct quotations from the narratives; see Tatum, *John the Baptist and Jesus*, p. 9, for a fuller description.

95. A complete listing of these 'rules of evidence' is including in Tatum, *John the Baptist and Jesus*, Appendix D, pp. 178-80.

96. Tatum, *John the Baptist and Jesus*, p. 120.

97. Tatum, *John the Baptist and Jesus*, p. 137.

98. Joan E. Taylor, *The Immerser: John the Baptist within Second Temple*

aim as providing John with a context,[99] and that context is Second Temple Judaism. In her analysis of the 'Immerser'—as she consistently designates John throughout the book—Taylor covers the usual topics related to the historical John, such as his possible connection with the Qumran community, his baptism, and his relationship to Jesus. However, Taylor's discussions of John as a teacher of righteousness and of his affinity with the Pharisees[100] constitute significant contributions to social-historical research on John.

Concerning methodology, Taylor does recognize the problem of using the Gospels as sources for historical data on John,[101] and she does consider the issues related to the reliability of some of the passages that she uses; see, for example, her discussions on John's ethical teachings in Lk. 3.10-14,[102] and on Jesus' assertion in Mt. 21.31-32 that, in contrast to the hard-heartedness of the chief priests and elders, prostitutes believed John.[103] Nevertheless, Taylor frequently cites passages from the Gospels with no consideration of whether or not they contain accurate historical data; see, for example, her use of Jesus' statement that John came 'neither eating bread nor drinking wine' (Lk. 7.33-34),[104] her use of descriptions from Mk 1.6 and Mt. 3.4 regarding John's diet and clothing,[105] and her use of John's admonition that those wishing to undergo his immersion must bear fruits worthy of repentance (Lk. 3.7-8).[106] Because of this inconsistent treatment of the sources for her historical reconstruction of John, Taylor's findings do not hold the same weight as those of Webb.

This survey of historical research on John the Baptist reveals that there has been a general unevenness in quality among the numerous offerings in the quest of the historical John; some efforts have definitely been more methodologically sound than others. Nevertheless, the enterprise as a whole demonstrates that scholarship has considered the primary motivation behind the Gospels as something other than the dissemination of historical data. Therefore, while the quest of the

Judaism (Grand Rapids: Eerdmans, 1997).

99. Taylor, *The Immerser*, p. 12.
100. Taylor, *The Immerser*, pp. 101-211.
101. Taylor, *The Immerser*, pp. 2-9.
102. Taylor, *The Immerser*, pp. 113-15
103. Taylor, *The Immerser*, pp. 119-20
104. Taylor, *The Immerser*, p. 32.
105. Taylor, *The Immerser*, p. 34.
106. Taylor, *The Immerser*, p. 82.

historical John may constitute an interesting exercise, it fails to consider the whole question of the early Church's use of John to propagate its message.

Redaction-Critical Analyses on John the Baptist

During the 1950s, a line of Gospel research developed that did place a focus on the Gospel writers' purposes in producing the Gospels. Redaction criticism attempted to discern the theological message of a given Gospel writer by analyzing his handling of the available traditions. The first major redaction-critical examination of John the Baptist in the Gospel of Matthew[107] still holds the place of distinction as the classic redaction-critical study on this topic: Wolfgang Trilling's 'Die Täufertradition bei Matthäus'.[108] For Trilling, the main point underlying Matthew's treatment of John is Matthew's denial of Israel's claim that it is the true people of God.[109] Trilling points out that the sixth woe against the scribes and Pharisees (23.29-36) and the parable of the vineyard (21.33-45) reveal a 'fate of the prophets' motif: in Israel, prophets are persecuted.[110] Further, he sees in the pericope depicting the death of John an example of a prophet facing this fate.[111]

Trilling finds in Matthew a tendency to assimilate John and Jesus.[112] On the basis of this tendency, Trilling concludes that the author wishes to suggest that Jesus too would encounter the same 'fate of the

107. Because the present study examines John the Baptist in the Gospel of Matthew only, this survey of research on redaction-critical studies of John is limited to those pertaining to the Gospel of Matthew. Prominent redaction-critical works on the figure of John the Baptist in the other Gospels include Hans Conzelmann, *The Theology of St. Luke* (trans. Geoffrey Buswell; New York: Harper & Row, 1961), pp. 18-27 (originally published in 1953); and Willi Marxen, *Mark the Evangelist: Studies on the Redaction History of the Gospel* (trans. James Boyce, Donald Juel, William Poehlmann and Roy A. Harrisville; Nashville; Abingdon Press, 1969), pp. 30-53 (originally published in 1956).

108. Wolfgang Trilling, 'Die Täufertradition bei Matthäus', *BZ* 3 (1959), pp. 271-89.

109. 'Die Täufertradition', p. 289.

110. 'Die Täufertradition', p. 274.

111. 'Die Täufertradition', pp. 272-73.

112. 'Die Täufertradition', pp. 282-86; Trilling also discerns a tendency to differentiate between John and Jesus in order to ensure that Jesus' unique position was not endangered (pp. 286-87).

prophets'.[113] Trilling points out that part of the assimilation process relates to the opponents of these two figures; both John and Jesus are depicted as facing a common front of opposition, designated 'die gottfeindliche Front' by Trilling.[114] Because this front consists of the leadership of the Jewish people,[115] its opposition to the prophets of God demonstrates the Jewish people's failure to qualify as the 'true Israel'.

In 1968, Walter Wink published *John the Baptist in the Gospel Tradition*,[116] the standard redactional analysis of John the Baptist. However, Wink's chapter on John in the Gospel of Matthew[117] is heavily dependent on Trilling's findings. At the beginning of the chapter, Wink admits this dependence: 'We are fortunate to have in [Trilling's article] a definitive study of Matthew's treatment of John. We shall therefore make the structure of his analysis our own and supplement on the basis of it.'[118] Unfortunately, his supplementation is meager; it consists of only two notable points. First, Wink asserts that Matthew's redactional activity on John is governed by the notion that John is Elijah.[119] Secondly, Wink rejects the view that Matthew's treatment of John is in the service of a polemic against the Baptist community.[120]

Another redaction critic who exhibits a strong reliance on Trilling is John Meier.[121] Like Trilling, Meier notes Matthew's tendencies to assimilate John and Jesus and also to subordinate John to Jesus.[122] Further, although Meier agrees with Trilling that Matthew has woven a motif of the 'fate of prophets in Israel' into his narrative,[123] he disagrees

113. Trilling, 'Die Täufertradition', p. 284.

114. Trilling, 'Die Täufertradition', pp. 274-75

115. That is: King Herod at the birth of Jesus; Archalaeus upon the return of Jesus from Egypt; Herod Antipas in relation to the execution of John; the Pharisees and Sadducees at the site of John's baptizing activity; the Pharisees, scribes, chief priests and elders at various points throughout the adult life of Jesus.

116. Walter Wink, *John the Baptist in the Gospel Tradition* (Cambridge: Cambridge University Press, 1968).

117. Wink, *Gospel Tradition*, pp. 27-41.

118. Wink, *Gospel Tradition*, p. 27.

119. Wink, *Gospel Tradition*, p. 40.

120. Wink, *Gospel Tradition*, pp. 40-41; this concern to reject the hypothesis that John was absorbed into the Gospels as a witness against his own disciples is found throughout Wink's book in his treatment of each of the four Gospels.

121. John P. Meier, 'John the Baptist in Matthew's Gospel', *JBL* 99 (1980), pp. 383-405.

122. Meier, 'John the Baptist', p. 386.

123. Meier, 'John the Baptist', p. 399.

with Trilling's conclusion that this motif explains Matthew's assimilating-yet-subordinating tendency.[124] Instead, Meier finds the explanation for this tendency in Matthew's conception of salvation history,[125] a three-stage conception involving: (1) the time of the prophets; (2) the time of Jesus; and (3) the time of the Church. In placing John in the second stage with Jesus,[126] Meier argues:

> The birth of the King necessarily involves a fuller coming of the kingdom, from the birth of Jesus onwards. For that reason, when the Baptist appears on the stage in Chapter 3, he can hardly still belong to the old period of the law and the prophets. A new period, the mid-point of time, has already begun with the birth of Christ; and the Baptist necessarily stands within it by the inner logic of Matthew's schema. The Baptist's proclamation, rebukes, threats, fate, and martyrdom all reflect his place squarely within the central period of salvation history. This is the most important, indeed, the only adequate explanation for his being paralleled with Jesus.[127]

Although redaction-critical studies have uncovered significant insights into Matthew's use of John in this Gospel, they have left unanswered a number of questions related to Matthew's crafting of the story. What is the overall role that John plays within the plot of Matthew's story? Why is such an extensive description of John given in 3.1-10 when the focal point of ch. 3 is the pronouncement of Jesus as the Son of God? Why is John presented as fulfilling prophecy in 3.3 and then as fulfilling essentially the same prophecy again in 11.10? What is the significance of John's expression of doubt regarding the identity of Jesus in 11.3? Why is such a detailed account of John's execution given in 14.3-12? A different method is needed to answer questions such as these.

124. Meier, 'John the Baptist', p. 403.

125. Meier, 'John the Baptist', pp. 403-405.

126. Trilling also asserts that John was not to be included in the time of the prophets, although this assertion is subordinate to his main redactional finding: John as an illustration of the 'fate of prophets in Israel'.

127. Meier, 'John the Baptist', p. 404.

Chapter 2

METHODOLOGY

To examine these issues left unaddressed by historical and redaction-critical studies, it is useful to utilize a literary-critical approach. The field of literary criticism[1] is very wide, with many different—and even conflicting—methodologies. Therefore, it is necessary at the outset to establish the precise nature of the literary-critical methodology adopted by the present study. To this end, I survey the field,[2] and then narrow the focus onto the particular approach to be used in this study.

To analyze the developments in literary criticism of this century, it is useful to view the field against the backdrop of a schema presented by M.H. Abrams.[3] Abrams sets forth four elements of a work of art, and explains how each has been the focus of a different literary orientation: the 'mimetic',[4] according to which a work of art is an imitation of the universe; the 'pragmatic',[5] which focuses on the effects made on the audience; the 'expressive',[6] where the focus is on the artist's intentions; and the 'objective',[7] which analyzes the work itself in isolation from all other points of reference.

The middle decades of the twentieth century witnessed a distinct shift from an 'expressive' orientation toward literature emerging out of the

1. The designation 'literary criticism' is understood in two different ways by biblical scholars: (1) as a synonym for 'source criticism'; and (2) as a method involving the adoption of secular literary-critical theory for the study of biblical narratives. This study uses the designation 'literary criticism' in the latter sense.

2. This survey excludes treatment of structuralism and deconstruction.

3. M.H. Abrams, *The Mirror and the Lamp: Romantic Theory and the Critical Tradition* (New York: W.W. Norton, 1953).

4. Abrams, *The Mirror and the Lamp*, p. 8.

5. Abrams, *The Mirror and the Lamp*, p. 14.

6. Abrams, *The Mirror and the Lamp*, p. 21.

7. Abrams, *The Mirror and the Lamp*, p. 26.

Romantic era[8] to an 'objective' orientation, as seen in such movements as formalism,[9] structuralism, and New Criticism. Of the secular literary critics espousing this objective orientation, two have become favourites in the field of biblical literary criticism.[10] Wayne Booth and Seymour Chatman.

Booth, in his book *The Rhetoric of Fiction*,[11] breaks new ground with such discussions as his articulation of the unreliable versus the reliable narrator,[12] though this distinction has not been particularly prominent in Gospel studies since it has been generally accepted that the narrators of the Gospels are all reliable.[13] For biblical literary critics, Booth's discussions on the 'author' have been most influential. Given the name of his work, it is not surprising that Booth speaks in terms of 'pursuing the author's means of controlling his reader'.[14] However, does this not sound more like the agenda of the 'expressive' orientation with its focus on the author's intentions as opposed to the 'objective' orientation championed by Booth which brackets out those intentions? Despite this reference to 'the author's means of controlling his reader', Booth remains true to his formalist agenda, for when he speaks of the 'author', he does not mean the real flesh-and-blood author. Rather, he posits an 'implied author', conceptualized as follows:

8. Abrams, *The Mirror and the Lamp*, pp. 21-22.

9. While Russian Formalism flourished in the early decades of the twentieth century, Peter Widdowson notes that it did not have a major impact until the late 1960s and 1970s when the works of Russian Formalists were rediscovered and translated, and so '[i]n this sense the Russian Formalists "belong" to this later moment of their *reproduction*': Raman Selden and Peter Widdowson, *A Reader's Guide to Contemporary Literary Theory* (Lexington: The University Press of Kentucky, 3rd edn, 1993), p. 5 (emphasis original).

10. While literary criticism has been practised by both Old Testament and New Testament scholars, the following analysis will focus on the latter.

11. Wayne C. Booth, *The Rhetoric of Fiction* (Chicago: University of Chicago Press, 2nd edn, 1983); the first edition was published in 1961.

12. See, for example, his discussions on pp. 6-7, 158-59.

13. However, Stephen D. Moore, *Literary Criticism and the Gospels: The Theoretical Challenge* (New Haven: Yale University Press, 1989), pp. 30-34, sees in James Dawsey, *The Lukan Voice: Confusion and Irony in the Gospel of Luke* (Macon, GA: Mercer University Press, 1986), a case for characterizing the narrator of Luke as unreliable, though Dawsey himself does not use the terminology 'unreliable narrator'.

14. Dawsey, *The Lukan Voice*, p. xiii.

> As [the real author] writes, he creates not simply an ideal, impersonal 'man in general' but an implied version of 'himself' that is different from the implied authors we meet in other men's work...The 'implied author' chooses, consciously or unconsciously, what we read; we infer him as an ideal, literary, created version of the real man; he is the sum of his own choices.[15]

Therefore, we have a version of the author that is entirely encoded in the text, befitting a formalist approach.

Even more influential than Booth has been Chatman's most prominent work, *Story and Discourse*.[16] Chatman conceptualizes a narrative text as consisting of a story—the 'what', or the events and existents[17] of the narrative—and a discourse—the 'how', or the means by which the story is presented[18]—and then proceeds to examine issues related to each of these component parts. In the course of his discussion of discourse, Chatman sets forth a narrative-communication model that draws on Booth's distinction between real author and 'implied author', but also makes the same distinction on the other side of the communication process, that is, between real reader and 'implied reader',[19] that is, the reader presupposed by the text.[20] Adding narrator and narratee, the model appears as follows.[21]

	Narrative text	
Real author →	Implied author → (Narrator) → (Narratee) → Implied reader	→ Real reader

The introduction, starting in the 1970s, of concepts such as these into the study of the Gospels represented a radical departure from the

15. Dawsey, *The Lukan Voice*, pp. 70-71, 74-75.

16. Seymour Chatman, *Story and Discourse: Narrative Structure in Fiction and Film* (Ithaca, NY: Cornell University Press, 1978).

17. Chatman uses the term 'existents' to cover characters and settings (Chatman, *Story and Discourse*, p. 19).

18. Chatman, *Story and Discourse*, pp. 9, 19.

19. This designation was first coined by Wolfgang Iser, *The Implied Reader: Patterns of Communication in Prose Fiction From Bunyan to Beckett* (Baltimore: The Johns Hopkins University Press, 1974), though Booth was already using the concept, without this designation, thirteen years earlier (see Booth, *Rhetoric of Fiction*, pp. 137-38).

20. Chatman, *Story and Discourse*, pp. 149-50.

21. Chatman, *Story and Discourse*, p. 151.

redaction-critical approach then in vogue. A redaction critic has a tendency to fragment the text of a Gospel, thus losing sight of the Gospel as a whole, while a literary critic treats the whole text as an integrated unit. This holistic focus, however, was not an entirely new innovation, for composition criticism—a subcategory of redaction criticism—also emphasizes the text as a whole.

A more basic distinction between biblical literary criticism and redaction criticism has to do with the object of inquiry underlying each of these two approaches. Redaction criticism—including composition criticism—has as its object of inquiry the theology of the evangelist. Therefore, a redaction critic analyzes the redactional work evident in the text in an attempt to discern the theological interests of the evangelist. Biblical literary critics, on the other hand, are not concerned with the theological interests of the historical author. In fact, biblical literary critics bracket out all historical questions in conceptualizing a 'story world' totally separate from the real world. In contrasting a literary-critical approach to the Gospel of Mark with the historical-critical method, David Rhoads writes:

> Other approaches tend to fragment, in part because their purpose is to put elements of the text into contexts outside the text; so, for example, biblical scholars may identify the feeding of the five thousand as a historical event in Jesus' time or as an oral story emerging from the early church or as vehicle for a theological truth...or as a story which reveals the author's intention, or as instructions to Mark's community. Narrative criticism brackets these historical questions and looks at the closed universe of the story-world.[22]

Without question, this shift away from the search for historical data represented a radical departure from the way in which Gospel studies had been conducted for centuries. Yet the works of these formalist literary critics retain at least one characteristic of significance from redaction criticism. Stephen D. Moore points out that, with redaction criticism,

> the exegete's overview of the total message of the biblical work becomes the primary control in interpeting any portion of it...
>
> Precise comparative and analytic methods, redaction criticism in particular, require that the words of the text be present all at once.[23]

22. David Rhoads, 'Narrative Criticism and the Gospel of Mark', *JAAR* 50 (1982), pp. 411-34 (413).

23. Moore, *Literary Criticism and the Gospels*, pp. 79, 86.

Therefore, a redaction critic analyzes any given passage with a knowledge of not only everything that precedes the passage, but also with a knowledge of everything that follows it. It is this type of full knowledge of the text that Moore finds also in formalist literary-critical analyses of the Gospels.[24] Committed to a holistic approach stressing the unity of the narrative of a Gospel, critics of this persuasion posit the text as a static object, laid out in its entirety for examination. Typical of this type of literary-critical approach is the position of Robert C. Tannehill later in his career,[25] as reflected in the introduction to his narrative commentary on the Gospel of Luke:

> the discussion that follows is not simply an expanded reading; it is a commentary. It represents part of what might be said after reading a second, third, or fourth time. It is not confined to what is happening when reading for the first time, with much of the text still unknown.[26]

Positing an analysis executed after multiple readings of the whole text, Tannehill clearly envisions an analysis informed by full knowledge of every detail in the text. However, the appropriateness of this static approach to literary criticism—what will be designated 'narrative criticism' for the purposes of this study[27]—is thrown into question by the findings of research in the field of orality in the ancient world.

It has been widely noted that reading in antiquity was almost always done aloud.[28] The New Testament era is characterized by what Pieter

24. Moore, *Literary Criticism and the Gospels*, p. 86.

25. Earlier in his career, Tannehill espoused a significantly different position. For an example of his earlier position, see Robert C. Tannehill, 'The Disciples in Mark: The Function of a Narrative Role', *JR* 57 (1977), pp. 386-405.

26. Robert C. Tannehill, *The Narrative Unity of Luke–Acts: A Literary Interpretation*. I. *The Gospel According to Luke* (Philadelphia: Fortress Press), p. 6.

27. The term 'narrative criticism' has been used in a number of different ways by practitioners of biblical literary criticism. In this study, it is used to designate this type of static approach to literary criticism, as opposed to the more dynamic, audience-oriented approach discussed below (see p. 74).

28. See, for example, Paul Saenger, 'Silent Reading: Its Impact on Late Medieval Script and Society', *Viator* 13 (1982), pp. 367-414 (370); David E. Aune, 'The Apocalypse of John and the Problem of Genre', *Semeia* 36 (1986), pp. 65-96 (77); Gilbert L. Bartholomew, 'Feed My Lambs: John 21.15-19 as Oral Gospel', *Semeia* 39 (1987), pp. 69-96 (72); Thomas E. Boomershine, 'Peter's Denial as Polemic or Confession: The Implications of Media Criticism for Biblical Hermeneutics', *Semeia* 39 (1987), pp. 47-68; Paul J. Achtemeier, '*Omne verbum sonat*: The New Testament and the Oral Environment of Late Western Antiquity',

Botha calls 'scribal culture', that is, 'culture familiar with writing but in essence still significantly, even predominantly oral... [in which] reading is largely vocal'.[29] Paul J. Achtemeier notes that this type of phenomenon results from a cultural bias of the oral over the written.[30] Achtemeier also observes that documents lacked systematic punctuation and visible indications of paragraphs, sentences, or even words.[31] Documents of this type would be difficult to read silently, as the following comments by Paul Saenger on ancient Latin writing—which apply also to the Greek manuscripts of the New Testament—make clear:

> Latin writing, which consisted of undivided rows of capital letters or their cursive equivalents, was entirely phonetic and had no ideographic value. Since in ancient books verbal concepts were not represented by recognizable images, the Romans developed no clear conception of the word as a unit of meaning. Instead, Roman grammarians considered the letter and syllable to be basic to reading. The Roman reader, reading aloud to others or softly to himself, approached the text syllable by syllable in order to recover the words and sentences conveying the meaning of the text.[32]

One text from the New Testament illustrates this practice of reading aloud to oneself. In Acts 8.26-28, Philip is directed by an angel of the Lord to the Gaza Road where Philip sees an Ethiopian eunuch seated in a chariot and reading what turns out to be a manuscript of the prophet Isaiah. In v. 30, we are told that Philip approached the chariot, and 'heard' the eunuch reading, thus indicating that the eunuch must have been reading aloud.[33]

A short passage from Augustine's *Confessions* provides even stronger support for the assertion that virtually all reading in antiquity was done aloud:

> Now, as [Ambrose] read, his eyes glanced over the pages and his heart searched out the sense, but his voice and tongue were silent... Perhaps he

JBL 109 (1990), pp. 3-27 (15).

29. Pieter J.J. Botha, 'Mute Manuscripts: Analyzing a Neglected Aspect of Ancient Communication', *Theologia Evangelica* 23 (1990), pp. 35-47 (42).

30. Achtemeier, '*Omne verbum sonat*', pp. 10-11.

31. Achtemeier, '*Omne verbum sonat*', p. 10.

32. Saenger, 'Silent Reading', pp. 370-71.

33. Scholars who draw this conclusion include: Bartholomew, 'Feed My Lambs', p. 72; Boomershine, 'Peter's Denial', p. 53; Achtemeier, '*Omne verbum sonat*', p. 16.

> was fearful lest, if the author he was studying should express himself vaguely, some doubtful and attentive hearer would ask him to expound it or discuss some of the more abstruse questions, so that he could not get over as much material as he wished, if his time was occupied with others. And even a truer reason for his reading to himself might have been the care for preserving his voice, which was very easily weakened.[34]

These comments by Augustine obviously reflect a person who is very unaccustomed to witnessing someone reading silently, so much so that he feels compelled to speculate as to the reason for this phenomenon. Therefore, we have further evidence that reading in antiquity was almost always done aloud.

The foregoing discussion addresses the case of an individual person reading alone. However, evidence from antiquity suggests that such a scenario would not have been commonplace. First, written materials during this era were relatively scarce. In this age predating the printing press, all documents had to be hand-produced, a long and arduous task. As a result, relatively few New Testament manuscripts would have existed.[35] Therefore, not many members of the early Church would have had direct access to these writings. Further, the level of literacy in this era was low,[36] and so, even if members of the early Church were fortunate enough to come upon some New Testament manuscripts, there was no guarantee that they would be capable of reading them. Given the relative scarcity of the manuscripts and the high level of illiteracy during this era, it is likely that access to the contents of the New Testament manuscripts for most members of the early Church would have been restricted to listening to oral readings from the texts.

Achtemeier finds in the texts of the New Testament pieces of evidence that suggest that the documents were written for just such an

34. Augustine, *Confessions* 6.3.

35. William A. Graham, *Beyond the Written Word: Oral Aspects of Scripture in the History of Religion* (Cambridge: Cambridge University Press, 1987), p. 124; Boomershine, 'Peter's Denial', p. 54; George A. Kennedy, *New Testament Interpretation through Rhetorical Criticism* (Chapel Hill: University of North Carolina Press, 1984), p. 5.

36. Werner H. Kelber, *The Oral and the Written Gospel: The Hermeneutics of Speaking and Writing in the Synoptic Tradition, Mark, Paul, and Q* (Philadelphia: Fortress Press, 1983), p. 17; Jack Goody, *The Domestication of the Savage Mind* (Cambridge: Cambridge University Press, 1977), pp. 152-53; Botha, 'Mute Manuscripts', p. 42.

oral–aural communication. In particular, he cites features of the text designed to guide a hearer in determining when one unit of thought is ending and when another is beginning. These signals of organization include: alliteration;[37] anaphora,[38] that is, statements beginning with the same word or words; parallelism;[39] and inclusio,[40] including the Marcan technique of intercalating stories where one story functions as an inclusio for a second story.[41] Achtemeier finds these features in operation in both narrative and epistolary literature, but sees them as especially necessary in the latter, for letters do not possess the flow of narrative to aid the audience, and they also often contain long and complex arguments.[42]

The foregoing discussion suggests that the New Testament writers wrote with a hearer, rather than a reader, in mind.[43] From a literary-critical perspective, this recognition influences the way in which the 'implied reader' is conceptualized. Since the implied reader is defined as the reader presupposed by the text, and the evidence outlined above suggests that the text presupposes a hearer rather than a reader, then our implied reader is not a 'reader' at all; rather, he or she should be understood as an 'implied hearer'. This understanding, in turn, has some significant implications. Readers, once they have read a given passage, are able to read it over again, flip back to compare it with earlier passages, and even flip forward to see how it fits with the story's outcome. Hearers, on the other hand, do not have the physical words before them; for hearers, the words are not so much objects existing in space as they are events existing in time.[44] Hearers experience words only as they encounter them in sequence, with no way to check back

37. Achtemeier, '*Omne verbum sonat*', pp. 22, 25.
38. Achtemeier, '*Omne verbum sonat*', pp. 21, 23-24.
39. Achtemeier, '*Omne verbum sonat*', p. 24.
40. Achtemeier, '*Omne verbum sonat*', pp. 24-25.
41. Achtemeier, '*Omne verbum sonat*', p. 21.
42. Achtemeier, '*Omne verbum sonat*', pp. 22, 25.
43. Cf. Aune, 'Apocalypse of John', p. 78. The same assertion, but addressing the Gospel of Mark alone, is made by the following scholars: Mary Ann Beavis, 'The Trial before the Sanhedrin (Mark 14.53-65): Reader Response and Greco-Roman Readers', *CBQ* 49 (1987), pp. 581-96 (593); Joanna Dewey, 'Mark as Interwoven Tapestry: Forecasts and Echoes for a Listening Audience', *CBQ* 53 (1991), pp. 221-36 (235); Boomershine, 'Peter's Denial', pp. 53-54.
44. Moore, *Literary Criticism and the Gospels*, p. 86.

other than through mental recall or to check forward other than through anticipation.

Conceptualizing the audience of a narrative work in this way totally changes the way in which the literary-critical endeavour is executed. In place of the audience envisioned by Tannehill later in his career—an audience approaching the text for the second or third or fourth time who is thus armed with a thorough knowledge of the whole narrative—now we have a first-time audience proceeding through the text sequentially without a thorough knowledge of what lies ahead. With this type of literary analysis, the critic is no longer examining the text as a static entity. Rather, the critic is engaging in a dynamic enterprise, following the experience of the audience as they proceed through the narrative. Moore calls this a 'story of reading' which he describes as follows:

> the interpreter, approaching the evangelist's story as if for the first time, narrates a tale of anticipations and reversals, of puzzles, enigmas, and the struggles to solve them, of beliefs and presuppositions challenged and overthrown.[45]

In other words, the interpreter chronicles the ways in which the text impacts the audience at each step throughout the narrative.

Some insights from research into the orientation toward literature of antiquity support this approach as appropriate for the analysis of the narratives of the Gospels. Of Abrams's four orientations toward works of art outlined earlier,[46] the 'pragmatic' orientation dominated during the era in which the New Testament documents were produced.[47] This being the case, the texts of the New Testament should be understood as literature designed to impact its audience. Further, George A. Kennedy notes that the era of the New Testament writings was an age of rhetoric.[48] In contrasting this age of rhetoric to our modern age, Robert M. Fowler writes, 'moderns tend to be preoccupied with *what* is said (story), whereas the ancients were preoccupied with *how* something was said and *how* it affected the hearer (discourse)'.[49] Because this

45. Moore, *Literary Criticism and the Gospels*, pp. 80-81.

46. See p. 33 above.

47. Abrams, *The Mirror and the Lamp*, pp. 20-21, notes that from the late first century BC through the eighteenth century AD, attitudes towards works of art were dominated by a 'pragmatic' orientation.

48. Kennedy, *New Testament Interpretation*, p. 5.

49. Robert M. Fowler, *Let the Reader Understand: Reader-Response Criticism*

strong orientation toward impacting the audience underlies the texts of the New Testament, it follows that, in analyzing these writings, one should use a methodology sensitive to this dimension of the texts.

This approach of presupposing a first-time audience—almost always termed a first-time 'reader'—has been adopted by many biblical literary critics[50] who undertake to analyze the narratives of the Gospels in a more dynamic fashion than their narrative-critical cousins. Further, just as the practitioners of narrative criticism trace their roots to secular literary critics—that is, Booth and Chatman—these audience-oriented literary critics also draw on the works of secular literary critics. By far, the most popular of these has been Wolfgang Iser.

Iser's essay 'The Reading Process: A Phenomenological Approach'[51] lays out his approach. Iser advocates

> the phenomenological theory of art [which] lays full stress on the idea that, in considering a literary work, one must take into account not only the actual text but also, and in equal measure, the actions involved in responding to that text.[52]

and the Gospel of Mark (Minneapolis: Fortress Press, 1991), p. 23 (emphasis original).

50. See, for example, Robert M. Fowler, *Loaves and Fishes: The Function of the Feeding Stories in the Gospel of Mark* (Chico, CA: Scholars Press, 1981); Fred W. Burnett, 'Prolegomenon to Reading Matthew's Eschatological Discourse: Redundancy and the Education of the Reader in Matthew', *Semeia* 31 (1985), pp. 91-109; Richard A. Edwards, *Matthew's Story of Jesus* (Philadelphia: Fortress Press, 1985); Jouette M. Bassler, 'The Parable of the Loaves', *JR* 66 (1986), 157-72; J. Lee Magness, *Sense and Absence: Structure and Suspension in the Ending of Mark's Gospel* (Atlanta: Scholars Press, 1986); Lyle Eslinger, 'The Wooing of the Woman at the Well: Jesus, the Reader and Reader-Response Criticism', *Journal of Literature & Theology* 1 (1987), pp. 167-83; Jeffrey Lloyd Staley, *The Print's First Kiss: A Rhetorical Investigation of the Implied Reader in the Fourth Gospel* (Atlanta: Scholars Press, 1988). The analysis by Moore, *Literary Criticism and the Gospels*, pp. 73-78, of Tannehill, 'Disciples in Mark', finds that this work presupposes a first-time reader, a finding particularly interesting in light of Tannehill's position nine years later in *The Narrative Unity of Luke-Acts: A Literary Interpretation*. I. *The Gospel According to Luke* (Philadelphia: Fortress Press, 1986) (see p. 37 above).

51. Wolfgang Iser, 'The Reading Process: A Phenomenological Approach', in *The Implied Reader: Patterns of Communication in Prose Fiction from Bunyan to Beckett* (Baltimore: The Johns Hopkins University Press, 1974), pp. 274-94; originally published in *New Literary History* 3 (1972), pp. 279-99.

52. Iser, 'Reading Process', p. 274.

In fact, Iser goes so far as to assert that the literary work 'is more than the text, for the text only takes on life when it is realized...The convergence of text and reader *brings the literary work into existence*'.[53] Therefore, unlike a formalist approach—with its focus exclusively on the text as a repository out of which meaning is to be extracted—Iser's approach conceptualizes meaning as coming into existence only upon the interaction of the reader with the text. Therefore, any given text is capable of holding different meanings for different readers.[54]

According to Iser, this possibility of multiple meanings for a given text results from the fact that any literary work is characterized by omissions or gaps that must be filled by the reader. Further, since these gaps will be filled differently by different readers, a variety of realizations will occur.[55] Iser likens this process to star-gazing:

> two people gazing at the night sky may both be looking at the same collection of stars, but one will see the image of a plough, and the other will make out a dipper. The 'stars' in the literary text are fixed; the lines that join them are variable.[56]

This approach to literary analysis, as it has been practised by biblical literary critics, has been called 'reader-response criticism'. However, Stanley E. Porter argues that much of what has gone under this title does not technically qualify as reader-response criticism.[57] Porter's definition of this methodology is extracted from the work of Stanley Fish; Porter chooses Fish's work because of its stature in the development of this approach.[58] Porter sets out five characteristics of reader-response criticism:

> First, reader-response criticism explicitly shifts the centre of authority from the text itself...or the author...to the reader, not an historical first reader or any particular subsequent reader...but a contemporary reader...Second, the reader is involved in a complex interplay with the text, which chronicles his or her struggle to comprehend. Third, meaning

53. Iser, 'Reading Process', pp. 274-75 (emphasis added).

54. Iser, 'Reading Process', p. 280

55. Iser, 'Reading Process', pp. 279-80.

56. Iser, 'Reading Process', p. 282.

57. Stanley E. Porter, 'Why Hasn't Reader-Response Criticism Caught on in New Testament Studies?' *Journal of Literature & Theology* 4 (1990), pp. 278-92 (280).

58. Porter, 'Why Hasn't Reader-Response Criticism Caught on?', p. 279.

> is not a single thing—a propositional truth—but the reader's making and then responding to the text. Fourth, the result of the abandonment of independent meaning is that the meaning which one produces cannot be checked against some objective standard but is the product of a reading strategy. Fifth, those who hold to similar reading strategies constitute 'interpretive communities'.[59]

Fish's position is clearly distinguishable from that of Iser on some points. For example, Iser has no concept of interpretative communities. Further, Porter points out that, while Iser sees the words of a text as relatively stable, with only the gaps between the words to be filled in, Fish holds that the words themselves are open to interpretation.[60] However, on the essential elements of this method, the two critics agree: both hold that meaning does not reside in the text, but rather is created through a reader's interaction with the text, thus resulting in the potential of a different meaning for each different reader approaching a given text.

Porter measures the works of five biblical literary critics who claim to be practitioners of reader-response criticism—Robert Fowler,[61] Norman R. Petersen,[62] Mary Ann Beavis,[63] Jeffrey Lloyd Staley[64] and Alan Culpepper[65]—against his five-point definition, and finds each of them wanting. While his comments on the five critics differ, a common thread runs through all five critiques: each of these scholars has retained a formalist conception of the reader. In other words, Porter finds in each of these scholars a presupposition that the reader's experience of the text is dictated by the text itself or by the author's—presumably the 'implied' author's—intention. Therefore, there is a complete lack of recognition of participation by the reader in the production of meaning, a concept central to reader-response criticism.

It is not surprising to find such a reluctance among biblical literary

59. Porter, 'Why Hasn't Reader-Response Criticism Caught on?'. This summary reflects the position of Stanley Fish later in his career, after he abandoned the position he held earlier. His earlier position will be outlined below at pp. 45-47.

60. Porter, 'Why Hasn't Reader-Response Criticism Caught on?', p. 279.

61. Fowler, *Loaves and Fishes*.

62. Norman R. Petersen, 'The Reader in the Gospel', *Neot* 18 (1984), pp. 38-51.

63. Beavis, 'Trial before the Sanhedrin'.

64. Staley, *Print's First Kiss*.

65. R. Alan Culpepper, *Anatomy of the Fourth Gospel* (Philadelphia: Fortress Press, 1983).

critics to embrace whole-heartedly this reader-response paradigm. Even a cursory glance at the corpus of literary analyses of biblical narratives makes it clear that the agenda of almost all of these works is the utilization of literary theory in the service of exegesis. To put it another way, the ultimate goal of these studies is to determine what the elements of the text say, or, in the case of pragmatic-oriented exegetes, how the elements of the text impact the audience. In either case, the text is understood as a repository of information waiting to be extracted. Reader-response criticism, on the other hand, presupposes that there is nothing absolute in the text waiting to be extracted, for meaning will vary from reader to reader as the interaction of each individual reader with the text results in a different meaning. Therefore, for a discipline dominated by a preoccupation with probing the text for insights hidden therein, it only makes sense that reader-response criticism would not be able to make serious inroads, even among biblical literary critics with a pragmatic orientation.

The present study shares this prevailing preoccupation with probing the text for insights; therefore, a reader-response approach as outlined above is not appropriate. Rather, it is necessary to establish a methodology that utilizes reader-response criticism's dynamic approach to the text—conceiving of a first-time audience proceeding sequentially through the text—while at the same time presupposing that texts do contain meaning to be sought by means of exegesis. For these purposes, Stanley Fish—or, more specifically, 'early' Stanley Fish—is helpful.

The summary of Fish's position outlined above[66] represents his views from the mid-1970s on. Earlier in his career, however, he posited a different understanding of the reading process, as reflected in an essay published in 1970 entitled 'Literature in the Reader: Affective Stylistics'.[67] Fish notes that when one approaches a text, one ordinarily asks such questions as 'what does this sentence mean?' or 'what is it about?' or 'what is it saying?'[68] It is presupposed with this approach that 'meaning is located (presumed to be imbedded) *in* the utterance, and

66. See pp. 43-44 above.

67. Stanley E. Fish, 'Literature in the Reader: Affective Stylistics', in Jane P. Tompkins (ed.), *Reader-Response Criticism: From Formalism to Post-Structuralism* (Baltimore: The Johns Hopkins University Press, 1980), pp. 70-100; originally published in *New Literary History* 2 (1970), pp. 123-62.

68. Tompkins, 'Literature in the Reader', p. 71.

the apprehension of meaning is an act of extraction'.[69] Fish suggests that, instead of asking such questions, one should be asking, 'what does this word, phrase, sentence, paragraph, chapter, novel, play, poem, *do*?'[70] Therefore, the goal of this approach is '*an analysis of the developing responses of the reader in relation to the words as they succeed one another in time*'.[71] What constitutes the 'meaning' of a text? Fish asserts:

> the information an utterance gives, its message, is a constituent of, but certainly not to be identified with, its meaning. It is the experience of an utterance—*all* of it and not anything that could be said about it, including anything I could say—that *is* its meaning.[72]

The position outlined thus far would fit comfortably into the reader-response methodology. However, about halfway through the essay, Fish feels obliged to address the objection that this method of analysis 'leads one away from the "thing itself" in all its solidity to the inchoate impressions of a variable and various reader'.[73] It is in answering this objection that Fish drifts away from a pure reader-response position.

Fish draws on the work of Ronald Wardhaugh from the field of modern linguistics, specifically, the concepts of 'linguistic competence' and 'semantic competence'. For a definition of the former, Fish quotes Wardhaugh: 'the idea that it is possible to characterize a linguistic system that every speaker shares'.[74] Fish then argues:

> If the speakers of a language share a system of rules that each of them has somehow internalized, understanding will, in some sense, be uniform; that is, it will proceed in terms of the system of rules all speakers share. And insofar as these rules are constraints on production—establishing boundaries within which utterances are labeled 'normal', 'deviant', 'impossible', and so on—they will also be constraints on the range, and even the direction, of response; that is, they will make response, to some extent, predictable and normative.[75]

69. Tompkins, 'Literature in the Reader', p. 75 (emphasis original).
70. Fish, 'Literature in the Reader', p. 73 (emphasis original).
71. Fish, 'Literature in the Reader', p. 73 (emphasis original).
72. Fish, 'Literature in the Reader', pp. 77-78 (emphasis original).
73. Fish, 'Literature in the Reader', p. 82.
74. Fish, 'Literature in the Reader', p. 83, quoting Ronald Wardhaugh, *Reading: A Linguistic Perspective* (New York: Harcourt, Brace and World, 1969), p. 60.
75. Fish, 'Literature in the Reader', p. 84.

On the concept of semantic competence, Fish again quotes from Wardhaugh who makes a case for a set of rules that would 'characterize just that set of facts about English semantics that all speakers of English have internalized and can draw upon in interpreting words in novel combinations'.[76] Armed with these two concepts, Fish concludes:

> Obviously, the intersection of the two systems of knowledge would make it possible to further restrict (make predictable and normative) the range of response; so that one could presume (as I have) to describe a reading experience in terms that would hold for all speakers who were in possession of both competences.[77]

By means of this analysis, Fish has succeeded in answering the objection of an uncontrolled variety of responses emerging from a given text. However, in the process, Fish has had to abandon a concept central to reader-response criticism, that is, that a reader brings his or her own individuality to a text, and it is the interaction of reader and text that creates meaning, distinctive to that particular reader. In essence, Fish's analysis in the second half of the essay cancels out the reader-response methodology advanced in the first half; he is forced to admit: 'This [analysis]...commits me to a monistic theory of meaning.'[78] In the end, Fish's position reflects a formalist reliance on the text as the arbiter of meaning.

This resulting position provides a model for the present study. Its radically dynamic orientation fits well with the discussion above on how the prominence of orality in the New Testament era relates to how we conceptualize the Gospel narratives.[79] Further, its formalist orientation suits the agenda of the present study, that is, to probe the texts of Matthew's Gospel related to John the Baptist in search of literary insights. Regarding a name for this approach, its radically dynamic orientation distinguishes it from 'narrative criticism' as defined earlier,[80] and its formalist orientation distinguishes it from 'reader-response criticism'. Further, the name must avoid the term 'reader' since it posits a hearer, rather than a reader, as the audience. Since this approach is so heavily oriented toward following the

76. Fish, 'Literature in the Reader', quoting Wardhaugh, *Reading*, p. 90.
77. Fish, 'Literature in the Reader', pp. 84-85.
78. Fish, 'Literature in the Reader', p. 97.
79. See pp. 37-41 above.
80. See p. 37 above.

experience of the audience as it proceeds through the narrative, it is designated 'audience-oriented criticism'.

Because this study adopts a formalist orientation, it is not concerned with discerning the meaning intended by the original author, that is, the original historical author. Rather, it is concerned with the intentions of the implied author/narrator.[81] This study proceeds sequentially through the text, tracing the narrator's efforts to influence the implied hearer/narratee's[82] experience of the story.

Naturally, this study considers the story level of Matthew's narrative; it is attentive to the plot of the story and to the characters—particularly John the Baptist—who inhabit this story world. However, since this study adopts a pragmatic orientation toward the narrative, it is especially attentive to the discourse level, that is, to the means by which the narrator attempts to impact the narratee. What follows is a sketch of some basic literary concepts pertinent to the analysis of both the story level and the discourse level of a narrative. This sketch does not purport

81. Booth, *Rhetoric of Fiction*, p. 4, points out that most narratives until recent times have been characterized by a reliable narrator; see also Robert Scholes and Robert Kellogg, *The Nature of Narrative* (New York: Oxford University Press, 1966), pp. 264-65. Specifically on the Gospel of Matthew, Jack Dean Kingsbury, *Matthew as Story* (Philadelphia: Fortress Press, 2nd edn, 1988), p. 31, asserts that the narrator of this work is reliable. (Most biblical literary critics hold that the narrators of the Gospels are reliable: Mark Allan Powell, *What is Narrative Criticism?* [Minneapolis: Fortress Press, 1990], p. 26; Elizabeth Struthers Malbon, 'Narrative Criticism: How Does the Story Mean?', in Janice Capel Anderson and Stephen D. Moore [eds.], *Mark and Method: New Approaches in Biblical Studies* [Minneapolis: Fortress Press, 1992], p. 28; but cf. Moore, *Literary Criticism and the Gospels*, pp. 30-34, who demonstrates that J.M. Dawsey [*The Lukan Voice*] posits an unreliable narrator for the Gospel of Luke, though without using the designation 'unreliable narrator'.) By definition, a reliable narrator is in accord with the impled author; therefore, for practical purposes, the terms 'narrator' and 'implied author' can be used interchangeably. In this study, the implied author/narrator will be designated 'the narrator'.

82. Most biblical literary critics also find little or no difference between the implied readers and narratees of the Gospels: Malbon, 'Narrative Criticism', p. 28. Therefore, these terms may also be used interchangeably. As indicated, this study conceptualizes an implied 'hearer' rather than an implied 'reader' (see p. 40 above). Because the term 'implied hearer' is not part of common parlance, it will be avoided. Rather, the term 'narratee' will be used to designate the implied hearer/narratee.

to be exhaustive;[83] rather, it covers only those concepts that are especially relevant to the present study.

One of the main focuses of analysis on the *story level* is 'plot'. However, analysis of plot may take different shapes, the most significant distinction being between plot analysis using a static approach versus a dynamic approach to the text, or, to put it another way, between presupposing a second- or third- or fourth-time audience versus presupposing a first-time audience.

The significance of this distinction is aptly demonstrated by Fowler's analysis of the relationship between Mark's accounts of the feeding of the multitudes on the one hand, and his account of the Last Supper on the other hand.[84] A redaction-critic—presupposing multiple readings of the text, and thus a full knowledge of every detail of the Gospel—would undoubtedly read eucharistic significance into the feeding stories. Fowler, on the other hand, comes to a different conclusion by positing a first-time reader:

> Often the verbal similarities between 6.41, 8.6 [the feedings] and 14.22 [the Last Supper] are noted and used to justify the discovery of 'eucharistic' overtones in the two feeding stories. Regrettably, to argue in this fashion is to stand the gospel on its head. *As the author has structured his work, Jesus' last meal with his disciples in Mark 14 presupposes the earlier feeding stories and not vice versa.* Here we are making a conscious decision to adhere to the internal chronology of the author's story, according to which the last meal is preceded by, and read in the light of, the previous meals in Mark.[85]

Therefore, Fowler's sequential reading of Mark produces a vastly different interpretation than that produced by static readings of the text.

Because the present study constitutes an analysis of a character, John the Baptist, 'characterization' is significant. In an analysis of characterization, it is important to distinguish between the approach of narrative criticism and that of the audience-oriented criticism adopted by this study. As noted above,[86] a narrative-critical methodology presupposes

83. For a thorough discussion of these concepts, see especially Fowler, *Let the Reader Understand*; see also David Rhoads and Donald Michie, *Mark as Story: An Introduction to the Narrative of a Gospel* (Philadelphia: Fortress Press, 1982); Culpepper, *Anatomy of the Fourth Gospel*; Kingsbury, *Matthew as Story*; Powell, *What Is Narrative Criticism?*

84. Fowler, *Loaves and Fishes*.

85. Fowler, *Loaves and Fishes*, pp. 134-35 (emphasis original).

86. See p. 37 above.

multiple readings of a narrative resulting in a full knowledge of every detail in the text. Therefore, a narrative-critical approach to characterization tends to draw together data on a given character from throughout a narrative to produce an integrated portrait of that character. In contrast, the audience-oriented criticism of this study yields a different approach to characterization. Instead of pulling together data from every part of the narrative to produce an integrated portrait of a character, the approach of this study analyzes data on the character in a sequential manner in order to discover how a first-time audience would experience the character at various points in the narrative.

In discussing this type of analysis, John A. Darr stresses that '*character is cumulative*',[87] that is, an audience's experience of a character involves a process in which the image of the character grows and evolves over time as new pieces of information are revealed. Darr demonstrates, with a revealing analysis of the Pharisees in Luke–Acts, how a sequential approach to characterization can yield significantly different interpretations than those emerging from the traditional static approach.[88]

Darr points out that studies using a static approach to characterization have invariably come to two conclusions:

> (1) Luke's Pharisees are a heterogeneous amalgamation of negative *and* positive traits (with the former appearing mostly in the Gospel, the latter in Acts), but that (2) we should weight the positive characterizations more heavily because they indicate editorial 'upgrading' from the way the Pharisees are handled in Luke's sources.[89]

Darr explains that this mixed—as opposed to consistently negative—portrait of the Pharisees results from beginning one's analysis with the

87. John A. Darr, *On Character Building: The Reader and the Rhetoric of Characterization in Luke–Acts* (Louisville, KY: Westminster/John Knox Press, 1992), p. 42 (emphasis original).

88. This analysis constitutes a chapter of *On Character Building*, pp. 85-126; the chapter is entitled 'Observers Observed: The Pharisees and the Rhetoric of Perception'.

89. Darr, *On Character Building*, p. 86. As is readily apparent from the second conclusion, these findings have resulted from redaction-critical, and not literary-critical, analyses of the Pharisees in Luke–Acts. However, Darr notes that literary analyses of Luke–Acts using a static approach have come to the same characterization of the Pharisees; he cites as an example D.B. Gowler, 'A Socio-Narratological Character Analysis of the Pharisees in Luke–Acts' (PhD dissertation; Southern Baptist Theological Seminary, 1989).

data in Acts and then proceeding to the data in Luke. The book of Acts contains a number of passages that depict the Pharisees in at least a neutral, and perhaps even a positive, light (5.34-42; 15.5; 22.3; 23.1-10; 26.5). With this portrayal as background, certain details in the Gospel of Luke pertaining to the Pharisees begin to appear laudable: they are absent from the Passion Narrative; they plot against Jesus, but their plotting does not include efforts to destroy him; they warn Jesus of Herod's desire to kill him; they invite Jesus to be a dinner guest on three separate occasions. Therefore, despite clearly anti-Pharisaic sentiments in the Gospel of Luke—for example, the woes pronounced by Jesus against them—the overall portrait of the Pharisees is, at worst, mixed.[90]

Darr counters this characterization with one resulting from a sequential reading of the narrative, that is, one that first encounters the negative traits in the Gospel and, only after that, witnesses the relatively positive ones in Acts. For Darr, this shift in approach yields a radically different portrait of the Pharisees:

> the Pharisees appear to be more completely and consistently *distanced* (negative) and more complex in terms of their narrative functions than biblical critics have heretofore realized. In this story the Pharisees are consistently drawn as a group character which serves as a *paradigm of imperceptiveness*. Laden with irony, they continuously observe (*paratereo*) Jesus and other agents of God and yet utterly fail to recognize the significance of either the persons and events they see or the messages they hear.[91]

The present study follows Darr's lead in approaching characterization in a sequential manner.

Apart from analysis of the story level of Matthew's narrative, the present study is also attentive to its *discourse level*, that is, the techniques that make up the way in which the story is presented to the audience. For an analysis of a narrative's discourse level, when presupposing a first-time audience proceeding sequentially through the text, the work of Menakhem Perry provides some helpful insights.[92] Actually, Perry specifically states that the process he outlines 'is definitely based

90. Darr, *On Character Building*, pp. 88-89.

91. Darr, *On Character Building*, pp. 86-87 (emphasis original).

92. Menakhem Perry, 'Literary Dynamics: How the Order of a Text Creates its Meanings', *Poetics Today* 1 (1979), pp. 35-64, 311-61; originally published in Hebrew in 1974.

on a second or third reading'.[93] Therefore, at first glance, it appears that Perry's whole approach would be incompatible with the approach of the present study. However, a closer look at Perry's work reveals that such is not the case.

Unlike literary critics such as Tannehill, who posit a second- or third- or fourth-time reader in order to establish a static view of the text,[94] Perry posits a second- or third-time reader only because he feels compelled to do so in order to establish the necessary vantage point from which to solve a problem he has regarding surprises in the text. He explains:

> The reading process described in this article is therefore from the vantage-point of the whole. It is a process of a 'reconstructed first reading'. Only from this vantage-point can one make the selection between relevant and accidental surprises. An actual first reading of a text is a gradual process of selection. The more the construction of the whole nears its completion, the more the reader is able to tell accidental surprises from functional ones.[95]

This problem of distinguishing between relevant and accidental surprises arises in the experience of an 'actual first reading', that is, the reading by an actual reader approaching the text for the first time. Perry feels it necessary to eliminate all accidental surprises from consideration, and he conceptualizes the audience as a second- or third-time reader in order to do so. Perry calls the resulting reading process a 'reconstructed first reading', that is, a first-time reading without accidental surprises. In positing this second- or third-time reader who eliminates all accidental surprises in order to leave only relevant surprises for consideration, Perry is, in essence, describing the experience of an 'implied reader'. Kingsbury defines the 'implied reader' as follows:

> the term 'implied reader' denotes no flesh-and-blood person of any century. Instead, it refers to an imaginary person who is to be envisaged, in perusing Matthew's story, as responding to the text at every point with whatever emotion, understanding, or knowledge the text ideally calls for.[96]

93. Perry, 'Literary Dynamics', p. 59.

94. See p. 37 above.

95. Perry, 'Literary Dynamics', p. 357.

96. Kingsbury, *Matthew as Story*, p. 38, addressing the implied reader of the Gospel of Matthew.

The implied reader, defined in this way, responds ideally to the text at every point. Therefore, he or she feels the impact of relevant surprises, but does not even notice what Perry calls 'accidental surprises', for such so-called 'surprises' are not part of the ideal response intended by the implied author. In the end, then, Perry's 'reconstructed first reading'—that is, a first-time reading with accidental surprises eliminated—is functionally equivalent to a first-time reading by the implied reader, the process underlying the present study. Therefore, Perry's insights can be used in the formulation of the present study's methodology.

Perry's emphasis on the sequential nature of the text is evident in the following passage:

> [The literary text's] verbal elements appear one after another, and its semantic complexes (e.g., scenes, ideas, characters, plot, value-judgments) build up 'cumulatively', through adjustments and readjustments. That a literary text cannot yield its information all at once is not just an unfortunate consequence of the linear character of language. Literary texts may effectively utilize the fact that their material is grasped successively; this is at times a central factor in determining their meanings. The ordering and distribution of the elements in a text may exercise considerable influence on the nature, not only of the *reading process*, but of the *resultant whole* as well: a rearrangement of the components may result in the activation of alternative potentialities in them and in the structuring of a recognizably different whole.[97]

In his discussion of the ordering and distribution of elements in a text, Perry asserts that elements at the beginning of a message hold more weight than subsequent ones, the so-called 'primacy effect'.[98] In support of this assertion, he draws upon two psychological experiments which involve the reading of sets of details to subjects, with the opening details suggesting one conclusion and the closing details suggesting the opposite conclusion. Both experiments find that the opening details hold much more weight in the formulation of a conclusion than do the subsequent opposing details.[99] Perry appeals to these experiments for

97. 'Literary Dynamics', p. 35 (emphasis original). On pp. 40-41, Perry outlines numerous ways in which material can be distributed along the text-continuum in order to affect the reader in various ways.

98. Perry, 'Literary Dynamics', p. 52-53.

99. The first was the work of S.E. Asch, 'Forming Impressions of Personality', *Journal of Abnormal and Social Psychology* 41 (1946), pp. 258-90, cited in Perry, 'Literary Dynamics', pp. 54-55. Asch read out a set of six personality traits—

the light they can shed on how people process information received sequentially. Of course, these experiments are not totally analogous to the reading process presupposed by Perry; he envisions people reading details from a printed page, whereas these experiments involve people having details read to them. Because these experiments involve a hearing audience, they are actually more analogous to the methodology of the present study—which presupposes a first-time hearer as the audience—than to the methodology of Perry. For the purposes of my analysis of John the Baptist in the Gospel of Matthew, the insights derived from these experiments dictate that special attention be paid to the beginning of Matthew's narrative and to its earliest references to John.

Perry is careful to point out that this primacy effect does not produce impressions that necessarily survive the entire literary work:

> rather than being constructed according to the dictates of its initial material a literary text is based on the *tension* between forces resulting from the primacy effect and the material at the *present* point of reading. The primacy effect never works in isolation. If the text intends the effect of its initial stage to prevail throughout, it must keep reinforcing it.[100]

Perry even goes so far as to assert that the primacy effect can be intentionally subverted:

> What happens in a literary text is that the reader retains the meanings constructed initially *to whatever extent possible*, but the text causes them

arranged with positive traits at the beginning and negative traits at the end—to one group, and then read out the same six traits in reverse order to a second group. Perry describes the results as follows: 'Group A saw him primarily as an able person having certain shortcomings which did not, however, overshadow his merits. Group B on the other hand, saw him as a "problematic" person whose abilities were hampered by his difficulties.' The second experiment was conducted by Abraham Luchins, 'Primacy-Recency in Impression Formation', in Carl I. Hovland (ed.), *The Order of Presentation in Persuasion* (New Haven: Yale University Press, 1957), cited in Perry, 'Literary Dynamics', p. 55. In this experiment, two lists of a person's activities were formulated, the first presenting activities generally associated with an extroverted person and the second outlining activities typical of an introverted person. Of those to whom the first and then the second list were read, 78 per cent felt that the person was friendly, while only 18 per cent of those to whom the second and then the first list were read came to the same conclusion. (Of those to whom only the first list was read, 95 per cent saw the person as friendly, while of those to whom only the second list was read, only 3 per cent came to the same conclusion.)

100. Perry, 'Literary Dynamics', p. 57 (emphasis original).

> to be modified or replaced. The literary text, then, *exploits* the 'powers' of the primacy effect, but ordinarily it sets up a mechanism to oppose them, giving rise, rather, to a recency effect.[101]

The present study is attentive to the workings not only of the primacy effect, but also of the recency effect as I proceed through the text of the Gospel of Matthew.

Another interest of Perry is the retrospective action in the reading process. He contends that, while the reading process involves a forward progression sentence by sentence, a reader's mind also undertakes backward activity with earlier material.[102] Perry presents two types of backward activity—the previous material's shedding light on the new material, and the new components' illuminating the earlier ones—but comments almost exclusively on the latter only.[103]

Because Perry's analysis assumes an actual reader, he allows for the possibility of a reader's going back and re-reading earlier passages in response to a text's retrospective action of recalling an earlier text.[104] With this view of the reader, it is not surprising that he specifically states that the process he envisions is based on a second or third reading.[105] However, his comments on retrospective action in the reading process are not dependent on the possibility of multiple readings. Indeed, Iser—whose work on retrospective action is foundational in the world of literary theory—discusses this concept apart from presupposing multiple readings of the text.

Iser describes the mechanics of 'retrospection'—as well as the related concept of 'anticipation'—as follows:

> Whatever we have read sinks into our memory and is foreshortened. It may later be evoked again and set against a different background with the result that the reader is enabled to develop hitherto unforeseeable connections. The memory evoked, however, can never reassume its original shape, for this would mean that memory and perception were identical, which is manifestly not so. The new background brings to light new aspects of what we had committed to memory; conversely these, in turn, shed their light on the new background, thus arousing more complex anticipations.[106]

101. Perry, 'Literary Dynamics', p. 57 (emphasis original).
102. Perry, 'Literary Dynamics', p. 58.
103. Perry, 'Literary Dynamics', pp. 58-61.
104. Perry, 'Literary Dynamics', p. 59.
105. Perry, 'Literary Dynamics', p. 59.
106. Iser, 'Reading Process', p. 278.

From this excerpt, it is evident that Iser understands retrospection primarily as a process in which a later text influences the reader's perception of an earlier text. Note, however, that Iser also speaks of an influence exerted by the earlier text on the reader's understanding of the later text; he asserts that the things committed to memory—that is, the details of the earlier text—'shed their light on the new background'. Therefore, Iser does allow for the possibility that the earlier text could influence the understanding of the later text, though he makes no effort to develop this idea.

Fowler adopts Iser's understanding of retrospection[107] and uses it in his analysis of the Gospel of Mark. Like Iser, Fowler envisions retrospection primarily as a dynamic in which a later text influences the understanding of an earlier text.[108] His analysis of Mark's account of Jesus' trial, however, demonstrates the possibility that an earlier text could influence the understanding of a later text, although he never explicitly articulates this. Fowler writes:

> The priests and elders lose control of themselves and start to abuse the condemned man: 'And some began to spit on him, and cover his face, and to strike him, saying to him, "Prophesy!"' (14.65). 'Prophesy what?' we might ask. The answer is by no means clear...In the instant that Jesus is challenged to 'prophesy!' in the story, the reader realizes that Jesus' most significant prophecy in the Gospel, the prediction of his suffering and death, is in the process of being fulfilled in the story, even though no one in the story takes note of such fulfillment.[109]

According to Fowler, this challenge to prophesy in Mk 14.65 prompts retrospection to earlier passages in which Jesus is seen as prophesying his suffering and death. Further, Fowler explains how these earlier passages influence the implied reader's understanding of this later challenge to prophecy. Therefore, Fowler's analysis of Mk 14.65 illustrates the use of retrospection in prompting the implied reader to draw on earlier texts to enrich the understanding of a later text. The present study identifies the same dynamic in the Matthean narrator's use of John the Baptist.

One concept that is foundational to any discussion of the discourse

107. Fowler, *Let the Reader Understand*, p. 43.

108. See Fowler's discussions on retrospection on pp. 139, 166, 169, 202, 238, 241-42 and 248.

109. Fowler, *Let the Reader Understand*, p. 199.

level of a narrative is 'point of view'. Moore provides a solid definition of this concept:

> Point of view denotes the rhetorical activity of an author as he or she attempts through the medium of a narrator (or more precisely, by an act of narration), and from his or her position within some socially shared system of assumptions, beliefs, and values to impose a story-world upon a reader (or listener).[110]

Among biblical literary critics, the most popular system of analyzing point of view is that of Boris Uspensky as outlined in *A Poetics of Composition*.[111] Uspensky discusses point of view as it is manifested on five different levels or planes: ideological, phraseological, spatial, temporal and psychological.[112]

Concerning point of view on the ideological, or 'evaluative', plane, the main issue is 'whose point of view does the author assume when he evaluates and perceives ideologically the world which he describes'.[113] Uspensky notes that this point of view may be that of the author, or that of the narrator—assuming an unreliable narrator whose ideological point of view is at odds with that of the author—or that of one of the characters, with the possibility of a variety of ideological points of view being present in a given narrative.[114] However, concerning the narrative under investigation in the present study, the Gospel of Matthew, Kingsbury correctly asserts that the implied author adopts a single evaluative point of view—that of God—as normative for the whole narrative.[115] Uspensky rates this type of single, dominating point of view as the simplest, and least interesting, case on the ideological plane,[116] and describes how it works as follows:

110. Moore, *Literary Criticism and the Gospels*, p. 26.

111. Boris Uspensky, *A Poetics of Composition: The Structure of the Artistic Text and Typology of a Compositional Form* (trans. Valentina Zavarin and Susan Wittig; Berkeley: University of California Press, 1973).

112. Uspensky devotes a chapter to each of the ideological, phraseological and psychological planes. However, he deals with both the spatial and temporal planes in one chapter; indeed, he sometimes speaks in terms of the 'spatio-temporal' level. In this study, the spatial and temporal planes are seen as sufficiently distinctive to warrant separate treatments.

113. Uspensky, *Poetics of Composition*, p. 8.

114. Uspensky, *Poetics of Composition*, p. 8.

115. Kingsbury, *Matthew as Story*, p. 34.

116. Uspensky, *Poetics of Composition*, p. 8.

> if some other point of view should emerge, nonconcurrent with the dominant one (if, for example, some facts should be judged from the point of view of one of the characters), this judgment will be reevaluated from the more dominant position, and the evaluating *subject* (the character), together with his system of ideas, will become the *object*, evaluated from the more general viewpoint.[117]

To communicate to the narratee an evaluation of a character's ideological point of view, the narrator may simply declare the evaluation in the form of explicit commentary. Alternatively, the narrator may lead the narratee to identify with, or distance him- or herself from, a given character; in this way, the character is established as positive or negative, and thus as a reliable or unreliable source of the narrator's ideological point of view.

The differentiation of points of view on the phraseological plane is evident in distinctions in speech characteristics. Uspensky describes how point of view on this plane can shift:

> Let us assume that an event to be described takes place before a number of witnesses...Each of the observers may offer his own description of the events; presumably these versions would be presented in the form of direct discourse (in the first person). We would then expect these monologues to be distinct in their particular speech characteristics...
>
> Theoretically, the author, constructing his narrative, may use first one and then another of these various narrations. These narrations, originally assumed to be in direct discourse, may merge and be transposed into authorial speech. Within the authorial speech the shifting from one point of view to another is expressed in different uses of forms from someone else's speech.[118]

Of course, the narrator possesses particular speech characteristics as well. Therefore, characters may have their points of view aligned with, or distanced from, that of the narrator when their speech utilizes, or fails to utilize, speech characteristics of the narrator. This is particularly evident in the use of names,[119] an issue of phraseological point of view that is relevant in the present study.

Point of view on the spatial plane has to do with the spatial relationship between the narrator and the characters in the story. The narrator may first establish a position following one character, but then shift to

117. Uspensky, *Poetics of Composition*, p. 9 (emphasis original).

118. Uspensky, *Poetics of Composition*, pp. 17-18.

119. Uspensky presents a lengthy discussion of 'naming'; see *Poetics of Composition*, pp. 20-32.

positions following other characters in successive episodes; this strategy results in a balanced focus among the various characters. On the other hand, the narrator may maintain a position close to a single character over an extended stretch of the narrative; this strategy has the effect of bestowing a sense of significance on that character. The narrator's choices regarding spatial position are influential for the narratee's experience of the narrative, as this study demonstrates.

The narrator also manipulates spatial point of view through controlling the distance from which the narratee experiences the action of the story.[120] The narrator may narrate one part of a pericope from a distance, thus de-emphasizing those details of the passage. Alternatively, the narrator may draw in close to the action in another part of the pericope—not unlike a movie camera zooming in on one part of a scene—thus emphasizing that part of the passage. The present study analyzes such narrative moves to discern what the narrator wishes to emphasize and de-emphasize.

On the temporal plane, the narrator may manipulate point of view in a number of different ways to influence the narratee's experience of the narrative. Most narratives are narrated from a point subsequent to the final event of the story;[121] the story is related retrospectively with the use of past-tense verbs. Occasionally, however, a narrator may choose a position concurrent with the action of the story by abandoning the past tense in favour of the present tense. Uspensky explains the effect of such a narrative move:

> Each time the present tense is used, the author's temporal position is synchronic—that is, it coincides with the temporal position of his characters...The purpose of this device is to take the [audience] directly into the action of the narrative, and to put him into the same position as that occupied by the characters of the story.[122]

In such a case, the narrator's temporal point of view is internal to the narrative, whereas a narrator who is narrating from the future—looking back at the characters' present—has a temporal point of view that is external to the narrative.[123] This distinction between points of view external and internal to a narrative is significant to a narratee's experi-

120. Norman R. Petersen, '"Point of View" in Mark's Narrative', *Semeia* 12 (1978), pp. 97-121 (112).

121. Chatman, *Story and Discourse*, p. 80.

122. Uspensky, *Poetics of Composition*, p. 71.

123. Uspensky, *Poetics of Composition*, p. 67.

ence of a narrative. An external point of view prompts a sense of estrangement,[124] while an internal point of view brings about a sense of identification.[125] Therefore, a narrator may shift from past to present tense in order to draw the narratee into a position internal to the narrative, where he or she identifies with a certain character, or characters, in the story.

On the temporal plane, the narrator may also cause a deviation from a strict sequential presentation of the events of the story, that is, a divergence of plotted time from story time. The narrator may plot a given episode either before or after it actually occurs in the story-line, thus enhancing the impact of that episode on the narratee. In the present study, this technique is examined in connection with the account of John the Baptist's execution (Mt. 14.1-12).

Also relevant to point of view on the temporal plane is pacing; discourse time may be slower than, the same as, or faster than, story time. Gérard Genette sets out four possible narrative speeds: (1) 'ellipsis', where discourse time halts, but story time continues; (2) 'summary', where discourse time is shorter than story time; (3) 'scene', where discourse time and story time are equal; and (4) 'pause', where story time halts, but discourse time continues.[126] Chatman adds a fifth possibility: 'stretch', where discourse time is longer than story time.[127] In the present study, 'summary' and 'scene' are especially significant for our analysis. Genette points out that summary constitutes 'the 'background' against which scenes stand out'.[128] Therefore, this analysis determines the material in the narrative that the narrator de-emphasizes by reporting it in summary narrative, and the material that the narrator emphasizes by using scene narrative.

Point of view on the psychological plane has to do with the degree to

124. Uspensky, *Poetics of Composition*, p. 131.

125. Uspensky, *Poetics of Composition*, p. 88.

126. Gérard Genette, *Narrative Discourse: An Essay in Method* (trans. Jane E. Lewin; Ithaca, NY: Cornell University Press, 1980), pp. 93-95.

127. Chatman, *Story and Discourse*, pp. 72-73; Genette (*Narrative Discourse*, p. 95) asserts that where discourse time is longer than story time, it is because extra-narrative elements have extended the scene or descriptive pauses have interrupted, and not because the scene has been slowed down, or 'stretched', as Chatman would designate it; therefore, Genette does not include this phenomenon as a separate category.

128. Genette, *Narrative Discourse*, p. 97; Genette makes this comment concerning literature produced up to the end of the nineteenth century.

which the narrator relies on the consciousness of the characters in the story.[129] The narrator may choose to describe a character strictly from the perspective of an outside observer, that is, adopt a point of view external to the character. Alternatively, the narrator may choose a point of view internal to the character. Uspensky describes this as follows:

> behaviour may be described from the point of view of the person himself or from the point of view of an omniscient observer who is permitted to penetrate the consciousness of that person. In this kind of description we find revealed the internal processes (thoughts, feelings, sensory perceptions, emotions) which are not normally accessible to an external observer (who can only speculate about such processes, projecting his own experience onto the external manifestations of someone else's behavior).[130]

Such descriptions from a point of view internal to the character are most often revealed with the use of *verba sentiendi*, that is, verbs such as 'thought', 'felt', 'knew' and 'recognized' which indicate the workings of a character's mind.[131]

According to Uspensky, the effect of a psychological point of view strictly external to a character is a sense of alienation.[132] Of course, this view is based on the study of the modern novel which is characterized by frequent and lengthy descriptions of a character's thoughts and feelings; in the context of the modern novel, the complete absence of any internal descriptions of a major character is noteworthy. Unlike the modern novel, however, the Gospels are characterized by a complete lack of extensive descriptions of what is going on in a character's mind. In fact, the Gospels contain relatively little in the way of any description at all of a character's thoughts and feelings. Therefore, for the analysis of the Gospel narratives, the absence of internal descriptions of a given character should not be interpreted as an attempt by the narrator to alienate the narratee from that character.

On the other hand, since internal descriptions are used so sparingly in the Gospels, their presence when they do occur should be taken as significant. Booth designates these internal descriptions 'inside views', and suggests that use of them has the effect of evoking sympathy from

129. Uspensky, *Poetics of Composition*, p. 81.
130. Uspensky, *Poetics of Composition*, p. 83.
131. Uspensky, *Poetics of Composition*, p. 85.
132. Uspensky, *Poetics of Composition*, p. 94.

the audience.[133] Of course, a single, short inside view will not necessarily have this effect; if an isolated inside view of a given character is clearly at odds with the norms of the narrative, it will have the effect of alienating, as opposed to evoking sympathy from, the audience. However, Booth convincingly demonstrates that prolonged inside views of a character, whether positive or negative, can have the effect of prompting sympathy for that character. He discusses Jane Austen's *Emma* as an example. Booth asserts that if Emma was described only from an external point of view, she would come across as an unpleasant person who evokes no sympathy from the audience; the narrator here presents a heroine with serious faults which lead her to be unkind to a number of other characters. However, Booth points out that most of the story is shown through Emma's eyes, and this sustained inside view results in the audience's hoping for good fortune for her rather than holding her in disdain.[134]

Apart from this sympathy-evoking quality of extensive inside views, even short and isolated inside views are useful to the narrator, for they have the capacity of functioning as powerful tools in the service of characterization in the narrative. Rather than having to be restricted to how characters appear or to what characters say or do, the narrator can also present their thoughts and feelings for the purposes of portraying them in a certain way to the narratee. The narrator is able to engender a sense of affinity with a character through an inside view in harmony with the dominant ideological point of view of the narrative, or a sense of distance through an inside view at odds with that dominant point of view. The present study analyzes inside views to determine their effect on the narratee's experience of the narrative.

This overview of point of view has focused on aspects of this concept that are especially pertinent to the present study.[135] Because this study

133. Booth, *Rhetoric of Fiction*, p. 12.

134. Booth, *Rhetoric of Fiction*, pp. 245-49.

135. Uspensky, *Poetics of Composition*, provides an extensive discussion of point of view, covering numerous aspects of this concept not dealt with here. For an alternative typology of point of view, see Chatman, *Story and Discourse*, pp. 151-58. For discussions of point of view as it pertains to the Gospels, see Janice Capel Anderson, 'Point of View in Matthew: Evidence' (paper presented at the Symposium on Literary Analysis of the Gospels and Acts; Society of Biblical Literature, 21 December 1981); Petersen, '"Point of View" in Mark's Narrative'; James L. Resseguie, 'Point of View in the Central Section of Luke (9.51–19.44)', *JETS* 25 (1982), pp. 41-47; Culpepper, *Anatomy of the Fourth Gospel*, pp. 20-34.

adopts a strictly sequential approach to the narrative, my analysis of point of view is strictly sequential as well; I proceed through the text, noting shifts in point of view on the various planes, and analyzing the significance of these shifts for the unfolding narrative.

Chapter 3

STRUCTURE

For the purposes of structuring the following analysis, the structure of Matthew's Gospel could be used as an organizing principle, if Matthew's Gospel does in fact have a discernible structure. Decades of debate have resulted in a great diversity of suggestions for conceptualizing the structure of Matthew's Gospel, but three stand out from the rest: (1) a structure patterned after the Pentateuch; (2) a chiastic structure; and (3) a tripartite structure formed by the twice-repeated phrase 'From that time Jesus began... '.[1] I will examine each of these proposed structures from the perspective of the audience-oriented critical methodology adopted by the present study, and thus determine if any of them may be used to structure my analysis of John the Baptist in Matthew.

The *Pentateuchal theory* of Matthew's structure was first established

1. A fourth prominent way of conceptualizing the structure of Matthew's Gospel has been through the analysis of Matthew's stance on salvation history. See, for example: Rolf Walker, *Die Heilsgeschichte im ersten Evangelium* (Göttingen: Vandenhoeck & Ruprecht, 1967); Wolfgang Trilling, *Das Wahre Israel: Studien zur Theologie des Matthäus-Evangeliums* (Munich: Kösel, 1968); Georg Strecker, *Der Weg der Gerechtigkeit: Untersuchung zur Theologie des Matthäus* (Göttingen: Vandenhoeck & Ruprecht, 3rd edn, 1971); Hubert Frankemölle, *Jahwebund und Kirche Christi: Studien zur Form- und Traditiongeschichte des 'Evangeliums' nach Matthäus* (Münster: Aschendorff, 1973); William G. Thompson, 'An Historical Perspective in the Gospel of Matthew', *JBL* 93 (1974), pp. 243-62; John P. Meier, 'Salvation History in Matthew: In Search of a Starting Point', *CBQ* 37 (1975), pp. 203-13. However, the focus of these studies is to discern a theological point: Matthew's understanding of salvation history; unlike the works represented in the other three categories, these analyses are not primarily concerned with the demarcation of fixed boundaries between sections making up the structure of the Gospel. For this reason, these studies are not included in the present discussion on the structure of the narrative.

by Benjamin W. Bacon.[2] Bacon points out the way in which Matthew gathers most of his teaching material into five lengthy discourses: (1) the Sermon on the Mount (chs. 5–7); (2) the discourse on mission and martyrdom (ch. 10); (3) the discourse on the Kingdom of Heaven (ch. 13); (4) the discourse on church administration (chap. 18); and (5) the discourse on eschatology (chs. 23–25), with the conclusion of each discourse marked by a variation of the formula: 'And when Jesus finished these sayings…'.[3] In addition, each discourse joins with the narrative section preceding it[4] so that the two sections form a single unit; therefore, the text from ch. 3 to ch. 25 is made up of five 'books' to correspond to the five books of the Pentateuch, with chs. 1–2 acting as a prologue and chs. 26–28 acting as an epilogue.

Bacon's basic premise of the alternation between narrative and discourse sections has been adopted by many scholars. On the other hand, the details of Bacon's analysis have been challenged on numerous fronts,[5] though the present critique will limit itself to only one issue: how Bacon's suggested structure fares from an audience-oriented critical perspective, that is, a perspective presupposing a first-time narratee proceeding sequentially through the text.

Bacon posits the first two chapters of the Gospel as a prologue, with 3.1 marking the beginning of Matthew's first 'book'. For a narratee, proceeding sequentially through the text, to take 3.1 as such a major transition, there needs to be something substantial in the narrative to signal to the narratee that he or she is entering into a new section of the narrative. However, 3.1 contains nothing substantial enough to accomplish this task. As a result, the narratee would not recognize the material following 3.1 as a new section of the narrative.

Once the narratee has gone through the narrative section of Bacon's first book (3.1–4.25) and moves a significant distance into ch. 5, he or

2. Benjamin W. Bacon, 'The "Five Books" of Matthew against the Jews', *Expositor* 15 (1918), pp. 56-66; Bacon's thesis is developed in more detail in his *Studies in Matthew* (New York: Henry Holt, 1930).

3. Cf. Mt. 7.28-29; 11.1; 13.53; 19.1 and 26.1-2.

4. With the Sermon on the Mount: chs. 3–4; with the discourse on mission and martyrdom: chs. 8–9; with the discourse on the Kingdom of Heaven: chs. 11–12; with the discourse on church administration: chs. 14–17; and with the discourse on eschatology: chs. 19–22.

5. For a thorough, but concise, summary of these challenges, see David R. Bauer, *The Structure of Matthew's Gospel: A Study in Literary Design* (Sheffield: Almond Press, 1988), pp. 30-35.

she will undoubtedly notice the shift from narrative to discourse. If the narratee is to take this narrative section and this discourse section together as two parts of the same unit, there needs to be prominent links in the text between these two sections to alert an unsuspecting narratee to this fact. Such links, however, are lacking in the text. Therefore, once the narratee has encountered the concluding formula in 7.28-29 and moves on into the narrative section of Bacon's second book, it is inconceivable that the narratee would recognize the material from 3.1 to 7.29 as a discrete unit.

As the narratee proceeds through the text, the narrative sections will not catch his or her attention; the Gospel began with four straight chapters of narrative, thus conditioning the narratee to expect this type of text throughout. The discourse sections, on the other hand, do stand out because of their distinctive nature. Further, once the narratee has encountered a few of these discourses, it is entirely plausible that he or she will start to notice a pattern, especially since each discourse concludes with the same type of formula. Nevetheless, as in the case of the first discourse, each of these later discourses lacks the requisite clues to signal to the narratee that it is to be taken together with the preceding narrative as a set. Because the narratee does not see each narrative-plus-discourse as a unit, he or she cannot recognize the material from 3.1 through 25.46 as a series of five discrete books. Moreover, while en route, there is no way for the narratee to know that these discourses will number five in the end, and so any thought of a parallel to the Pentateuch simply would never come to mind.

From an audience-oriented critical perspective, Bacon's pentateuchal theory suffers from a fatal flaw: it presupposes a static approach to the text. Bacon's analysis requires the narrative to be an object existing in space, something that can bc examined all at once. Only in this way would Bacon be able to become aware of the details in the text needed to formulate his parallel to the Pentateuch. The adoption of a dynamic approach to the narrative, on the other hand, never allows the narratee to see the whole narrative as an object that can be examined all at once. Because the narratee is limited to a strictly sequential progress through the narrative, without the ability to check back or check forward, he or she would simply never perceive the structure proposed by Bacon.

Various scholars have suggested a *chiastic structure* as the organizing principle of the Gospel of Matthew, though these variations all tend to rely on the alternation of narrative and discourse sections as an underlying premise. Typical of these suggestions is the structure proposed by Peter F. Ellis,[6] which can be diagrammed as follows:

	narrative	*sermon*	*narrative*	*sermon*	*narrative*	*sermon*
A	chs. 1–4					
B		chs. 5–7				
C			chs. 8–9			
D				ch. 10		
E					chs. 11–12	
F						ch. 13
E′					chs. 14–17	
D′				ch. 18		
C′			chs. 19–22			
B′		chs. 23–25				
A′	chs. 26–28					

David Bauer provides a narrative-critical evaluation of the chiastic structures proposed by Ellis and also that proposed by H. Benedict Green.[7] Bauer asserts that, for a chiastic structure to be effective as a literary device, it must be relatively clear and discernible, and, in his opinion, the chiastic structures proposed by Ellis and Green are not. From Bauer's perspective, a chiastic structure for Matthew is not even clear enough for Ellis and Green to be able to agree on basic issues such as how the chiasm achieves its purpose and the location of its central turning point.[8]

In the end, Bauer concludes that Ellis and Green have failed to meet the burden of proof: chiastic structures must be relatively clear

6. Peter F. Ellis, *Matthew: His Mind and his Message* (Collegeville, MN: Liturgical Press, 1974), p. 12. Others who have engaged in chiastic analyses include: Charles H. Lohr, 'Oral Techniques in the Gospel of Matthew', *CBQ* 23 (1961), pp. 403-35; H. Benedict Green, 'The Structure of St. Matthew's Gospel', in Frank L. Cross (ed.), *Studia Evangelica IV: Papers Presented to the Third International Congress on New Testament Studies*. I. *The New Testament Scriptures* (Berlin: Akademie Verlag, 1968), pp. 47-59, though Green partially abandons this suggestion in *The Gospel According to Matthew* (Oxford: Oxford University Press, 1975); H.J. Bernard Combrink, 'The Structure of the Gospel of Matthew as Narrative', *TynBul* 34 (1983), pp. 61-90.

7. Bauer, *Structure of Matthew's Gospel*, p. 40; Bauer examines Green's ideas as they stood in 1968, but Green had already partially abandoned those ideas by the time Bauer wrote this critique; see note 6 above.

8. Bauer, *Structure of Matthew's Gospel*, p. 40.

and discernible, and each of these scholars has simply failed to supply the evidence necessary to make his case. Yet it is interesting to note that, in evaluating Ellis and Green in this way, Bauer does not preclude the possibility of a chiastic structure for the Gospel of Matthew. From an audience-oriented critical perspective, is a chiastic structure for Matthew's narrative, in fact, a possibility? Could a first-time hearer—proceeding sequentially through the text without the capacity of checking back or checking forward—grasp a chiastic structure encompassing the whole narrative? I shall use Ellis's suggested structure for the purposes of testing this out.

The narratee begins the journey through the Gospel with passage after passage of narrative text, a narrative flow that is interrupted by a discourse beginning in ch. 5. By the time the narratee finishes this lengthy speech and continues onto the narrative of ch. 8, would he or she recognize the material already covered as two discrete units, each with its own themes, and this new narrative material as a third? Such is perhaps conceivable. On the other hand, it is just as conceivable that the narratee would understand this new narrative material as nothing more than a resumption of the narrative interrupted by the discourse, and not as a third discrete unit in the text. Further, as the narratee continues to go through narrative (ch. 8–9), and then discourse (ch. 10), and then narrative (chs. 11–12), and then discourse (ch. 13), he or she could perhaps see in this material a series of discrete units, as Ellis suggests. On the other hand, the narratee could just as well understand the whole of the text up to this point as one continuous narrative which is interrupted by a number of discourses. The foregoing would indicate that, regarding Ellis's treatment of the material up through ch. 13, the jury is still out. Regarding the material beyond ch. 13, however, there is no doubt as to the jury's ultimate verdict.

According to Ellis, the discourse of ch. 13 represents the central turning point of the chiastic structure, after which each new section of the text matches, in reverse order, the sections preceding ch. 13. However, from the perspective of a first-time narratee proceeding sequentially through the text, this suggestion is problematic, for there is nothing in ch. 13 to signal to the narratee that the central turning point of the Gospel has been encountered. This, in itself, is not fatal for Ellis's case; if it can be shown that the following section contains markers prominent enough to alert an unsuspecting narratee to the fact that this new section matches the one immediately preceding the discourse of ch. 13—thus rendering this discourse a turning point in the Gospel—Ellis's theory has a chance for survival. Unfortunately for Ellis, the text does not contain markers prominent enough to accomplish this task.

Even if we assume that the narratee could somehow recognize such a match, adoption of Ellis's theory places upon the narratee expectations that are beyond all possibility. As the narratee proceeds through the narrative section of chs. 14–17 and into the discourse of ch. 18, he or she is now expected to recognize this discourse as a match for the fourth last section encountered, all without being able to check back. Further, with each successive section, the narratee is expected to make the match with a previous section even farther in the recesses of his or her memory: clearly an impossible task.

A chiastic structure of the magnitude proposed here requires the narratee to recognize connections between sections that grow progressively farther and farther apart, the last set separated by a staggering 22 chapters! Clearly, this theory necessitates the ability to view the whole narrative at one time. The approach adopted by the present study, however, precludes such a viewing. It presupposes a narratee who has a clear view of only the most recently encountered material, with a more nebulous mental image of what precedes that, and an even more nebulous mental image of material farther back still. For this reason, the narratee would not be capable of matching a new section with a previous one any significant distance back in the narrative, a capacity essential for the conception of a chiastic structure that encompasses the entire narrative. This is not to say that a dynamic approach to the narrative allows for no chiastic structures at all. The narrator may arrange a certain number of lines, sentences, or even paragraphs in such a way as to lead the narratee to perceive a chiasm.[9] However, it is not reasonable to posit a narrator who arranges all of the details of the narrative to form a single gigantic chiastic structure, and a narratee—proceeding

9. See, for example, the chiasm in Mt. 7.6:

A Do not give what is holy to dogs
  B And do not throw your pearls before swine
  B′ Or they will trample them under foot
A′ And turn and maul you

sequentially through the text—who grasps the significance of the arrangement.

While the theory of a *tripartite structure* for the Gospel of Matthew has been suggested by many scholars,[10] its most prominent proponent has been Jack Dean Kingsbury. Back in the mid-1970s, Kingsbury used redaction criticism to support this position.[11] He notes the use of the formula ἀπὸ τότε ἤρξατο [ὁ] Ἰησοῦς in 4.17 and 16.21,[12] and asserts that 'Matthew, by combining the phrase *apo tote* with the verb *archomai*, has succeeded in creating an expression that strongly denotes the beginning of a new phase in the "life of Jesus"'.[13] Further, after arguing for 1.1 not to be understood as the title for the whole Gospel, but rather as the superscription for the first section of the Gospel,[14] Kingsbury posits a structure for the Gospel which can be outlined as follows: 'the person of Jesus Messiah (1.1–4.16), the proclamation of Jesus Messiah (4.17–16.20), and the suffering, death, and resurrection of Jesus Messiah (16.21–28.20)'.[15] With his transition from redaction criticism to literary criticism, Kingsbury retained his position on a tripartite structure for the Gospel of Matthew, though he has not written a major work defending this position from a literary-critical perspective.[16] That task has been taken up by David Bauer.[17]

Bauer states his objectives as follows: '(a) to determine the major units and sub-units within the Gospel, and (b) to identify the structural relationships within and between these units'.[18] To accomplish these tasks, Bauer focuses on certain rhetorical features, or compositional relationships, of the text. In an introductory chapter, he provides a brief description of several such compositional relationships: repetition,

10. See Bauer, *Structure of Matthew's Gospel*, p. 153 n. 37, for a list of scholars who have adopted this tripartite structure.

11. Jack Dean Kingsbury, *Matthew: Structure, Christology, Kingdom* (Philadelphia: Fortress Press, 1975).

12. Kingsbury, *Structure, Christology, Kingdom*, p. 7.

13. Kingsbury, *Structure, Christology, Kingdom*, p. 8.

14. Kingsbury, *Structure, Christology, Kingdom*, pp. 9-11.

15. Kingsbury, *Structure, Christology, Kingdom*, p. 25.

16. Kingsbury has outlined this position in literary-critical terms, such as in his section on 'The Structure of Matthew and its View of the History of Salvation', in *Matthew as Story* , pp. 40-41.

17. Bauer, *Structure of Matthew's Gospel*.

18. Bauer, *Structure of Matthew's Gospel*, p. 13.

contrast, comparison, causation and substantiation, climax, pivot, particularization and generalization, statement of purpose, preparation, summarization, interrogation, inclusio, interchange, chiasm, and intercalation.[19] However, in his treatment of the text itself, Bauer uses only a few of these—repetition, contrast, comparison, causation, particularization, climax, and inclusio—and even admits that the findings of two whole chapters, one on 'Repetition of Comparison' and the other on 'Repetition of Contrast', concern themes repeated throughout the Gospel, and so have no direct bearing on the divisions within the Gospel.[20]

Bauer's basic position on the structure of Matthew's narrative emerges from an analysis which he terms: 'repetition of particularization and climax with preparation and causation'.[21] Bauer asserts that 1.1, 4.17 and 16.21 represent general statements, or superscriptions, with each particularized in the text following it; this results in three sections, each initiated by a statement indicating the nature of its content, and each building toward a climax near its conclusion. Further, the first section acts as preparation for the second, while the second provides causation for the third.

With this analysis, Bauer concludes with the same tripartite structure as that emerging out of Kingsbury's redaction-critical work, but now with the support of literary-critical concepts. However, it remains to be seen if this structure can stand up under the scrutiny of the particular literary-critical approach adopted by the present study. Would a narratee, starting from the beginning and proceeding sequentially through the text, recognize 1.1, 4.17 and 16.21 as superscriptions, or headings, and the text following each as particularization of the themes contained in that heading?

The opening verse of the Gospel—'The book of the genealogy of Jesus Christ, Son of David, Son of Abraham'—does possess the nature of a heading, and so could very well be taken as such by the narratee. Nevertheless, this verse does not contain sufficient clues to signal to the narratee that this statement constitutes the heading of an initial section of the narrative only, as opposed to the heading of the narrative as a whole. Further, as the narratee continues past 1.1 and into the following

19. Bauer, *Structure of Matthew's Gospel*, pp. 13-19.
20. Bauer, *Structure of Matthew's Gospel*, p. 138.
21. Bauer, *Structure of Matthew's Gospel*, pp. 73-108.

narrative, he or she would undoubtedly notice, throughout the early chapters of the Gospel, particularization of the themes of 1.1, as Bauer asserts. But again, there is nothing to inform the narratee that this particularization is peculiar to an initial section of the narrative alone; from the perspective of a narratee who has experienced only the early chapters of the narrative, this particularization of the themes of 1.1 could very well be a feature of the whole Gospel.

Upon reaching 4.17, would the narratee recognize a transition into a new section? Admittedly, the content of 4.17 does indicate a transition; however, the narratee would not necessarily view this as a transition into a new section of the Gospel. Narratives such as this are expected to contain transitions, and clearly not every transition constitutes the demarcation of a new section in the structure of the narrative. Therefore, in the absence of some feature that causes this transition to stand out, it would not be taken by the narratee as significant. Of course, advocates of the tripartite structure theory could argue that this transition does contain just such a feature: a striking similarity to the transition in 16.21. However, because our narratee is defined as a first-time audience proceeding sequentially through the text, this striking similarity is irrelevant, for when the narratee encounters the transition in 4.17, he or she is totally unaware of this later transition's existence. As a result, the narratee would not see the transition in 4.17 as exceptional, and so would have no reason to take 4.17 as a heading of a new section. Therefore, as the narratee passes through 4.17 and into the following narrative, he or she would not recognize elements in the text as particularization of 4.17, simply because the theme of 4.17 has not been impressed upon the narratee as significant enough to warrant particularization.

This critique of Bauer's position demonstrates the basic incompatibility between his approach and the methodology adopted by the present study. In contrast to this study's dynamic approach to the narrative, Bauer utilizes a static approach, one that presupposes the ability to view the whole narrative at one time. Bauer's appropriation of this approach is evident in his description of literary criticism as a method that 'focuses upon the form of the final work as a literary *object*'.[22]

This is also evident in the way he uses data from the Gospel in support of points that he makes. For example, as evidence of Matthew's

22. Bauer, *Structure of Matthew's Gospel*, p. 12 (emphasis added).

particularization of the theme 'Christ' in the first section of the narrative, Bauer asserts: 'The fulfillment quotations which cluster in this material point to Jesus as the Christ who forms the climax of and gives meaning to salvation history.'[23] For Bauer, the existence of this clustering of fulfilment quotations here, in contrast to their isolated occurrences later in the narrative, is to be taken as significant for the purposes of signalling to the audience that particularization is taking place. It should be noted, however, that, while a narratee proceeding sequentially through the text would undoubtedly notice these fulfilment quotations, he or she would not necessarily see them as being clustered here in the opening of the narrative. The narratee is not aware at this point that these fulfilment quotations appear much more sparsely later in the narrative; for all the narratee knows, these quotations continue at this rate throughout the entire narrative. Only a static approach to the narrative would equip the narratee with an awareness that the concentration of fulfilment quotations being experienced here in the text is unique to the early chapters of the Gospel.

As further evidence of Matthew's particularization of the theme 'Christ' in the first section of the narrative, Bauer states: 'John the Baptist refers to Jesus as "the coming one" (3.11), meaning the Christ (11.2).'[24] Would the narratee necessarily see this designation 'the coming one' in 3.11 as referring to 'the Christ'? It is true that the narrator's crafting of 11.2-3 does indicate that John the Baptist uses the designation 'the coming one' for the Christ. However, when the narratee comes across this designation in 3.1, he or she is not aware that John uses it for the Christ, simply because the contents of 11.2-3 have not yet been encountered. Again, only by means of a static approach to the narrative would the narratee be able to read into 3.11 John's identification of 'the coming one' with the Christ in 11.2-3.

To summarize, Bauer's static approach to the narrative allows him to examine all of the data of the whole Gospel in service of his analysis of any given passage. In fact, his central thesis of 'superscriptions particularized in the following text' is premised on the ability to do just that. With the whole text of the Gospel available from the outset, 1.1, 4.17 and 16.21 could be taken as the headings of three sections, each lying open to the observer who is able to scan back and forth over their

23. Bauer, *Structure of Matthew's Gospel*, p. 76.

24. Bauer, *Structure of Matthew's Gospel*, p. 76.

contents, searching for examples of particularization of each section's themes.

On the other hand, the narratee presupposed by the present study is limited to a strictly sequential progress through the narrative, and so does not have the vantage point of the text presupposed by Bauer; as a result, he or she is not able to see the structuring features that Bauer sees. In fact, it is questionable whether a narratee, proceeding sequentially through a narrative, is ever able to discern a structure that encompasses a whole narrative, such as the three reviewed in this study. Robert C. Tannehill addresses this issue as follows:

> The outline of a Gospel has...been a subject of frequent study. This usually results in a topical outline with neat divisions. Such an outline may be appropriate to a well-constructed essay, but it is not necessarily appropriate to a narrative. There are special aspects of *narrative* composition which biblical scholars will continue to ignore if there is not greater awareness of how stories are told and how they communicate.[25]

All such proposed outlines, including the three examined here, emerge from studies that presuppose full knowledge of every detail of the narrative from the outset. Indeed, the very concept of 'structure' supposes an object with discernible parts. In contrast, the dynamic approach adopted by the present study does not envision a narrative as an object to be observed in space, but rather as an event. This approach focuses on the efforts of the narrator to influence the narratee's experience as he or she encounters detail upon detail in the flow of the narrative.

Certainly, the narrator can—and does—employ structuring devices as part of a full array of narrative tools used to bring about various effects upon the narratee. However, the structures formed by such devices are limited in scope to that which the narratee can readily notice while proceeding sequentially through the text.[26] Proposed structures for the entire text of Matthew are of a significantly different

25. Tannehill, 'Disciples in Mark', p. 387 (emphasis original). These comments reflect Tannehill's position while still an advocate of a dynamic, as opposed to a static, approach to the text; later in his career, he would adopt a static approach to the text, as reflected in his *Gospel According to Luke*, p. 6.

26. For example, in Mt. 5, the narrator concludes a beatitude in v. 3 with the words ὅτι αὐτῶν ἐστιν ἡ βασιλεία τῶν οὐρανῶν, and, after several other beatitudes, concludes an eighth with exactly the same wording; in this way, the narrator forms an inclusio, a structuring device that spans less than 75 words.

type, for they exceed what a narratee, proceeding sequentially through the text, can be reasonably expected to comprehend. For these reasons, it is concluded that, from an audience-oriented critical perspective, the text of Matthew's narrative does not contain an overarching structure that can be laid out in outline form, such as a Pentateuchal structure, a chiastic structure or a tripartite structure. The present study, lacking such an outline around which to organize its analysis, commences simply from the beginning of the narrative and examines, in sequence, each passage relevant to an understanding of the role that John the Baptist plays in the narrative of Matthew.

Part II

Exegesis

The first mention of John the Baptist in the Gospel of Matthew does not occur until the account of his ministry of preaching and baptizing as presented in Chapter 3. I cannot, however, simply begin my analysis at that point in the text; by the time the narratee encounters that passage, he or she has already been exposed to two complete chapters of narrative details, and this exposure cannot help but influence the narratee's experience of the first passage on John the Baptist.[1] The material in the first two chapters of the narrative acts as pre-information for my analysis of John, and this pre-information must be examined in order to determine what the narratee carries into his or her encounter with John.

1. Cf. Dorothy Jean Weaver, *Matthew's Missionary Discourse: A Literary Critical Analysis* (Sheffield: JSOT Press, 1990) p. 31.

Chapter 4

PRE-INFORMATION

As noted in Chapter 2, the implied author/narrator of Matthew adopts a single, dominating ideological point of view as normative for the narrative. Because the narrative contains a number of different ideological points of view, the narrator needs some way of communicating to the narratee which of these are aligned with the normative ideological point of view of the narrative and which are not. Therefore, perhaps the single most important task undertaken by the narrator in the opening chapters of the Gospel is the conditioning of the narratee to be able to discern between reliable and unreliable sources of the narrator's own normative ideological point of view.

The narrator begins this task in the opening verse of the Gospel: Βίβλιος γενέσεως Ἰησοῦ Χριστοῦ υἱοῦ Δαυὶδ υἱοῦ Ἀβραάμ (1.1). With this verse, the narrator clearly establishes Jesus as the protagonist of the story. Having established this fact, it is tempting to conclude further that Jesus' status as protagonist automatically qualifies him as a reliable source of the narrator's ideological point of view. However, such is not the case, for it is possible for a narrator to cast an unreliable character as the protagonist of a story.[1] Therefore, it is necessary to examine the narrator's treatment of Jesus in these opening chapters to determine whether the narrator establishes Jesus as a reliable protagonist or not.

As we have just seen, the narrator's treatment of Jesus begins in the opening verse of the Gospel with an ascription to him of the designations 'Messiah', 'Son of David' and 'Son of Abraham'. Each of these designations portrays Jesus in a very positive light, as a significant figure in his people's history. Further, the following genealogy (1.2-16)

1. For example, in Charles Dickens's *A Christmas Carol*, Ebenezer Scrooge is the protagonist, yet for most of the story his ideological point of view does not reliably reflect that of the implied author.

enhances Jesus' significance in this history; the genealogy has Abraham as its first entry and Jesus as its final entry, thus depicting Jesus as the culmination of Israel's history. Through this positive depiction of Jesus right at the outset of the narrative, the narrator begins the process of conditioning the narratee to perceive Jesus as a reliable source of the narrator's own ideological point of view, a process that Booth terms the conferral of the 'badge of reliability'.[2]

The narrator continues this process in the material following the genealogy with a series of formula quotations, each introduced with a variation of 'This took place in order that what had been spoken by the Lord through the prophet might be fulfilled'.Therefore, the narrator uses these formula quotations to present Jesus as fulfilling the following prophecies: (1) the circumstances surrounding Jesus' conception fulfil the prophecy cited in 1.23; (2) the flight to Egypt fulfils the prophecy cited in 2.15; and (3) the move to Nazareth fulfils the prophecy cited in 2.23.[3]

It should be noted, however, that the mere citation of a character's fulfilling prophecy does not necessarily establish that character as a reliable source of the narrator's ideological point of view; the nature of the prophecy fulfilled is crucial in making a determination on reliability. For example, in 2.17-18, Herod's slaughter of the children in and around Bethlehem is cited as fulfilling prophecy. This operates toward establishing Herod as a negative character, and thus as an unreliable source of the narrator's ideological point of view. In contrast, the citations in the first two chapters related to Jesus as fulfilling prophecy do not reflect negatively on Jesus at all; in fact, the first two—Jesus as 'Emmanuel' (1.23) and Jesus as God's son (2.15)—reflect very positively on him. As a result, Jesus' participation in fulfilling prophecy operates toward establishing him as a positive character. Therefore, we have further efforts by the narrator early in the narrative to establish Jesus as a reliable source of the narrator's ideological point of view.

Depicting Jesus in this way provides the narrator with a powerful

2. Booth, *Rhetoric of Fiction*, p. 8.

3. A fourth formula quotation in this section of the narrative—Herod's slaughter of the children of Bethlehem as fulfilling the prophecy quoted in 2.18—does not cite Jesus as fulfilling prophecy. Whether 2.5-6 qualifies as a fifth formula quotation is debated; see W.D. Davies and Dale C. Allison, Jr, *A Critical and Exegetical Commentary on the Gospel According to Saint Matthew* (3 vols.; Edinburgh: T. & T. Clark, 1988), I, p. 241.

tool for influencing the narratee's experience of the narrative. Once the narrator has succeeded in establishing Jesus as a reliable source of the narrator's own ideological point of view, then the narrator's options for communicating ideologically with the narratee are dramatically increased. In addition to the use of explicit commentary as a means for communicating his own ideological point of view, the narrator may now use Jesus as a mouthpiece for accomplishing this task. This, in turn, is significant for the present study for, in attempting to discern the narrator's ideological point of view on John the Baptist, Jesus' words with and about John can now be taken as reliable reflections of that point of view. Further, John's own ideological point of view can be measured against that of Jesus as a means of determining whether John is a reliable or unreliable source of the narrator's ideological point of view.

Besides the task of conditioning the narratee to be able to make judgments as to the reliability of the characters in the story, the narrator also uses these opening chapters, and particularly the opening verse of the Gospel, to establish his own phraseological point of view on the name of the story's protagonist: 'Jesus', 'Messiah', 'Son of David' and 'Son of Abraham'. Having established this phraseological point of view, the narrator is able to use nomenclature throughout the rest of the narrative as a way of influencing the narratee into identifying with some characters and feeling alienated from others. For example, by having a character use one of the designations presented in 1.1, the narrator creates an alignment of that character's point of view with his own—the normative point of view of the narrative—thus arousing within the narratee a sense of affinity with that character.[4] On the other hand, a character's consistent use of designations other than those established as the narrator's own phraseological point of view has the effect of arousing within the narratee a sense of distancing from that character. The present study examines John the Baptist's phraseological point of view as it pertains to the naming of Jesus in order to determine what effect this has on the narratee's experience of John.

4. A character's use of one of these designations would not bring about an alignment of the character's and the narrator's points of view if the context—for example, a context of irony—clearly indicates that such is not in accord with the intentions of the narrator.

Chapter 5

JOHN: ALIVE AND WELL

The Introduction of John

At the beginning of ch. 3, the narratee witnesses the appearance of a new character: 'In those days, John the Baptist appeared in the wilderness of Judea' (3.1). The way in which the narrator presents John is striking, for, up to this point in the narrative, the narrator has hardly ever attached titles to characters' names as he has done here.[1] The infrequency of this practice suggests that the narrator reserves the bestowal of titles for situations where the content of the title contributes significantly to the characterization of the character so designated.

Here in 3.1, the narrator prompts the narratee to anticipate that John's significance in the story will be connected with a ministry of baptism. As the narratee begins to proceed through this section of the narrative, however, he or she does not find John executing a ministry of baptism. Rather, the narratee finds a preacher of repentance; John is depicted as proclaiming the message 'Repent, for the Kingdom of Heaven has drawn near' (3.2). Therefore, in the first two verses of ch. 3, the narrator sends the narratee mixed signals. On the one hand, the narrator leads the narratee to expect to see John's engaging in a ministry of baptism only to withhold that picture of John in favour of one showing John as a preacher of repentance. What does the narrator accomplish through this narrative move? By creating the expectation of seeing John as baptist but then withholding fulfilment of this expectation, the narrator builds within the narratee a sense of anticipation. Therefore, when the narratee finally does encounter the passage focusing on John as baptist, it will have a greater impact on the narratee, for he or she will

1. Apart from the triple ascription of titles to Jesus in the opening verse of the narrative, titles have been attached to names on only three occasions: 'King' to 'David' in 1.6, and 'King' to 'Herod' in 2.1 and 2.3.

encounter it with a sense of anticipation. The narrator's crafting of the narrative in this way indicates that the narrator holds the passage that finally does depict John as baptist to be of great importance.

The opening verses of ch. 3 exhibit some significant narrative moves by the narrator on the spatial plane. The first two verses of ch. 3 consist of one sentence with a main clause followed by two participial phrases. The main clause reads, 'John the Baptist appeared in those days...'; with this clause, the narrator begins this account of John with a very general picture, one bereft of spatial bearings.[2] With the first participial phrase, the narrator provides John with a spatial context: '...preaching in the wilderness of Judea...'. To this point, however, John remains a lone figure preaching off in the distance in a vast wilderness area. With the second participial phrase, the narrator draws considerably closer to the lone figure, for the narratee is now close enough to John to hear his actual words: 'Repent for the Kingdom of Heaven has drawn near' (3.2).

To summarize, in these two verses, the narrator begins his presentation of John by depicting him with no spatial context, and then provides John with a spatial context far off in the distance, and then draws in on John close enough to hear some of his words. Note, however, that only a summary of his message is given at this point; from the perspective of point of view on the spatial plane, the narrator has drawn in on John close enough to enable the narratee to hear the gist of his message, but not yet close enough to hear any more than that.

By drawing in on John step by step in this way, the narrator leads the narratee to expect one more step and an actual encounter with John. Again, however, the narrator sets up an expectation only to withhold its fulfilment; the narrator leads the narratee step by step toward an encounter with John, but then holds the narratee back just as he or she is on the verge of the encounter. By forcing the narratee to wait for the fulfilment of this expectation, the narrator builds on the sense of anticipation already initiated through the designation of John as baptist followed by the withholding of a depiction of him fulfilling that role, as noted above.

In place of an actual encounter with John, the narrator inserts a block

2. Cf. the introduction of the Magi (2.1): to describe the appearance of the Magi, the narrator uses the same verb (παραγίνομαι) as that used to describe the appearance of John, but also includes two prepositional phrases which specify that the Magi came 'from the east' and 'to Jerusalem'.

of material introduced by the conjunction γάρ that signals to the narratee entry into an explanatory note.[3] This note begins with a citation of John as fulfilling a prophecy regarding the way-preparer of the Lord:

> The voice of one crying out in the wilderness:
> 'Prepare the way of the Lord,
> Make straight his paths' (3.3).

Because the contents of the cited prophecy are clearly positive in nature, this assertion by the narrator of John's fulfilling this prophecy serves to begin the process of establishing John as a positive character, and thus a reliable source of the narrator's ideological point of view.[4] In addition, this fulfilment quotation impresses on the narratee the theme of John as the forerunner of Jesus. Further, because this theme is presented by means of a fulfilment quotation—an assertion that God's word through a prophet has now been fulfilled—it makes an exceptionally strong impression on the narratee. Clearly, the narrator has plans to develop this theme later in the narrative.

The narrator continues this explanatory note with a description of John's clothing and diet (3.4). An analysis of this verse from the perspective of point of view on the temporal plane suggests that the narrator does not hold the information contained in it to be especially important; this information is presented in summary narrative, as opposed to scene narrative, thus indicating that it is to be considered mere background material.[5] Nevertheless, this information does have a role to play in the development of the narrative, and so must be examined.

Regarding John's clothing, the narrator states, 'John had a garment of camel's hair and a leather belt around his waist' (3.4). Many commentators see in this verse a clear allusion to the description of Elijah in 2 Kgs 1.8.[6] It is true that the reference to John's belt matches the

3. See Fowler, *Let the Reader Understand*, pp. 92-98, for a discussion of parenthetical γάρ clauses as they are used in the Gospel of Mark.

4. Cf. the discussion on the narrator's similar treatment of Jesus in the opening chapters of the Gospel, pp. 78-80, above.

5. See the discussion on scene versus summary narrative on p. 60, above.

6. For example, Daniel J. Harrington, *The Gospel of Matthew* (Collegeville, MN: Liturgical Press, 1991), p. 51; Frederick Dale Bruner, *Matthew: A Commentary* (2 vols.; Dallas: Word Books, 1990 [1987]), I, p. 72; Francis W. Beare, *The Gospel According to Matthew* (Peabody, MA: Hendrickson, 1981), p. 90; David Hill, *The Gospel of Matthew* (Grand Rapids: Eerdmans, 1972), p. 91.

reference to Elijah's belt in the second half of 2 Kgs 1.8.[7] Unfortunately, the reference to the garment of camel's hair in Mt. 3.4 does not appear to match the description of Elijah as a 'hairy man' in conventional English translations of 2 Kgs 1.8.[8] However, Gwilyn H. Jones points out that the Hebrew of 2 Kgs 1.8 could be rendered, 'a man with garment of hair'.[9] Jones writes:

> In support of this latter kind of interpretation, reference can be made to the importance attached to Elijah's mantle (1 Kg. 19:19; 2 Kg. 2:8, 13ff.), and to later allusions implying that such a garment was one of the prophetic insignia.[10]

With this interpretation, both halves of the depiction of John in Mt. 3.4 match the two halves of the depiction of Elijah in 2 Kgs 1.8. This being the case, it is evident that the narrator is using this description of John to intimate an identification between John and Elijah. This identification, however, is not developed at this point in the narrative; the narrator gives just a hint of it here to prepare the narratee for a more thorough treatment of it later in the narrative.

Regarding John's diet, the narrator states that 'his food was locusts and wild honey'. Unlike the description of John's clothing, these words do not constitute an allusion to an Old Testament passage. Like the description of John's clothing, however, the significance of these words does not lie solely within the confines of this passage. The narrator does present this description of John's diet to fill out this introduction of John by depicting him as a person who practised subsistence living in the wilderness.[11] At the same time, the narrator gives this description to provide the narratee with information that will help him or her to interpret a passage later in the narrative.[12]

7. Cf. ζώνην δερματίνην περὶ τὴν ὀσφὺν αὐτοῦ (Mt. 3.4) with ζώνην δερματίνην περιεζωσμένος τὴν ὀσφὺν αὐτοῦ (2 Kgs 1.8 LXX).

8. For example, NASB, NEB, NRSV and the Tanakh.

9. Gwilyn H. Jones, *1 and 2 Kings* (2 vols.; Grand Rapids: Eerdmans, 1984), II, p. 378. Modern English translations that adopt this interpretation include RSV, JB, NJB, NAB and NIV.

10. Jones, *1 and 2 Kings*, II, p. 378; Jones finds Old Testament support for his second point in Zech. 13.4.

11. Cf. Hill, *Matthew*, pp. 90-91; Robert H. Gundry, *Matthew: A Commentary on his Literary and Theological Art* (Grand Rapids: Eerdmans, 1982), p. 45; Harrington, *Matthew*, p. 51.

12. See the treatment of Mt. 11.18 on p. 124 below.

After the narrator's explanatory note citing John's fulfilling prophecy (v. 3) and describing John's clothing and diet (v. 4), the narrator then describes the people's response to John: 'Then Jerusalem and all Judea and all the region around the Jordan were going out to him' (3.5). This response resumes the narrative following the parenthetical commentary by the narrator. Therefore, the response of the people is not prompted by John's clothing and diet, but by his message: 'Repent, for the Kingdom of Heaven has drawn near' (v. 2). Further, the narrator presents this information in summary narrative, thus indicating to the narratee that this is to be considered a continuation of the background material of v. 4.

As the people were going out to John, 'they were being baptized in the Jordan River by him confessing their sins' (3.6). In this clause, we have the first description of John's ministry of baptism. Recall that the narrator's crafting of the opening verses of ch. 3 serves to build within the narratee a sense of anticipation of seeing John finally as baptist.[13] Therefore, because this clause in 3.6 contains a reference to John's baptizing activity, it has the effect of prompting within the narratee a sense of closure for that anticipation, for the expectation of seeing John as baptist is now fulfilled.

A closer look at this text, however, suggests that the narrator intends this sense of closure to be a fleeting one. Note that the narrator offers this reference to John's baptizing activity in summary, and not scene, narrative; therefore, this reference constitutes mere background material, and not the prominent display of John as baptist which the narratee has been led to expect. Note also that this description of John's baptizing activity begins and ends with this clause; the narrator makes no attempt to develop this component of John's ministry beyond this simple description. What, then, is behind the narrator's insertion of this reference at this point? By leading the narratee to believe that he or she has achieved closure for the anticipation building since the beginning of this account on John, but then snatching that closure away, the narrator intensifies that sense of anticipation even further. The fact that the narrator goes to such an extent to intensify the impact of the passage finally presenting John as baptist shows the degree of importance this passage holds for the development of the narrative.

In the following verse, the narration slows down markedly; an examination of v. 7 reveals that the time taken to describe the action here

13. See pp. 81-82, above.

approximately equals the time-lapse of the action itself. Therefore, the narratee here witnesses the transition from summary narrative to scene narrative. With this transition, the narrator ends the background material on John and shifts now to the encounter with John anticipated by the narratee since v. 2 where he or she was left hanging at the end of a step-by-step approach toward John for which the narrator provided no closure. Further, with the fulfilment of this anticipation of having a significant encounter with John, the narratee would also expect this account to fulfill the anticipation of seeing John as baptist. However, the narratee is again disappointed, for this encounter depicts John in his role as preacher of repentance, and not in his role as baptist. As a result, the narratee's sense of anticipation on this point is intensified even further.

This encounter with John begins Ἰδὼν δὲ πολλοὺς τῶν Φαρισαίων καὶ Σαδδουκαίων ἐρχομένους ἐπὶ τὸ βάπτισμα αὐτοῦ(3.7a). This portion of the verse is often translated with the sense, 'When he saw many of the Pharisees and Sadducees coming for the purpose of his baptism' (3.7).[14] It is questionable, however, whether such a translation captures the sense intended by the narrator. It should be pointed out that the only clear instance of someone coming to John for the purpose of being baptized by him is the case of Jesus in 3.13, and there the narrator does not use the preposition ἐπί with the noun βάπτισμα, but rather the genitive article τοῦ plus the infinitive form of the verb βαπτίζω. Further, the noun βάπτισμα is used only one other place in the narrative,[15] and there it refers to John's general practice of baptizing, as opposed to an individual act of baptizing. For these reasons, I conclude that ἐπὶ τὸ βάπτισμα αὐτοῦ should not be translated 'for the purpose of his baptism'. Instead, a spatial sense of the preposition ἐπί should be adopted, rendering the translation 'to his baptism'. Therefore, the narrator here presents a picture of these Pharisees and Sadducees as coming out to John for the purpose of observing his practice of baptism.[16]

14. For example NASB, RSV, NRSV, JB and NJB; NAB has the equivalent 'for his bath'.

15. In the pericope on the controversy over the source of Jesus' authority, Jesus asks the chief priests and the elders, 'From what source was the baptism of John?' (21.25).

16. Commentators who come to this conclusion include Alan Hugh McNeile, *The Gospel According to St. Matthew* (Grand Rapids: Baker Book House, 1915), pp. 26-27; Gundry, *Matthew*, p. 46; Davies and Allison, *Saint Matthew*, I, pp. 303-304.

This mention of 'Pharisees and Sadducees' as acting together poses a problem for historical critics, because historically these two Jewish groups were rivals and thus were very unlikely to act in concert. From a narrative-critical perspective, however, this problem does not exist. Kingsbury notes that, when the Gospel of Matthew is analyzed using a narrative-critical approach,

> the phrase 'the Pharisees and Sadducees' refers exclusively to characters within the story of Matthew and is not additionally pressed to become a source from which to derive information about the Pharisaic Judaism that existed outside the story in the world of the first evangelist.[17]

The content of John's address to these Jewish leaders begins with the vocative 'Brood of vipers!' (3.7b). In this way, the narrator uses John to launch a negative characterization of the Jewish leaders.[18] Because of this negative characterization, the narratee is conditioned to view the Jewish leaders as unreliable sources of the narrator's ideological point of view.

In his address to the Jewish leaders, John continues, 'Who warned you to flee from the coming wrath?' (3.7c). This question represents an instance of verbal irony;[19] John's words imply that the Jewish leaders are coming to him for baptism in order to escape judgment, but the tenor of John's whole address to them clearly indicates John's belief that they have no intention of submitting to his baptism of repentance. Therefore, John's question to them constitutes a sarcastic taunt aimed at their unrepentant attitude.

John follows this taunt with a pair of exhortations: the first is given in the positive, telling these Jewish leaders what they must do, and the second in the negative, telling them what they must stop doing. The

17. Jack Dean Kingsbury, 'Reflections on "The Reader" of Matthew's Gospel', *NTS* 34 (1988), pp. 442-60 (457).

18. It could be argued that this negative characterization of the Jewish leaders begins earlier in the narrative, with the chief priests' and scribes' participation in Herod's plot to destroy Jesus (cf. 2.4-6). I contend, however, that their participation in that plot does not necessarily characterize them negatively, since they do nothing more than answer Herod's inquiry about the birthplace of the Messiah. Further, the text does not indicate that they are even aware of Herod's plot. Therefore, I conclude that, just as the Magi's participation in Herod's plot (cf. 3.7-9) is not sufficient to render them as negative characters, so the participation of the chief priests and scribes is not enough to render them as negative characters.

19. For discussions on verbal irony, see Fowler, *Let the Reader Understand*, pp. 11-13; and Rhoads and Michie, *Mark as Story*, pp. 59-60.

first exhortation reads, 'Bear fruit worthy of repentance' (3.8). The most natural way to take this aorist imperative is as an ingressive aorist.[20] Interpreted in this way, John's words are understood as an exhortation directing the Jewish leaders to change the way they were living: 'Start bearing fruit'. However, this imperative could simply be taken as expressing à command with a punctiliar sense: 'Bear fruit'. Interpreted in this way, John's words are understood as a sarcastic taunt, daring the Jewish leaders to produce—even one time—fruit that reflects repentance.

Regardless of which interpretation is adopted, this exhortation serves to intensify the negative characterization of the Jewish leaders; in either case, the exhortation presupposes that they are not living the way they should. However, the latter interpretation results in the characterization being significantly more negative. Further, its biting sarcasm matches the biting sarcasm of John's question to the Jewish leaders in the preceding verse. For these reasons, I conclude that the second interpretation should be adopted; this exhortation is a sarcastic taunt that adds significantly to the negative characterization of the Jewish leaders.

The second exhortation is a negative one: 'Do not think to say among yourselves, "We have Abraham as a father"' (3.9a). These words are significant from the perspective of point of view on the psychological plane, for they imply that John is privy to the Jewish leaders' thoughts.[21] Therefore, John is here depicted as possessing the ability to read minds. This depiction is significant, for, up to this point in the narrative, the only person who has demonstrated this capacity has been the narrator himself: see, for example, the narrator's report on Joseph's thoughts on learning that Mary was with child (1.19).[22] Because John exhibits a degree of omniscience through this display of mind-reading abilities, his reliability is enhanced in the eyes of the narratee.

Immediately following this second exhortation, John provides the rationale for his assertion that the Jewish leaders should not rely on

20. For a description of this sense of the aorist imperative, see BDF, p. 173 par. 337(1).

21. Anderson, 'Point of View in Matthew', p. 18, calls this a complex inside view, 'where the narrator implies or tells the readers that [a character] has an inside view of a third party'.

22. Later in the narrative, Jesus is also depicted as possessing this ability to read minds. See Kingsbury, *Matthew as Story*, pp. 36-37, for examples of the narrator's and Jesus' use of this capacity.

their descent from Abraham. His reason is introduced with the words 'I say to you' (3.9b). Although this formula appears many times in the phraseology of Jesus, it is used by John only here. In their discussion of Jesus' use of this formula, Davies and Allison assert that it 'reflects at least Jesus' implicit claim to be God's prophetic spokesman, and one should compare the Old Testament legitimation formula, "Thus says Yahweh"'.[23] Because the narrator has already presented John as fulfilling a prophecy concerning a prophetic voice crying out in the wilderness, John's use of the formula 'I say to you' would be taken in the same way as that specified by Davies and Allison for Jesus. As a result, the narratee views John's following statement as a declaration of a prophetic spokesperson of God.

John declares, 'God is able from these stones to raise up children to Abraham' (3.9b). The aorist infinitive ἐγεῖραι conveys a punctiliar sense, thus suggesting a one-time demonstration of God's abilities. For this reason, John's statement could be paraphrased, 'God is able to have people of God emerge from these stones *right now*'. John is saying, then, that God is not bound by the belief structure of the Jewish leaders, but has the power to raise up a people even from lifeless stones. In this way, the narrator uses John as a prophetic spokesperson of God to impress upon the narratee that God's election transcends the Jewish leaders' petty reliance on heredity.

In v. 10, the narrator has John begin a metaphor with the words, ἤδη δὲ ἡ ἀζίνη πρὸς τὴν ῥίζαν τῶν δένδρων κεῖται. Carl R. Kazmierski argues that these words clearly indicate that judgment has already begun.[24] For this interpretation to succeed, κεῖται must be understood as describing the swing of an axe at the root of the trees. An examination of this verb's usage in the New Testament, however, reveals that κεῖται is never used in this way. Here, it is either used intransitively ('lies'), or it serves as the passive for the transitive τίθημι[25] ('is laid'). In either case, the verb does not yield the image of an axe being swung; instead, the resulting image depicts an axe as lying beside[26] the root of

23. Davies and Allison, *Saint Matthew*, I, p. 490. In making these comments, they assume a functional equivalence between 'I say to you' and 'Truly I say to you'; for discussion on this latter formula, see pp. 113-14 below.

24. Carl R. Kazmierski, 'The Stones of Abraham: John the Baptist and the End of Torah (Matt 3,7-10 par. Luke 3,7-9)', *Bib* 68 (1987), pp. 22-39 (30).

25. 'κεῖμαι', BAGD, p. 426.

26. For this sense of the preposition πρός in πρὸς τὴν ῥίζαν τῶν δένδρων, see

the trees or being laid down beside the root of the trees. This being the case, judgment must still lie in the future. For this reason, it is a mistake to interpret this metaphor as depicting a judgment already under way.

Davies and Allison comment that, from the presence of the word ῥίζα ('root'), it is clear that 'not just the branches are to be cut but also the root'.[27] In presupposing an attack against the branches of the trees, Davies and Allison are inappropriately influenced by the image of Rom. 11.17 and 11.24 which involves the removal of branches; John's metaphor does not intimate in the least that branches are involved. Further, Davies and Allison argue that the use of the word ῥίζα makes plain that the root is to be cut. Their position, however, overlooks the possibility that an axe lying near the root of the trees could be used for chopping at something other than the root. Indeed, the use of the singular 'root' suggests that the narrator envisions something quite different.

The metaphor uses the plural 'trees' to designate the Jewish leaders and others aligned with their ideological point of view. To correspond to these plural 'trees', one would expect a reference to plural 'roots'. However, the metaphor speaks of a singular 'root'. Recall that, in the preceding verse, the Jewish leaders are depicted as claiming Abraham as their father. In other words, they are shown as claiming a descent back to a single source, to a single root. Therefore, John's charge that they not rely on their descent back to Abraham constitutes a major threat to the Jewish leaders, for it calls into question what they understand as the sustaining source of their peoplehood. In other words, John's charge threatens the Jewish leaders and adherents to their ideological point of view by threatening to sever them from their root. Therefore, the mention of the axe lying near the root of the trees does not envision an attack on the root. Instead, it envisions an attack on the trees themselves by which they are chopped down (cf. v. 10b) and thus severed from their root.

At this point in the narrative, the narratee has just encountered ten consecutive verses in which the focus has remained squarely on John. From the perspective of point of view on the spatial plane, these ten verses are striking because they constitute the first significant section of the narrative in which the narrator assumes a spatial position following a character other than Jesus. In fact, this section does not even contain a reference to Jesus. Since the narratee has been conditioned by the first

its second occurrence in Mk 4.1.

27. Davies and Allison, *Saint Matthew*, I, p. 309.

two chapters to view the story of this narrative as a story about Jesus, these first ten verses of ch. 3 stand out, for they apparently contribute nothing to the development of Jesus' story. Consequently, this detailed description of John appears to be wholly out of proportion to John's significance in the development of the plot. Because the significance of this material is obviously not to be found at the story level of the narrative, it must be sought at the discourse level as the narrative unfolds.

The narrator continues by providing the narratee with John's ideological point of view on himself (3.11). John begins with a comment on his own ministry of baptism: Ἐγὼ μὲν ὑμᾶς βαπτίζω ἐν ὕδατι εἰς μετάνοιαν (3.11a). Mention of his practice of baptism is modified by two prepositional phrases. The first, ἐν ὕδατι ('with water'), indicates mode. The sense of the second, εἰς μετάνοιαν, is not so clear. Davies and Allison list three possible understandings for this phrase: (1) baptism effects repentance; (2) baptism demands or summons repentance; and (3) baptism presupposes and expresses repentance. Davies and Allison indicate a preference for the third option.[28] Nigel Turner expresses the same opinion, using the term 'causal' to classify this usage of the preposition εἰς; he translates this phrase, 'because of repentance'.[29] This interpretation coordinates well with the picture of John's ministry of baptism presented to this point in the narrative; in 3.6, people are described as submitting to his baptism as they confess their sins, thus suggesting that the baptism is administered because of their repentance.

John then contrasts himself with a person he designates 'the one coming after me'. John asserts that the one coming after him is greater than he is (3.11b). Because John has already been depicted as possessing a high status (3.3), his statement grants an exceedingly high status to this one coming after him. In the mind of the narratee, this one who is coming after John must be Jesus. First, the opening two chapters of the narrative clearly establish Jesus as the central character of the story. Therefore, the lack of any reference to Jesus in the first ten verses of ch. 3 builds within the narratee a growing expectation to witness Jesus' reappearance into the story-line. In light of this growing expectation to see Jesus, John's mention of one coming after him is taken by the narratee as a reference to Jesus. Secondly, the first two chapters of the

28. Davies and Allison, *Saint Matthew*, I, p. 312.

29. Nigel Turner, *A Grammar of New Testament Greek*. III. *Syntax* (ed. James Hope Moulton; Edinburgh: T. & T. Clark, 1963), p. 266.

narrative present Jesus as Messiah (1.1, 16, 17, 18) and Son of God.[30] Therefore, when the narrator describes John as fulfilling a prophecy regarding the way-preparer of the Lord, the narratee understands John to be the way-preparer of Jesus. As a result, the narratee takes John's reference in 3.11 to the one coming after him as a reference to Jesus.

It is interesting to note the designation used by John in referring to Jesus: 'the one coming after me' or, in a simpler form which John uses later in the narrative, 'the coming one' (11.3). If John had used 'Jesus', 'Messiah', 'Son of David' or 'Son of Abraham', his phraseological point of view would have been aligned with that of the narrator established in the opening verse of the Gospel. However, the narrator has John use an entirely different designation, and thus denies John alignment with the narrator on the phraseological plane.

This move by the narrator is surprising, given the way in which he has presented John in a consistently positive light to this point in the narrative, thus leading the narratee to accept John as a reliable source of the narrator's own ideological point of view. What type of effect would this narrative move have on the narratee? An analysis of the operation of the primacy and recency effects[31] is helpful here. The primacy effect prompts the narratee to grant more significance to the elements of John's characterization encountered first. As we have seen, John is introduced in a very positive light, especially with the citation of his fulfilling the prophecy pertaining to the way-preparer of the Lord. Therefore, against the weight of this glowing introduction, his deviation from the narrator's phraseological point of view at this point in the narrative would not make a significant impact on the narratee. Nevertheless, this deviation does produce some tension, as the recency effect begins to contend with the primacy effect. In continuing our examination of John, it becomes imperative to pay close attention to the narrator's treatment of John in order to determine if the primacy effect is partially, or even totally, overcome during the course of the narrative.

30. In the account of the events leading up to Jesus' birth, the narrator indicates that Mary conceives 'by means of the Holy Spirit' (1.18), an assertion that is repeated by an angel of the Lord in its interaction with Joseph (1.20). Also, the narrator specifies that Jesus' escape to Egypt (2.13-14) was for the purpose of fulfilling a prophecy in which God says, 'Out of Egypt I have called *my son*' (2.15; emphasis added). Further, in two addresses to Joseph (2.13, 20), an angel of the Lord refers to Jesus not as 'your child', but as 'the child', thus emphasizing that Jesus is the son of a father other than Joseph. Cf. Kingsbury, *Matthew as Story*, p. 54.

31. For a discussion of these concepts, see pp. 53-55 above.

John's statement on the one coming after him continues: 'He will baptize you with the Holy Spirit and with fire' (3.11c).[32] To the narratee, baptism with the Holy Spirit is taken in a positive light, as a blessing; the only two references to the Holy Spirit in the narrative thus far both have the connotation of 'life-giving'.[33] Baptism with fire, on the other hand, may be taken either positively, as an experience of purification, or negatively, as an experience of judgment. Given the context, however, this reference to a baptism with fire is clearly a reference to judgment, for, in the immediately preceding verse, 'fire' is depicted as a means of judgment. Therefore, John presents a picture of the one coming after him as a bringer of blessing, but also as a bringer of judgment.

John elaborates on this image with the relative clause, οὗ τό πτύον ἐν τῇ χειρὶ αὐτοῦ (3.12a), thus describing the one coming after him with an object designated a πτύον in his hand. Through depicting this person as ready for action, John conveys a sense of imminence regarding the blessing and judgment to come. The nature of the action for which this person is ready, however, only becomes clear with an examination of the word πτύον.

The noun πτύον is almost universally understood as a farming utensil used in the winnowing process: grain is tossed into the air with it, allowing the heavier wheat to fall to the ground while the lighter chaff blows away. Because πτύον is understood in this sense, it is usually translated 'winnowing fork'.[34] Robert L. Webb, however, asserts that

32. For discussions on the issue of whether John originally referred to 'spirit' and 'fire', 'wind' and 'fire', or just 'fire', and on the issue of whether John was signifying salvation and judgment, or only judgment, see Ernest Best, 'Spirit Baptism', *NovT* 41 (1960), pp. 236-43; James D.G. Dunn, 'Spirit-and-Fire Baptism', *NovT* 14 (1972), pp. 81-92; Arthur Gerald Patzia, 'Did John the Baptist Preach a Baptism of Fire and the Holy Spirit?', *EvQ* 40 (1968), pp. 21-27.

33. In 1.18 and 1.20, the Holy Spirit is depicted as the agent of conception in the narrative of Jesus' birth.

34. This translation is used by the RSV, NRSV, NASB and NIV. It has also been adopted by Davies and Allison, *Saint Matthew*, I, p. 318; Hill, *Matthew*, p. 95; Bruner, *Matthew*, I, p. 81; Harrington, *Matthew*, p. 59; Ulrich Luz, *Matthew 1–7: A Commentary* (trans. Wilhelm C. Linss; Minneapolis: Augsburg, 1989), p. 172; John P. Meier, *Matthew* (Collegeville, MN: Liturgical Press, 1990), p. 25; Richard B. Gardner, *Matthew* (Scottdale: Herald Press, 1991), p. 63. Beare, *Matthew*, p. 97, and McNeile, *St. Matthew*, p. 29, conceptualize this instrument as a 'shovel' used to toss grain into the air in the winnowing process.

the imagery of 3.12 does not depict the winnowing process.[35] Webb points out that none of the words commonly used to depict the activity of winnowing is used here.[36] Instead, words carrying the sense of cleansing are used in both the Lukan and Matthean versions of this image.[37] Further, Webb looks to Gustaf Dalman[38] for details on Palestinian agricultural practices and finds that two different tools were evidently used in activity at a threshing floor. The first was a θρῖναξ, a fork used to separate the wheat from the chaff through winnowing. The second was a πτύον, a shovel used to heap the grain in preparation for winnowing, to gather the wheat and the chaff into separate piles following winnowing, and to clear the floor of the wheat and the chaff at the completion of the winnowing process.

This information provides an alternative to the traditional understanding of the image of v. 12. Given that a πτύον is used before and after the winnowing process, but not in the winnowing process itself, John envisions that the one coming after him will be doing something other than separating the wheat from the chaff. Further, given that v. 12 speaks of the one coming after John as poised to gather the wheat and to burn the chaff, John envisions that the winnowing process has already been accomplished. On the basis of these considerations, Webb presents a convincing argument for a new understanding of the image of v. 12. He asserts that this image depicts the one coming after John as having two piles before him, one of wheat and one of chaff. This figure uses a shovel (πτύον) to gather the wheat into his barn, an action that represents the blessing of the baptism of the Holy Spirit. He also uses the shovel to throw the chaff into the unquenchable fire, an action that represents the judgment of the baptism of fire. Webb asserts further that the wheat and the chaff came to be separated through John's repentance preaching, which resulted in two groups: the repentant and the unrepentant.[39] Therefore, John's ideological point of view of himself

35. Robert L. Webb, 'The Activity of John the Baptist's Expected Figure at the Threshing Floor (Matthew 3.12 = Luke 3.17)', *JSNT* 43 (1991), pp. 103-11.

36. Webb, 'The Activity of John', p. 106; he cites λικμάω, διασπείρω and διασκορπίζω as the verbs commonly used to describe winnowing.

37. In Lk. 3.17, the word διακαθαίρω is used, while in Mt. 3.12, the word διακαθαρίζω is used.

38. Gustaf Dalman, *Arbeit und Sitte in Palästina*, III (Hildesheim: Georg Olms, 1964), pp. 116-24, 201, 253-54, cited in Webb, 'Threshing Floor', p. 107.

39. Dalman, *Arbeit und Sitte in Palästina*, III, pp. 108-109.

involves an understanding of his own ministry as a process of separating the repentant from the unrepentant—the wheat from the chaff—in preparation for the conferral of blessing, or the execution of judgment, by the one coming after him.

This description of the threshing floor scene concludes a lengthy speech by John that begins with 3.7. On the conclusion of this speech, the narrator does not present any response emanating from John's audience. This lack of 'uptake' at the story level[40] indicates that John's discourse on the imminent judgment and on the one coming after him who is to execute it, does not find its significance at the story level so much as it does at the discourse level. Therefore, although these words are ostensibly directed at the Pharisees and Sadducees (cf. 3.7), their primary significance lies in the impact that they make on the narratee. With them, the narrator impresses on the narratee John's ideological point of view on the nature of Jesus' ministry: he comes as the eschatological judge.

John's Baptism of Jesus

In 3.13, Jesus finally makes his appearance. Because of John's immediately preceding depiction of the one coming after him, the narratee now expects to see Jesus entering the story-line as the eschatological judge, ready to perform a baptism of the Holy Spirit and a baptism of fire. In stark contrast to this expectation, the narratee actually witnesses Jesus as one who displays no characteristics of judgeship; he appears to have no intention of administering a baptism of the Holy Spirit or a baptism of fire but, instead, presents himself to have John's baptism administered to him.

The influence of the primacy effect leads the narratee to see John as a reliable source of the narrator's ideological point of view; John was introduced in glowing terms in the opening verses of ch. 3. However, we have already seen the primacy effect beginning to erode, as a new element in 3.11 initates a tension between the recency effect and the primacy effect; in that verse, John is denied alignment with the narrator on the phraseological plane as evidenced by John's use of a designation for Jesus that is not part of the narrator's own phraseological point of view. The tension triggered there now grows as John's reliability

40. That is, a lack of response by characters to something said in the story; see Fowler, *Let the Reader Understand*, pp. 21, 87 *et passim*.

becomes suspect when the narratee does not experience the Jesus that John has led him or her to expect. In fact, in vv. 14-15, John is shown openly contending with Jesus on the issue of John's baptizing Jesus. In v. 14, the narratee is presented with John's ideological point of view on Jesus' request for baptism: 'John tried to prevent[41] him, saying, "I need to be baptized by you, and do you come to me?"' Here, John discloses his expectation that Jesus execute his role as eschatological judge by baptizing him with the Holy Spirit. Immediately after this, however, the narratee is presented with Jesus' ideological point of view on this issue: 'Allow it now' (3.15). In contrast to John's view that he should not baptize Jesus, but rather that he should be baptized by Jesus, Jesus expresses in no uncertain terms the appropriateness of John's baptizing him.

In a contest between these two competing ideological points of view, the outcome is never in doubt. As we have seen above, the narrator makes numerous efforts in the opening chapters of the Gospel to establish Jesus' reliability;[42] clearly the narrator holds it to be of utmost importance that the narratee perceive Jesus as a reliable source of the narrator's own ideological point of view. The narrator also makes efforts to establish John as a reliable character.[43] However, these efforts pale in comparison with those afforded Jesus; the establishment of John's reliability is not nearly as important to the narrator as the establishment of Jesus' reliability. Therefore, in this contest between the competing ideological points of view of Jesus and John, Jesus' point of view easily wins out.

It should be noted, however, that John's ideological point of view is actually correct for the most part, being deficient on one point only. John's suggestion that Jesus should baptize him indicates that John understands Jesus as the eschatological judge who is now about to administer his baptism of the Holy Spirit and baptism of fire. The narrator gives no indication that John is incorrect in his understanding of Jesus as the eschatological judge. On this point, John's ideological point of view is aligned with that of the narrator; Jesus is indeed the eschatological judge. However, John does harbour a misunderstanding when it comes to the timing of Jesus' execution of this role. John

41. Conative imperfect; see Davies and Allison, *Saint Matthew*, I, p. 323; Beare, *Matthew*, p. 98; Luz, *Matthew 1–7*, p. 177.

42. See pp. 78-80 above.

43. See the discussions on 3.3 and 3.9a, above on pp. 83 and 88-89.

believes that Jesus is about to begin his role as the eschatological judge right then, as evidenced by John's expressed desire to receive the eschatological baptism of the Holy Spirit.

Notice Jesus' response. He does not attempt to correct John's understanding that he is the eschatological judge. Instead, he addresses the issue of timing: 'Allow it *now*' (3.15; emphasis added). In opposition to John's belief that he is here to begin his eschatological ministry of administering the baptism of the Holy Spirit and the baptism of fire, Jesus asserts that, *at the present time*, the appropriate course of action is for John to baptize him, never denying the possibility that he will administer a baptism of the Holy Spirit and a baptism of fire at some future time. Therefore, John's ideological point of view on Jesus is essentially correct; Jesus is indeed the eschatological judge. The defect in John's ideological point of view relates only to his understanding of when Jesus is to execute this role.

Because this defect is so minor in the scope of John's whole characterization, the narratee's assessment of him as a positive character is not negated; therefore, the narrator is able to continue to use John as a reliable source of his own ideological point of view. This defect does, however, influence the narratee's experience of the narrative in another way. It is John's belief that Jesus is here beginning his ministry as the eschatological judge that prompts him to ask, 'I need to be baptized by you, and do you come to me?' (3.14), and it is this question that provides Jesus with an opportunity to express his ideological point of view on the nature of his own ministry. He responds, 'for in this way it is fitting for us to fulfil all righteousness' (3.15b). On the meaning of the expression 'all righteousness', Ulrich Luz rightly asserts that here it designates 'the entirety of the divine will as the Matthean Jesus interprets it'.[44] Therefore, the narrator has John present a question that does not reflect the narrator's own ideological point of view in order to provide Jesus with an opportunity to make a statement concerning the nature of his messiahship: he is to fulfil the entirety of the divine will.

Jesus' statement in v. 15b does not pertain only to himself; he says that it is fitting for both himself and John to fulfil the entirety of the divine will for them. From the way in which Jesus and John have been presented in the narrative to this point, it is clear that Jesus' primary role within the divine will is to be the Messiah (cf. 1.1, 16, 17, 18; 2.4),

44. Luz, *Matthew 1–7*, p. 178; he notes the use of the adjective 'all' in support of this contention.

and John's primary role within the divine will is to be the way-preparer of the Messiah (3.3). Since Jesus is the Messiah—the 'Anointed One'—his anointing is basic preparation for his ministry as the Messiah. Therefore, as the way-preparer of the Messiah, John's administration of that anointing is basic to his ministry. Given this understanding, the act of baptism takes on an entirely different significance for Jesus than the significance it holds for others who are baptized by John. For the crowds, baptism is a symbol of repentance. For Jesus, however, it constitutes his anointing for his ministry as the Messiah.

John's response to Jesus in 3.15c reads τότε ἀφίησιν αὐτόν ('Then he allowed him'). Note that the verb used to describe John's response is the same verb used by Jesus in giving his instruction to John in the first place. Jesus gives the imperative ἄφες, and John's response is described as ἀφίησιν αὐτόν; Jesus speaks, and John does exactly what Jesus says. Here, the narrator uses diction to highlight the authority of Jesus.

The actual baptism of Jesus by John is not highlighted; only passing reference is made to it by means of a participial phrase using a passive participle. In fact, the narrator does not even specifically refer to John as playing a part in the baptism. Having been used to establish this baptismal scene as an anointing ceremony, and used to highlight Jesus' authority, John now fades away. From the perspective of point of view on the spatial plane, the narrator uses the meeting of John and Jesus in 3.13-15 to move from a position alongside John to a position alongside Jesus. In the process, John is effectively left behind. Given John's role at the story level—that of way-preparer for Jesus—the fact that he is left behind is not surprising; he has now fulfilled that role, and so, in the eyes of the narratee, he is no longer needed. With John's absence, the narrator is able to direct the full focus of the narratee on Jesus.

Because the present study is an analysis of John the Baptist, it is tempting to end the discussion of the present pericope at this point, since John is no longer mentioned. However, because John has been so instrumental in the development of this pericope, it is appropriate to continue the analysis to the pericope's climax. In leading the narratee to this climax, the narrator uses a number of rhetorical techniques. First, the description of Jesus' coming up from the water includes the adverb εὐθύς ('immediately', 3.16b). On the use of this adverb, Robert Fowler writes: '*Euthys* serves the pragmatic function of promoting the rapid forward progress of the narrative. It typifies a narrative that wants to catch us up and hurry us forward to an appointed destiny.'[45] By quickening the pace in this way, the narrator injects a sense of intensity into the flow of the narrative.

The narrator then introduces the following clause with the word ἰδού ('Behold!'); this demonstrative particle adds to the sense of intensity by grabbing the narratee's attention and focusing it on the following words 'the heavens were opened to him' (3.16c). These words create a striking image, for they suggest a direct heaven-to-earth interaction, something that has not taken place to this point in the narrative.[46] Further, the inclusion of the indirect object 'to him' suggests that Jesus is the only earthly recipient of this interaction. The remainder of v. 16 lends support to this view: it reads, 'and he saw the Spirit of God descending like a dove and coming upon him'. From the perspective of point of view on the psychological plane, the narrator here provides an inside view[47] of Jesus by allowing the narratee to see through the eyes of Jesus. By doing so, the narrator gives the narratee the impression that Jesus, and Jesus alone, is able to see the descent of the Spirit upon him.

At the beginning of v. 17, the narrator inserts another ἰδού, thus adding to the growing sense of intensity. This ἰδού focuses the narratee's attention on the noun φωνή ('voice'), a nominative that occurs here without a verb. This is an example of a nominative of exclamation, described by H.E. Dana and Julius R. Mantey as follows:

> When it is desired to stress a thought with great distinctness, the nominative is used without a verb. The function of designation, serving ordinarily as a helper to the verb, thus stands alone and thereby receives

45. Fowler, *Let the Reader Understand*, pp. 139-40.

46. In the Infancy Narrative, an angel of the Lord interacts with a human character, Joseph, on a number of occasions (1.20-21; 2.13, 19, 22). In each of these cases, however, a heavenly being has left the heavenly realm to interact with a human character in the earthly realm. The situation in the present verse is different. Here, the words 'the heavens were opened to him' indicate that actual interaction *between* the heavenly realm and the earthly realm is about to occur.

47. Fowler, *Let the Reader Understand*, pp. 120-26, adopts a categorization of inside views set out by Thomas E. Boomershine, 'Mark, the Storyteller: A Rhetorical-Critical Investigation of Mark's Passion and Resurrection Narrative' (PhD dissertation, Union Theological Seminary, New York, 1974), pp. 273-75, that divides inside views into 'perceptions', 'emotions', 'inner knowledge/motivation' and 'inner statements'. In this verse, the narrator presents a 'perception', that is, an insight into what a character sees or hears.

> greater emphasis...The nominative is the pointing case, and its pointer capacity is strengthened when unencumbered by a verb.[48]

By using a nominative of exclamation, the narrator further builds the intensity.

The description of this voice is qualified with the prepositional phrase 'from heaven', clearly indicating that this voice represents the voice of God. Up to this point in the story, God's ideological point of view has been expressed through the words of prophecy (1.23; 2.6, 15, 18, 23, 3.3), and through the agency of an angel of the Lord (1.20-23; 2.13, 20). Here, however, God's ideological point of view is to be expressed directly by the voice of God. Therefore, the building intensity now reaches its climax; what follows is a declaration of major proportions, certainly the most significant declaration thus far in the story.

By having God state, 'This is my son', the narrator presents God's own ideological point of view on the identity of Jesus, that he is the Son of God. Note that this statement is in the third person, apparently addressed to someone other than Jesus. An examination of the characters involved in this pericope, however, reveals that, by this point, Jesus is the only character present.[49] To determine the intended audience of this pronouncement by God, it is important to notice that the narrator includes no uptake at the story level. This indicates that God's declaration 'This is my son' is addressed directly to the narratee.

To summarize, the narrator uses various rhetorical devices—the adverb εὐθύς (v. 16b), the demonstrative particle ἰδού twice (vv. 16c, 17a), and the nominative of exclamation φωνή (v. 17a)—to provide for the narratee a sense of building toward a climax. In this way, the narrator attempts to impact the narratee as strongly as possible with the climactic pronouncement addressed directly to the narratee, that Jesus is the Son of God.

48. H.E. Dana and Julius R. Mantey, *A Manual Grammar of the Greek New Testament* (New York: Macmillan, 1941), p. 70.

49. From v. 13 on, the narrator makes mention of no one besides John and Jesus, thus giving the impression that they are alone. Further, from v. 16 on, not even John is mentioned, thus giving the impression that Jesus is now alone in this scene.

Chapter 6

JOHN: BOUND AND DETERMINED

This analysis of John's baptism of Jesus reveals that the narrator leaves John behind after the baptism, as the focus of the story shifts from John to Jesus. Despite this shift of focus, however, John does not disappear entirely from the narrative; in 4.12, the narrator states, 'When [Jesus] heard that John had been arrested, he withdrew into Galilee'. With this statement, the narrator marks the end of John's ministry; because he is imprisoned, John is no longer able to baptize. In this way, the narrator not only has John fade out of the picture after he baptizes Jesus, but here the narrator also has John shackled off-stage, thus ensuring that he is indisposed and thus unable to retake the limelight from Jesus. This leaves the stage clear for the narrator to present the inauguration of Jesus' ministry (4.17). Therefore, the narrator structures this section of the narrative to coordinate the end of John's ministry with the beginning of Jesus' ministry.[1] In this way, the narrator enhances the theme of John as forerunner of Jesus.

As Jesus embarks on his ministry, the narratee has no reason to expect to encounter John again in this narrative; John's role is that of way-preparer, and, now that the preparations for Jesus' ministry are completed, John's usefulness as way-preparer is exhausted. Yet the following chapters reveal that the narrator still considers John useful for the development of the narrative, even after he is locked away in prison.

The inauguration of Jesus' ministry occurs in 4.17: 'From that time Jesus began to preach and to say: "Repent, for the Kingdom of Heaven has drawn near"'. The narrator's use of diction here is significant. He has Jesus repeat verbatim the words that John used earlier to inaugurate his ministry (3.2). By doing so, the narrator prompts a retrospection to

1. Cf. Daniel Patte, *The Gospel According to Matthew: A Structural Commentary on Matthew's Faith* (Philadelphia: Fortress Press, 1987), p. 55.

the inauguration of John's ministry. It is interesting to note the tenacity of this character; John has just been removed as a character at the story level of the narrative (4.12), and yet he still makes himself useful at the discourse level, as the target of retrospection.

By prompting a retrospection to 3.2, the narrator influences the narratee's understanding of 4.17 in two ways. First, by inaugurating Jesus' ministry with the same words used to inaugurate John's ministry, the narrator begins to condition the narratee to expect elements of John's story to reappear later as part of Jesus' story.[2]

Secondly, by prompting the narratee to think back to ch. 3, the narrator brings to mind for the narratee the image of Jesus as the Son of God. As concluded in the above analysis of ch. 3, the material covering the preaching ministry of John and the baptism of Jesus builds to a climax in God's pronouncement of Jesus as the Son of God, by far the most significant declaration in the narrative to that point. Because the movement of ch. 3 is oriented so strongly toward this pronouncement, when the narratee is prompted by retrospection to think back to any point in ch. 3, his or her mind is drawn toward the climax at the end of the chapter. Therefore, while the wording of 4.17 prompts retrospection specifically to 3.2, the narratee's mind is immediately drawn toward the climax at the end of the chapter: the image of Jesus as the Son of God. As a result, the narratee views 4.17 against the backdrop of this image, and thus sees Jesus' embarking on his ministry with the authority of the Son of God. In this way, the narrator uses John at the discourse level of the narrative—as a target for retrospection—without even mentioning his name at the story level.

In the text covering Jesus' ministry, John comes up in a pericope in ch. 9. However, he makes himself useful earlier than that. In the section of warnings that concludes the Sermon on the Mount (7.13-27), the narrator has Jesus use the motif of trees bearing fruit (v. 19) in a warning to beware of false prophets. The narrator here manipulates Jesus' diction to have Jesus repeat the same words used by John in his

2. Trilling, 'Die Täufertradition', pp. 271-89, using a redaction-critical approach in his analysis of John the Baptist in the Gospel of Matthew, describes the connection between Jesus and John as 'Angleichung' ('assimilation'); see especially pp. 282-86. While Trilling is correct in noting an attempt to display similarities between John and Jesus, his analysis does not recognize the progression that the assimilation of Jesus to John undergoes through the course of the narrative. This progression is demonstrated later in the present study.

denunciation of the Pharisees and Sadducees in ch. 3.[3] In this way, the narrator again prompts retrospection to John's preaching ministry of ch. 3, and, in so doing, influences the narratee's understanding of 7.19. First, by having Jesus use exactly the same words uttered earlier by John, the narrator continues to condition the narratee to expect elements of John's story to reappear later as part of Jesus' story. Secondly, because the wording of 7.19 prompts retrospection to ch. 3, the climactic pronouncement of Jesus as the Son of God is drawn in as a backdrop against which Jesus' warnings of ch. 7 are to be viewed. As a result, the narratee sees Jesus as issuing these warnings with the authority of the Son of God. Therefore, as at 4.17, the narrator again uses John at the discourse level of the narrative—as a target for retrospection—without even mentioning his name at the story level.

The Question on Fasting

Because John has been arrested (4.12), he is no longer able to interact directly with Jesus. However, despite his imprisonment, John is still able to communicate with Jesus through his disciples. In fact, Darr points out that John's disciples 'are representative of their master and so function as a narrative extension of his character'.[4] As a result, their appearance in 9.14 does not represent the introduction of a new character group; instead, it represents the reappearance of John. For this reason, the following analysis of John's disciples treats them as if they were John himself.

The narrator's placement of this episode is significant. In the two passages immediately preceding this one, Jesus is seen facing opposition; in 9.3, the scribes accuse Jesus of blasphemy and, in 9.11, the Pharisees criticize Jesus for eating with tax collectors and sinners. Because the portrayal of John thus far in the narrative has been predominantly positive, the narratee expects this appearance of John's disciples to be a positive turn of events; in this context of opposition to Jesus' ministry, the narratee expects John's disciples to supply badly needed support for Jesus. Therefore, the question on fasting posed by

3. Cf. πᾶν δένδρον μὴ ποιοῦν καρπὸν καλὸν ἐκκόπτεται καὶ εἰς πῦρ βάλλεται (7.19) with πᾶν οὖν δένδρον μὴ ποιοῦν καρπὸν καλὸν ἐκκόπτεται καὶ εἰς πῦρ βάλλεται (3.10b).

4. Darr, *On Character Building*, p. 75. This assertion by Darr relates to the Lukan parallel to Mt. 9.14, but is equally applicable here.

John's disciples to Jesus shocks the narratee; rather than supply badly needed support for Jesus, John's disciples add to the opposition against Jesus by questioning the practice of his disciples.

Note the way in which John's ideological point of view has evolved to this point in the narrative. Back in ch. 3, John expressed an ideological point of view at odds with that of Jesus, though John's difference with Jesus was expressed in the most deferential way; when Jesus came to John for baptism, John said, 'I need to be baptized by you, and do you come to me?' (3.14). Here in 9.14, however, John's disciples exhibit no sign of deference; instead, they bluntly question Jesus on his disciples' failure to fast. Further, John's disciples go so far as to line up with the Pharisees over against Jesus on the issue of fasting: 'Why do we *and the Pharisees* fast often, but your disciples do not fast?' (9.14b; emphasis added). Since John's disciples act as representatives of John, their question effectively aligns John's ideological point of view with that of the Pharisees. This alignment is striking because the portrayal of John has been predominantly positive, whereas the Pharisees have been negatively characterized both through the way in which they were portrayed in ch. 3 (see above), as well as through the depiction of their opposition to Jesus in the passage immediately preceding the present one (9.10-13). Further, this alignment is all the more striking since it was John himself who launched the negative characterization of the Pharisees in the first place (see above). This shocking development highlights the fact that John's difference with Jesus has intensified.

It is interesting to note that, while John's disciples question the practice of Jesus' disciples, they do not question the practice of Jesus himself. If their concern were only the correct execution of the common custom of fasting, they would have included Jesus' own failure to fast in their inquiry. Instead, John's disciples exempt Jesus from their expectation of fasting. This exemption of Jesus suggests that the mention of fasting here does not refer to the common custom of fasting. To what, then, does this mention of fasting refer?

Recall that John's question to Jesus in the baptism scene demonstrated that John understood Jesus as the eschatological judge.[5] In fact, all that John declared about Jesus (3.11-12) as well as all that John said to Jesus (3.14) had to do with Jesus as the eschatological judge. From this, the narratee concludes that John's ideological point of view on Jesus is totally dominated by this conception of Jesus' task. Further,

5. See the discussion on 3.14 at p. 96 above.

since nothing in chs. 3–9 indicates that John's understanding on this issue has changed, the narratee has no reason to doubt that John's ideological point of view on Jesus is still dominated by this conception of him. This being the case, the question by John's disciples to Jesus should be viewed against the backdrop of this picture of Jesus as the eschatological judge that so dominates their understanding of Jesus. As a result, the narratee comes to see this mention of fasting not as a reference to the common custom of fasting, but rather as a reference to fasting as a sign of repentance in the face of eschatological judgment. This explains why John's disciples exempt Jesus from their expectation of fasting, for certainly the eschatological judge would not be required to fast as a sign of repentance in the face of the judgment that he himself is executing.[6]

What is the narrator attempting to accomplish through the inclusion of this passage at this point in the narrative? Although the narrator had John characterize Jesus as the eschatological judge back in 3.11-14, the chapters that follow focus on Jesus as a teacher and preacher (chs. 5–7) and as a healer (chs. 8–9), but not as a judge. As a result, by ch. 9, the image of Jesus as judge is in danger of fading completely from the narratee's mind. To ensure that this does not happen, the narrator introduces John's disciples into the story-line, and has them direct a question at Jesus that again casts him as the eschatological judge. In this way, the narrator refreshes this image of Jesus as judge in the narratee's mind through this long stretch of the narrative in which Jesus does not yet exercise this role.

We have already seen that, at Jesus' baptism, John correctly identified Jesus as the eschatological judge, but misunderstood the timing of Jesus' execution of that role. In the present pericope, when John's disciples question Jesus about fasting, they also correctly understand Jesus to be the eschatological judge. However, like John, they also possess a misunderstanding related only to the timing of Jesus' execution of that role. It is important to note that Jesus himself does not refute their belief that fasting in the face of eschatological judgment is appropriate. Instead, he challenges the appropriateness of fasting for the present time; in response to their inquiry, he asks, 'The bridegroom's attendants cannot mourn *as long as the bridegroom is with them*, can they?' (9.15a; emphasis added). With this rhetorical question, Jesus indicates that the position of John's disciples is

6. Cf. Patte, *Matthew*, p. 130.

incorrect, but only for the present time. With his next statement, Jesus makes it clear that, for a future time, their position is actually appropriate: 'Days will come when the bridegroom is taken away from them, and *then they will fast*' (9.15b; emphasis added). In this way, Jesus suggests that he will indeed execute the role of eschatological judge at some future time.

Back at Jesus' baptism, John's misunderstanding on the timing of Jesus' execution of his role as the eschatological judge provided Jesus with an opportunity to elaborate on the nature of his messiahship.[7] In like manner, this misunderstanding by John's disciples on the same issue in the present pericope provides Jesus with another opportunity to elaborate on this theme. Because John's disciples understand fasting as an appropriate response to Jesus, it is evident that they expect Jesus to usher in a kingdom characterized by judgment. Jesus, on the other hand, presents an entirely different picture of the Kingdom. Jesus speaks of the celebration of a wedding feast (cf. 9.15), thus indicating that his messiahship involves a celebratory, and not a fearful, inauguration of the Kingdom of Heaven.

John's Question on Jesus' Identity

At the beginning of ch. 11, John makes his first appearance in the storyline since his baptism of Jesus in 3.13-15. In 11.2-3, he responds to a report of the 'deeds of the Messiah'. This use of the title 'Messiah' is striking, for it is the first time this title has appeared in the narrative since its frequent usage in the opening two chapters of the Gospel.[8] In this way, the narrator prompts the narratee to view John's response within the context of the issue of Jesus' messiahship.

John's response reads, 'Are you "the coming one" or should we expect another?' (11.3). These words appear to indicate serious doubt on the part of John concerning Jesus' identity. Many commentators explain John's doubt by pointing to the disparity between John's expectation of Jesus as eschatological judge (cf. 3.11-12) and the works of Jesus as recorded in the narrative since the inauguration of Jesus' ministry in 4.17.[9] While these commentators are correct in identifying

7. See discussion on 3.14-15, above on p. 97.

8. The title 'Messiah' was used in 1.1, 16, 17, 18 and 2.4.

9. For example, David E. Garland, *Reading Matthew: A Literary and Theological Commentary on the First Gospel* (New York: Crossroad, 1993), p. 124;

this disparity as the cause of John's doubt, they do not adequately take into consideration the narrator's total treatment of John to this point in the narrative, for these commentators appear to proceed on the assumption that John's doubt arises as a direct result of what John now hears about Jesus' ministry.

This study has shown, however, that the sentiments that give rise to John's question in 11.3 are already evident long before this point in the narrative. As early as the baptismal scene (3.13-15), John expresses an uneasiness with Jesus for his coming to be baptized, rather than to execute his role as eschatological judge (see above). Then, in the pericope on the question of fasting (9.14-17), John's disciples exhibit an even greater uneasiness in response to Jesus' failure to direct his own disciples to fast in the face of eschatological judgment (see above), direction that would be expected of the eschatological judge. Therefore, John's expression of doubt in 11.3 does not simply arise from what John hears about Jesus at this point in the narrative. Rather, it represents the third instalment of a growing uneasiness in John's mind regarding Jesus' identity, an uneasiness first revealed politely in a deferential question (cf. 3.14), then expressed more seriously in a straightforward question (cf. 9.14), and now put bluntly in a question containing an actual expression of doubt (cf. 11.3).[10]

In spite of John's expression of doubt in 11.3, his ideological point of view on Jesus is still essentially correct: John believes that Jesus is the eschatological judge, which Jesus indeed is. The deficiency in John's ideological point of view here still relates only to the timing of Jesus' execution of that role.

Recall that John's uneasiness in 3.14 and the uneasiness of John's disciples in 9.14 each provided Jesus with an opportunity to elaborate on his messiahship. That same dynamic operates here as well, for Jesus again responds with a further description of his messianic role. Jesus begins his response by instructing John's disciples, 'Go and report to

Gundry, *Matthew*, p. 205; Bruner, *Matthew*, I, pp. 408-409; Meier, *Matthew*, p. 119; Gardner, *Matthew*, p. 186; John L. McKenzie, 'The Gospel According to Matthew', in Raymond E. Brown, Joseph A. Fitzmyer and Roland E. Murphy (eds.), *Jerome Biblical Commentary* (Englewood Cliffs, NJ: Prentice–Hall, 1968), II, p. 82.

10. Patte (*Matthew*, p. 159) recognizes that John (or John's disciples) demonstrate a misunderstanding on Jesus' messianic vocation in all three of these instances, but his analysis does not recognize the progression that takes place from one instance to the next.

John what you hear and see' (11.4b). Robert Gundry finds significance in the order of the two verbs, with hearing coming before seeing in order to stress Jesus' words, that is, his preaching and teaching.[11] Daniel Patte also finds in the verbs ἀκούω and βλέπω a distinction between Jesus' words and deeds.[12] Patte asserts that John doubts because he takes into account only Jesus' deeds (cf. 11.2); therefore, Jesus instructs John's disciples to report to John not only what they see—that is, the healing of the blind, the lame, the lepers and the deaf, and the raising of the dead—but also what they hear—that is, the good news preached to the poor. For both Gundry and Patte, then, the stress of this passage falls on Jesus' words.

A careful analysis of this passage, however, reveals that it focuses on both Jesus' words and deeds. The reference to what John's disciples *hear* most naturally relates to Jesus' own words about his activities as recorded in 11.5; John's disciples are instructed to report on what they hear Jesus say about his ministry. The reference to what John's disciples *see* most naturally relates to the activities themselves; John's disciples are instructed to report as witnesses of what they see Jesus do. Therefore, the narrator uses the clause 'what you hear and see' to establish a two-pronged witness to Jesus' activities. As a response to John's expression of doubt, John's disciples are to report to him Jesus' testimony on his own activities, and also their own testimony resulting from their observation of Jesus' activities. Far from setting Jesus' words over his deeds, the narrator gives equal weight to both.

What does the narrator intend for the narratee to see in the list of Jesus' activities recorded in 11.5? Most commentators hold that Matthew here recalls words from Isaiah.[13] It is clear that the narrator does not direct the narratee to one particular passage of Isaiah; no single passage in Isaiah refers to more than three of the six activities

11. Gundry, *Matthew*, p. 206; Gundry also points to 11.1 in support of this contention.

12. Patte, *Matthew*, pp. 158-59.

13. Beare (*Matthew*, p. 257) cites 35.4-6 and 61.1; Hill (*Matthew*, p. 198) cites 35.5-6 and 61.1-2; Harrington (*Matthew*, p. 156) cites 26.19, 35.5-6 and 61.1; Gundry (*Matthew*, p. 206) cites 26.19, 29.18-19, 35.5-6 and 61.1; Gardner (*Matthew*, p. 186) cites 26.19, 29.18-19, 35.5-6 and 61.1-2; Garland (*Reading Matthew*, pp. 124-25) cites 26.19, 29.18, 35.5-6, 42.18 and 61.1; Davies and Allison (*Saint Matthew*, II, pp. 242-43) cite 26.19, 29.18, 35.5-6, 42.7, 42.18 and 61.1.

mentioned in 11.5.[14] Instead, the narrator draws together in the list of v. 5 various blessings that Isaiah presents as manifestations of the eschatological salvation. It is important to notice that the particular blessings chosen by the narrator have been bestowed by Jesus upon characters earlier in the narrative.[15] Davies and Allison explain the effect of the narrator's list as follows:

> [Verse 5] contains more than a list of miracles: it also supplies a hermeneutical suggestion. Jesus' language directs one to Isaiah and is therefore an invitation to put Jesus' ministry and Isaiah's oracles side by side. Are not the promises of salvation being fulfilled? Is not eschatology in the process of being realized?[16]

By thus alluding to Isaiah, the narrator depicts Jesus as claiming to be the messianic bringer of salvation. In fact, this is Jesus' most explicit messianic claim to this point in the narrative. To provide a fitting lead for this weighty assertion by Jesus concerning his own messianic identity, the narrator uses John's strongest expression of uneasiness on that very issue.

Jesus concludes his list of messianic deeds with a beatitude: 'Blessed is the one who is not offended by me' (11.6). At the story level, this statement addresses John's situation; it directs him not to be offended by the nature of the messianic ministry he sees in Jesus, even though it does not meet John's own expectations. This statement, however, also has significance at the discourse level. The subject of this beatitude is indicated by the indefinite ὃς ἐάν ('whoever'). David Howell asserts

14. 29.18-19 refers to the deaf, the blind and the poor; 35.5-6 refers to the blind, the deaf and the lame; 42.18 refers to the deaf and the blind; 61.1-2 refers to the poor and the blind; 26.19 refers to the dead.

15. See 5.3 (beatitude on the poor in spirit); 8.1-4 (healing of a leper); 8.5-13 and 9.2-8 (healings of paralyzed people); 9.18-26 (raising of a dead girl); 9.27-31 (healing of two blind people). Up to this point in the narrative, Jesus has not been seen causing a deaf person (κωφός) to hear. It should be noted, however, that the word κωφός can be rendered either 'deaf' or 'mute', and Jesus has been seen causing a mute person (κωφός) to speak (cf. 9.32-34). It appears that the narrator intends the narratee to think back to the healing of the mute person in 9.32-34 when the narratee sees the reference to κωφός in the list. However, when it comes to choosing the wording for the list, the narrator selects words that speak of the deaf hearing, rather than the mute speaking, simply to assimilate the wording to the passages in Isaiah that all use the word κωφός to refer to the deaf (Isa. 29.18; 35.5; 42.18).

16. Davies and Allison, *Saint Matthew*, II, p. 243.

that 'whoever' statements, though addressing characters in the story, serve also to address the implied reader/narratee.[17] Therefore, the use of ὃς ἐάν in the beatitude of 11.6 indicates that the narrator intends to address this beatitude to the narratee. Support for this contention is found in the fact that there are no signs of uptake by any character in the story, thus indicating that the narrator intends this statement to be for the benefit of the narratee.

What type of effect does the narrator intend to have on the narratee by means of this statement? To this point, the narrator has presented an exalted portrait of Jesus the Messiah. The narrator has bestowed on him numerous honorific characterizations, such as 'Messiah, Son of David, Son of Abraham' (1.1), Saviour (1.21), 'Emmanuel' (1.23), eschatological judge (3.11-12), and Son of God (3.17). Against the backdrop of this exalted portrait, the narrator now shows the narratee a picture of Jesus the Messiah as one who spends his time among the blind, the lame, lepers, the deaf, corpses and the poor (cf. 11.4)—behaviour potentially offensive to someone who conceives of the Messiah only in exalted and glorious terms. Therefore, the narrator uses the beatitude of 11.5 to encourage the narratee to accept this characterization of Jesus' messianic ministry rather than to take offense because of it.

Jesus' Ideological Point of View on John

After having Jesus address John's question of 11.3, the narrator specifically states the topic to which Jesus now turns his attention: 'Jesus began to speak to the crowds *concerning John*' (11.7a; emphasis added). Jesus begins his comments on John with a series of questions addressed to the crowds, inquiring as to the reason behind their excursions into the wilderness. He asks if the crowds went out into the wilderness to see 'A reed shaken by the wind?' (11.7c)[18] or 'A person

17. David B. Howell, *Matthew's Inclusive Story: A Study on the Narrative Rhetoric of the First Gospel* (Sheffield: Sheffield Academic Press, 1990), p. 221; Fowler, *Let the Reader Understand*, p. 127 n. 1, designates this type of statement 'implicit commentary'.

18. Commentators have suggested several possibilities regarding the significance of the phrase 'a reed shaken by the wind': W.F. Albright and C.S. Mann, *Matthew* (Garden City, NJ: Doubleday, 1971), p. 136 (the reed as a symbol of vascillation by John); W.R. Farmer, 'John the Baptist', in *IDB*, II, pp. 955-62 (957) (the reed as a symbol of strength); David Flusser, *Die rabbinischen Gleichnisse und der Gleichniserzähler Jesus* (Bern: Peter Lang, 1981), pp. 52-53, cited in Edward J.

clothed in soft garments?' (11.8b).[19] Since Jesus is clearly speaking 'concerning John', the narratee knows that neither of these suggestions is even remotely close to the truth. Instead, the narratee takes these suggestions as rhetorical questions[20] leading toward the correct answer that ends the list: 'A prophet?' (11.9b). With this question, the narratee finally encounters a suggestion that resonates with John's characterization in the narrative: John in the prophetic role of calling the people to repentance and foretelling the coming of one mightier than himself.

The narrator reinforces this understanding of John by having Jesus confirm it, not only with the affirmative, 'Yes', but also with the supporting formula, 'I say to you' (11.9c). As pointed out in a previous discussion of this formula, these words signal a declaration made with the authority of a prophetic spokesperson of God.[21] Therefore, the presence of the formula 'I say to you' in the present context serves to endow Jesus' affirmation with a sense of divine authority. However, the narrator has Jesus immediately add to this characterization with the words, 'and more than a prophet'. While John has just been granted profound significance through his characterization as a prophet, this addition indicates that his significance transcends even that status.

The nature of John's true significance is evident in Jesus' assertion that John fulfills the prophecy, 'Behold, I send my messenger before your face who will prepare your way before you' (11.10). This citation of John as fulfilling this prophecy pertaining to the way-preparer of the Messiah does not constitute a new insight for the narratee, for the narrator presents essentially the same citation of John back in ch. 3 (3.3).

Young, *Jesus and his Jewish Parables: Rediscovering the Roots of Jesus' Teachings* (New York: Paulist Press, 1989), p. 238 (the reed as a symbol of the lack of compromise); Davies and Allison, *Saint Matthew*, II, p. 247 (the reed as a symbol of wonder-working).

19. Commentators have suggested several possibilities regarding the significance of the phrase 'a person clothed in soft garments': Alfred Plummer, *An Exegetical Commentary on the Gospel According to S. Matthew* (London: Elliot Stock, 1910), p. 161, and Garland, *Reading Matthew*, p. 126 (Herod Antipas); McNeile, *St. Matthew*, p. 153, and Gundry, *Matthew*, p. 207 (contrast to the prophet's hairy mantle); Beare, *Matthew*, p. 259 (effeminacy of the courtiers of Herod's palaces); Davies and Allison, *Saint Matthew*, II, p. 248 (worldly splendour).

20. Note that Jesus provides no opportunity for response to either of these questions.

21. See p. 89 above.

Why does the narrator repeat this citation at this point? The narrative since the first citation has revealed John as a way-preparer who does not fully comprehend the mission of the one whose way he is preparing (3.14; 9.14; 11.2-3). In fact, while the deficiency in John's ideological point of view relates only to the timing of Jesus as the eschatological judge, the deficiency has grown progressively more and more severe, even to the point now that John is openly questioning whether Jesus is truly the one whose way he is to be preparing. Therefore, while the primacy effect would have the narratee hold John as a capable way-preparer of the Lord, the recency effect now threatens to totally overwhelm this attitude toward John, thus rendering John useless as a way-preparer for the rest of the narrative. If the narrator wishes for the original characterization of John to survive, the narrator must reinforce it,[22] and it appears that the reiteration in 11.10 of John as the fulfilment of the prophecy regarding the way-preparer of the Messiah accomplishes this task; this reiteration serves to rehabilitate John in the eyes of the narratee. In this way, the narrator salvages John, and thus enables him to continue his function as way-preparer in the rest of the narrative.

Jesus continues his exposition on John with a statement introduced by the formula, 'Truly I say to you' (11.11a). Like the basic formula, 'I say to you', this one also signals that the following statement is made with the authority of a prophetic spokesperson of God. However, the addition of the word 'truly' enhances the solemnity of the statement; as David Hill asserts, 'In the Gospels...and in every strand of Gospel tradition, *amen* is used, without exception, to strengthen a person's own words'.[23] Therefore, while a statement introduced by 'I say to you' constitutes a weighty declaration, a statement introduced by 'truly I say to you' carries even more weight.[24] Robert Fowler describes the narrative significance of statements introduced by the latter formula as follows:

> They...function as pointed declarations originating from the hidden but ever present-narrator, aimed at the reader, and instructing the reader in

22. Cf. Perry, 'Literary Dynamics', p. 57.

23. David Hill, *New Testament Prophecy* (Atlanta: John Knox Press, 1979), p. 64.

24. Contra Davies and Allison, *Saint Matthew*, I, p. 490, who hold the two forms of the formula to be functional equivalents.

> the clearest of terms as to how to read the text. They are hermeneutical remarks aimed at shaping the reader's understanding of the narrative.[25]

At the beginning of v. 11, the augmented formula introduces the words, 'There has arisen no one among those born of women[26] greater than John the Baptist' (11.11a). This statement adds to the positive characterization of John resulting from Jesus' earlier assertions that John is 'more than a prophet' (11.9c) and that John fulfils a prophecy pertaining to the way-preparer of the Messiah (11.10). However, the question arises: for what reason does the narrator enhance this statement in v. 11a through the addition of the augmented formula? The narrator's purpose in highlighting this particular assertion becomes evident with a look at the following words: 'but the least in the Kingdom of Heaven is greater than he' (11.11b). Within v. 11, then, the narrator contrasts John's high position 'among those born of women' (v. 11a) with his position as lower than 'the least in the Kingdom of Heaven' (v. 11b). The words 'Truly I say to you' heighten the exalted characterization of John in the first half of the verse, thus magnifying the degree of contrast with the humbling characterization of John in the second half. In this way, the narrator accentuates John's lowly position.

Davies and Allison note three possible interpretations of 'the least in the Kingdom of Heaven'.[27] One interpretation holds that 'the least' refers to Jesus himself, 'with reference to his humility, to his being younger than John, or to his being John's disciple'. Davies and Allison correctly assert that Matthew would not likely think of Jesus as 'the lesser' or 'the least', and they add that this Gospel contains no evidence of Jesus' being John's disciple or of his being younger than John. A second interpretation identifies 'the least' as 'anyone now in the kingdom of Heaven'. Although Davies and Allison recognize this view as the most popular interpretation among modern commentators, they rightly refrain from adopting it, because it excludes John from participation in the Kingdom. A third possible interpretation identifies 'the least' as 'anyone in the kingdom of Heaven (when it comes)'. Davies and Allison explain this option by quoting J.C. O'Neill:

25. Fowler, *Let the Reader Understand*, p. 76.

26. Friedrich Büchsel, 'γεννητός', *TDNT*, I, p. 672, notes that γεννητοὶ γυναικῶν reflects a common Hebrew expression that 'denotes men as distinct from angels and God, i.e., as earthly creatures'.

27. Davies and Allison, *Saint Matthew*, II, pp. 251-52.

> Jesus is not contrasting all begotten [*sic*] of women, with John at their head, and some other group of men, the least of which is greater than John; he is contrasting the present state of the greatest of men with the future state of the least in the coming kingdom.[28]

Davies and Allison express a preference for this option, for it does not exclude John from the Kingdom and thus coincides with the following verse (11.12), which appears to include John in the Kingdom.[29]

This third interpretation proceeds on the assumption that the designation ὁ μικρότερος ('the least') refers to the person of lowest status among all those who participate in the Kingdom of Heaven. This assumption, however, is questionable. Earlier in the narrative, reference was made to the person of lowest status among those in the Kingdom (5.19), and the designation ἐλάχιστος...ἐν τῇ βασιλείᾳ τῶν οὐρανῶν ('least in the Kingdom of Heaven') was used. Because the narrator uses a different designation here in 11.11, it appears that the narrator intends this new designation as something other than merely a reference to the person of lowest status among those in the Kingdom.

To determine the narrator's intended meaning for the designation ὁ μικρότερος, it is important to note that the only other usage of the adjective μικρός to this point in the narrative occurs a mere 11 verses earlier.[30] It is used in its positive form in 10.42 where Jesus speaks of giving a cup of cold water to 'one of these little ones' (ἕνα τῶν μικρῶν τούτων). What is meant by this designation, 'little ones'? Note that the words ἕνα τῶν μικρῶν τούτων are followed by the prepositional phrase, εἰς ὄνομα μαθητοῦ. In the immediately preceding verse, a similar construction is used to describe receiving a prophet εἰς ὄνομα προφήτου. Dorothy Jean Weaver points out that εἰς ὄνομα should be translated 'because he is';[31] therefore, v. 41a speaks of one receiving a *prophet* because he is a *prophet*. Likewise, v. 41b uses the same prepositional phrase to speak of one receiving a *righteous person* because he is a *righteous person*. Finally, v. 42 uses the same prepositional phrase

28. J.C. O'Neill, *Jesus the Messiah: Six Lectures on the Ministry of Jesus* (Cambridge: Cochrane, 1980), pp. 10-11; cited by Davies and Allison, *Saint Matthew*, II, p. 251.

29. Davies and Allison also suggest that 11.9 might put John in the Kingdom as well (*Saint Matthew*, II, p. 252 n. 76).

30. Excluding the three usages of ἐλάχιστος, the irregular superlative form of μικρός; this form occurs in 2.6 and twice in 5.19.

31. Weaver, *Matthew's Missionary Discourse*, p. 210 n. 210.

to speak of one giving a drink to *one of these little ones* because he is a *disciple*, thus indicating that 'these little ones' are to be understood as disciples.

Because the narratee encounters the designation ὁ μικρότερος in 11.11 so soon after the use of ἕνα τῶν μικρῶν τούτων in 10.42, the narratee is prompted to make a connection between the two designations. As a result, the narratee understands ὁ μικρότερος to be a member of 'these little ones'. More specifically, this comparative—clearly to be understood as a superlative in this context—denotes the member of least prominence in that group. Therefore, 11.11 asserts that the person of least prominence among 'these little ones' is greater than John.

Does this mean that John is necessarily excluded from the Kingdom? Another look at the context of the reference to 'little ones' in 10.42 reveals that such is not the case. Jesus' statement in 11.11 does suggest that John is not to be considered as a member of the group designated 'little ones', for the person of least prominence within that group is greater than him. This, however, does not mean that John is necessarily excluded from the Kingdom. Back in 10.40-42, the reference to 'little ones' occurred in conjunction with references to 'prophets' and 'righteous persons', two other groups who obviously participate in the Kingdom along with the 'little ones'. Therefore, even though John is precluded by 11.11 from membership in the 'little ones', that does not necessarily preclude him from membership in some other group also participating in the Kingdom. Indeed, Jesus' statement about John as recorded in 11.9 indicates that he would certainly be a member of the 'prophets', and thus a participant in the Kingdom as well.

Now that it has been established that 11.11 does not function to exclude John from participation in the Kingdom, it remains to determine how 11.11 does, in fact, function. This verse contains the prepositional phrases, ἐν γεννητοῖς γυναικῶν ('among those born of women'), and ἐν τῇ βασιλείᾳ τοῦ οὐρανῶν ('in the Kingdom of Heaven'). It is important to note that these two phrases do not serve to separate all of humanity into those excluded from the Kingdom and those included in it. The phrase 'among those born of women' does not necessarily designate persons outside the Kingdom; the Gospel of Matthew does not include the Johannine distinction between that born of the flesh and that born of the Spirit (cf. Jn 3.6). Because no such distinction is evident in this narrative, the narratee would understand the phrase 'among those born of women' as a designation for all humanity. Therefore, the first half of v. 11 asserts that John is the greatest of all human beings.

The second half of v. 11 then asserts that the least prominent member of the 'little ones' is greater than John. The designation 'little ones', introduced in conjunction with designations as prominent as 'prophets' and 'righteous persons', emphasizes the lowly status of this group. In fact, the juxtaposition of these three designations in the span of a mere two sentences leads the narratee to consider the 'little ones' as the least prominent group in the whole Kingdom. Therefore, to claim that John is indeed a participant in the Kingdom, but at the same time assert that the 'littlest "little one"' is greater than him, defies logic. However, an examination of the way in which the narrator has crafted 11.11 suggests that he intends this verse to accomplish something beyond a mere comparison of the relative positions of these two figures.

In v. 11, the narrator uses the phrase ἐν γεννητοῖς γυναικῶν in the first half of the verse and the phrase ἐν τῇ βασιλείᾳ τοῦ οὐρανῶν in the second half. Note that both of these phrases begin with the preposition ἐν. It appears that the narrator is attempting to have the narratee see ἐν γεννητοῖς γυναικῶν and ἐν τῇ βασιλείᾳ τοῦ οὐρανῶν as parallel phrases.[32] The former phrase emphasizes the condition of humanness,[33] while the latter focuses on the Kingdom. In setting these two phrases in parallel, the narrator seems to be emphasizing a contrast between human perspective and the perspective of the Kingdom.

An examination of the content of v. 11 reveals the issue on which the human perspective is being contrasted with the perspective of the Kingdom. Note that each half of v. 11 contains the comparative μείζων, used in both cases to indicate that something is greater than something else: 'there has not arisen anyone among those born of women *greater* than John' (v. 11a) and 'the "littlest little one" is *greater* than he' (v. 11b). Apparently, the narrator has crafted this verse to contrast the human perspective on greatness with a perspective on greatness informed by the values of the Kingdom. This verse suggests that, while the prominence of John may qualify him for greatness by human standards, the values of the Kingdom are so radically different that greatness in the Kingdom is found in the least prominent member of the least prominent group. This saying then constitutes the first

32. Cf. Davies and Allison, *Saint Matthew*, II, p. 251.
33. See n. 26 above.

expression of the paradoxical truth: greatness in the Kingdom involves the opposite of what human wisdom would dictate.[34]

Jesus' next statement begins with the words ἀπὸ δὲ τῶν ἡμερῶν Ἰωάννου τοῦ βαπτιστοῦ ἕως ἄρτι ('From the days of John the Baptist until now'). The issue arises as to whether this statement is to be taken exclusively or inclusively, that is, indicating a period of time starting at John, and excluding him or including him. On this issue, Walter Wink points out, 'In almost every instance when Matthew uses ἀπὸ he gives it a temporal and inclusive sense, especially when used with ἕως.'[35] Davies and Allison also take this phrase with an inclusive sense: '[W]ould one not expect reference to a *point* in time rather than to a *span* of time ("the days of John") if the purpose were exclusion?'[36] Further, they assert, '11.9 makes John more than a prophet and therefore hints at his inclusion in a new period, the period after the law and the prophets (cf. 11.14-15)'.[37] Finally, Eduard Schweizer sees in Jesus' talk about himself and John together in 11.18-19 an indication that these two characters should be taken as members of the same era.[38] These points build a compelling case for taking the phrase 'From the days of John the Baptist until now' inclusively, denoting a period of time starting at John and including him.

The description of the state of the Kingdom during this period of time reads, ἡ βασιλεία τῶν οὐρανῶν βιάζεται καὶ βιασταὶ ἁρπάζουσιν αὐτήν (11.12b). This statement has given rise to a great deal of literature.[39] A proper understanding of this verse turns on two

34. This theme is developed further later in the narrative; see 18.4, 20.26 and 23.11.

35. Wink, *Gospel Tradition*, p. 29.

36. Davies and Allison, *Saint Matthew*, II, p. 254 (emphasis original).

37. Davies and Allison, *Saint Matthew*, II, p. 254.

38. Eduard Schweizer, *The Good News According to Matthew* (trans. David E. Green; Atlanta: John Knox Press, 1975), p. 263.

39. Davies and Allison (*Saint Matthew*, II, p. 254) describe this saying (with its Lukan parallel) as 'without a doubt, one of the NT's great conundrums'. Studies on this saying include Charles Stratton, 'Pressure for the Kingdom', *Int* 8 (1954), pp. 414-21; Franz Mussner, 'Der nicht erkannte Kairos', *Bib* 40 (1959), pp. 599-612; Georg Braumann, 'Dem Himmelreich wird Gewalt angetan (Mt 11 12 par.)', *ZNW* 52 (1961), pp. 104-109; Ernest Moore, 'ΒΙΑΖΩ, ΑΡΠΑΖΩ and Cognates in Josephus', *NTS* 21 (1975), pp. 519-43; P.W. Barnett, 'Who Were the "Biastai" (Matthew 11.12-13)?', *RTR* 36 (1977), pp. 65-70; Dieter Zeller, 'Die Bildlogik des Gleichnisses Mt 11 16-17/Lk 7 31-32', *ZNW* 68 (1977), pp. 252-57; David

issues: (1) whether the verb βιάζεται is to be taken as middle or passive; and (2) whether this verb carries a positive or negative connotation. Gottlob Schrenk[40] presents two different renderings for when βιάζεται is taken as middle and positive,[41] and two further renderings for when it is taken as passive and positive.[42] He sees, however, a significant problem with any interpretation that takes βιάζεται as positive:

> [T]he καὶ βιασταὶ ἁρπάζουσιν αὐτήν causes difficulty, since it is construed most naturally as an interpretation of the first part of the statement, βιασταί agreeing with βιάζεται. Since the reference...is obviously to a powerful hostile action, it seems better to seek an explanation which will better harmonize the two parts of the saying.[43]

Schrenk then discusses two different renderings for βιάζεται as passive and negative. The first reads, '[T]he rule of heaven is sought by unprincipled enthusiasts in violent action', which refers to the Zealots. Against this interpretation, Schrenk rightly argues that, because Matthew's concern here is with the prophets, the Law, the Baptist, Jesus and the Kingdom, a reference to the Zealots would be irrelevant. The second rendering reads, '[The divine rule] is contested, attacked or hampered by contentious opponents'. Schrenk adopts this interpretation, pointing out that it allows for the harmonization of the first and second halves of the saying, and that it corresponds to most of the linguistic parallels.

Ernest Moore's study of βιάζω and ἁρπάζω in the writings of Josephus lends support to Schrenk's contention that βιάζεται in 11.12

Catchpole, 'On Doing Violence to the Kingdom', *Journal of Theology for Southern Africa* 25 (1978), pp. 50-61; B.E. Thiering, 'Are the "Violent Men" False Teachers?' *NovT* 21 (1979), pp. 291-97; Rod Doyle, 'Mt 11.12: A Challenge to the Evangelist's Community', *Colloquium* 18 (1985), pp. 20-30; Peter Scott Cameron, *Violence and the Kingdom: The Interpretation of Matthew 11.12* (Frankfurt: Peter Lang, 2nd edn, 1988); Ernest Moore, 'Violence to the Kingdom: Josephus and the Syrian Churches', *ExpTim* 100 (1989), pp. 174-77. Davies and Allison (*Saint Matthew*, II, pp. 254-55), present a concise summary of the seven main interpretations of this verse.

40. Gottlob Schrenk, 'βιάζομαι, βιαστής', in *TDNT*, I, pp. 609-14 (610-11).

41. '[T]he rule of God breaks in with power, with force and impetus', or 'The kingdom of heaven compels or forces'.

42. '[T]he ardent pressure of needy souls from the time of the Baptist to "seize the kingdom as a prey"', or 'The dominion is powerfully advanced by God'.

43. Schrenk, 'βιάζομαι', I, p. 610.

should be taken with a negative connotation. Following an extensive examination of these verbs, and their cognates, Moore concludes: (1) 'The direct employment of physical violence is almost invariably implied in their usage, and particularly in their combined usage';[44] (2) 'The context of the two words often shows that an attempt is being made to force people or things, against their will or nature';[45] and (3) 'The context in which the words are used often implied (a) that the user of βία or ἁρπαγή has no right to the end for which it is exercised, and (b) that those against whom it is being used are being deprived of their rights'.[46] Based on the work of Schrenk and Moore, I conclude that the clause ἡ βασιλεία τῶν οὐρανῶν βιάζεται in 11.12 is to be taken with the sense 'the Kingdom of Heaven has been attacked'.

It remains to determine the identity of the βιασταί who have been attacking the Kingdom. In Schrenk's view, they are the human opponents of Jesus and John; Schrenk points to 'the forces which were opposed to [Jesus] in the Judaism of His day', and interprets 11.2 as follows: 'John as a βιαζόμενος is in the prison of the βιαστής [Herod]'.[47] However, given the narrative to this point, I contend that the narratee would not understand this mention of βιασταί in 11.12 as a reference to the human opponents of Jesus and John. The opening words of 11.12—'from the days of John the Baptist until now'—prompt the narratee to think back over the story from the appearance of John to this point in the narrative. With this stretch of the narrative as a backdrop, the narratee encounters the words 'the Kingdom of Heaven has been attacked'. Given the narrative to this point, the narratee would not understand this assertion as referring to violent attacks against the Kingdom by human opponents, for the narratee has witnessed no such attacks. Jesus has faced opposition to his ministry since the days of John,[48] but this opposition has not been sufficiently fierce to warrant the description 'the Kingdom of Heaven has been attacked'. Therefore, this assertion must be understood in some other way.

To this point, the whole story has been presented from the point of

44. Moore, 'ΒΙΑΖΩ', p. 534.
45. Moore, 'ΒΙΑΖΩ', p. 534.
46. Moore, 'ΒΙΑΖΩ', p. 536.
47. Schrenk, 'βιάζομαι', I, p. 612.
48. See, for example, 8.34 (the Gadarenes' begging Jesus to leave their region); 9.3 (the scribes' charging Jesus with blasphemy); and 9.11 (the Pharisees' opposing Jesus' practice of eating with tax collectors and sinners).

view of what might be called 'the physical realm'; it is a story that focuses on the exploits of human beings within history. It is clear from the narrative, however, that another realm exists, what might be called 'the spiritual realm'. An example of this other realm is seen in the Infancy Narrative where an angel interacts with Joseph on a number of occasions (1.20-21; 2.13, 19-20);[49] the actions of this angel represent incursions into the physical realm by a being who functions primarily in another realm.

The existence of this other realm sheds light on Jesus' assertion that the Kingdom of Heaven has been under attack since the days of John's ministry: the Kingdom has suffered attacks in warfare fought in the spiritual realm.[50] The narrative to this point contains evidence of the existence of such warfare involving spiritual beings. Immediately following the account of John's baptism of Jesus, Jesus encounters the devil (4.1-11); therefore, at the beginning of the period designated 'from the days of John the Baptist until now', a being from the spiritual realm makes a foray into the physical realm in order to oppose Jesus. Further, in the early stages of his ministry, Jesus casts out demons from two men in the region of the Gadarenes (8.28-34) and from a man unable to speak (9.32-34); again, within his ministry in the physical realm, Jesus confronts beings from the spiritual realm. These forays by beings from the spiritual realm into the physical realm to attack Jesus' efforts to further the Kingdom suggest that these spiritual beings are also attacking the Kingdom in their own native domain, the spiritual realm.

Perrin's analysis of 11.12 results in similar conclusions. He asserts that Mt. 12.28 and parallels interpret Jesus' exorcisms as a victory for the Kingdom in an eschatological struggle, and notes that v. 29 uses the verb ἁρπάζω to describe Jesus' actions against Satan in the eschatological struggle. Perrin then argues that the use of ἁρπάζω in 11.12 should be interpreted in the same way.[51] He summarizes this interpretation as follows: 'What we have here is the reverse of the situation envisaged in

49. Cf. also 2.12 and 2.22, in which warnings are given in dreams, presumably through the agency of an angel.

50. Cf. Kingsbury, *Structure, Christology, Kingdom*, p. 142; Kraeling, *John the Baptist*, p. 156; Amos N. Wilder, *Eschatology and Ethics in the Teachings of Jesus* (New York: Harper & Brothers, rev. edn, 1950), pp. 84, 182.

51. Norman Perrin, *The Kingdom of God in the Teaching of Jesus* (London: SCM Press, 1963), p. 173.

the interpretation of the exorcisms: there the Kingdom of Satan is being plundered, here that of God.'[52]

This understanding of 11.12 explains well how the Kingdom could be suffering violent attacks without the narratee witnessing them directly. On the basis of the foregoing analysis, I conclude that the clause 'the Kingdom of Heaven has been attacked' refers to assaults against the Kingdom in the spiritual realm at the hands of evil spiritual beings (βιασταί).[53] Therefore, Jesus uses this discourse on John as an opportunity to declare that the Kingdom has been under attack by evil spiritual beings from as early as the days of John's ministry up to the present.

Jesus continues, 'For all the prophets and the law prophesied until John' (11.13).[54] This statement is connected to the preceding verse by an explanatory γάρ,[55] and so constitutes the beginning of Jesus' own explanation of his claim that, from the days of John, the Kingdom has been under attack. The prophets and the law have been mentioned together twice in the narrative to this point (5.17; 7.12), and, in both cases, the law is mentioned before the prophets. For this reason, the reversal of their order in 11.13 stands out and specifically draws the narratee's attention to 'the prophets'. The narrator also has Jesus use ἐπροφήτευσαν ('prophesied') as the verb for this clause, and places it in a position of emphasis to enhance the theme of prophecy in this verse.

The continuation in v. 14 of Jesus' explanatory note focuses the general theme of prophecy onto a specific prophecy: John is identified

52. Norman Perrin, *Rediscovering the Teaching of Jesus* (London: SCM Press, 1967), p. 77.

53. While some may argue that the Jewish leaders also qualify as βιασταί, I contend that their opposition against the Kingdom is addressed in the immediately following pericope: the 'Parable of the Children' (11.16-19). See the discussion of this parable, below.

54. Commentators differ on the issue of whether the prepositional phrase 'until John' serves to exclude him from (e.g. Gundry, Harrington and Davies and Allison), or to include him in (e.g. Hill, Beare), the time of the prophets. The continuation in v. 14 of this explanatory note provides support for the former interpretation. It reads, 'and, if you are willing to receive it, he is "Elijah who is destined to come"'. In citing John as fulfilling the prophecy of Mal. 4.5, the narrator clearly sees John as belonging to the time of fulfilment, rather than the time of the prophets.

55. Davies and Allison, *Saint Matthew*, II, p. 257.

as the returning Elijah. This citation of John as fulfilling the prophecy of Mal. 4.5 serves to narrow John's characterization as way-preparer by characterizing him as the way-preparer for 'the great and terrible day of the Lord'.[56] Therefore, Jesus explains the attacks on the Kingdom by placing them within the context of eschatological warfare: John's arrival onto the scene constitutes the return of Elijah that is to precede the great and terrible day of the Lord, and, in the ensuing eschatological struggle, the Kingdom has been under attack.

Jesus concludes this speech on John with the words, 'Let the one who has ears hear' (11.15). On this statement, Davies and Allison assert, 'The point is that it takes more than an ear in order to hear with understanding. What is required is inner attention, concentration, discernment.'[57] With this statement of v. 15, then, the narrator closes Jesus' comments on John's relation to the Kingdom (vv. 11-15) with an exhortation to the narratee to pay special attention. Therefore, this section on John's relation to the Kingdom is bracketed by signals to pay special attention: 'Truly I say to you' at the beginning and 'Let the one who has ears hear' at the end. By constructing vv. 11-15 in this way, the narrator indicates that this section holds a special significance in the development of the narrative. The narratee, however, is left to determine the nature of this significance from the narrative as it unfolds.

The Parable of the Children

Immediately upon the close of this speech on John, the narrator has Jesus present a parable rebuking a group designated 'this generation'. To whom is Jesus referring with his use of this designation? In his explanation of the parable, Jesus identifies them as people who say of John, 'He has a demon'[58] (11.18), and of Jesus, 'Behold, a person who is a glutton and a drunkard, a friend of tax collectors and sinners' (11.19). The wording of the charge levelled against John does not help

56. Mal. 4.5 reads, 'Behold, I will send to you Elijah the prophet before the great and terrible day of the Lord comes'.

57. Davies and Allison, *Saint Matthew*, II, p. 259.

58. Kraeling (*John the Baptist*, pp. 11-13) argues that 'having a demon' does not mean 'being possessed by a demon', but rather 'having a demon at one's disposal'.

in the identification of 'this generation'; no character in the narrative has been shown making such an accusation against him. The wording of the charge levelled against Jesus, however, helps to identify 'this generation' as the Jewish leaders. In 11.19, Jesus claims that 'this generation' has accused him of being 'a friend of tax collectors and sinners'. In 9.10-14, Jesus is shown as being criticized for associating with tax collectors and sinners, and the criticism has its source among the Jewish leaders. Therefore, 'this generation' in 11.19 should be identified with the Jewish leaders and those aligned with their ideological point of view.

The parable itself presents two groups of children. The first group complains that the second group has not responded to their flute-playing with dancing nor to their dirge-singing with mourning (11.16b-17). Immediately following this parable, Jesus provides an explanatory note[59] indicating that the behaviour of these children represents the interaction of John and Jesus with their opponents.

In this explanatory note, John is mentioned first with the assertion that he came neither eating nor drinking (v. 18a). Recall that, back in ch. 3, the narrator gave a description of John's diet: 'His food was locusts and wild honey' (3.4). The discussion on this statement suggested that this description functions not only to fill out the introduction of John, but also to provide the narratee with information that would be helpful in interpreting a later passage.[60] With this parable, the narratee encounters that later passage. On its face, the assertion in 11.18 that John came neither eating nor drinking not only fails to fit the picture of John offered in the narrative up to this point, but it also appears to present a human impossibility: life without food or drink. However, by witnessing this assertion against the backdrop of the description of John's diet in 3.4, the narratee realizes that it is nothing more than a hyperbolic representation of John's ascetic lifestyle.

After this capsule description of John's lifestyle, Jesus then goes on to present the opponents' ideological point of view on John: 'He has a demon' (v. 18b). Because the narratee knows that John's eating habits stem from his commitment to an ascetic lifestyle, the narratee holds the opponents' suggestion that John has a demon to be totally preposterous. As a result, the opponents are held up to ridicule before the narratee.

59. Verses 18-19 are syntactically connected to the image of the children with an explanatory γάρ.

60. See pp. 84-85 above.

Verse 19 begins with a statement on Jesus' lifestyle—he came eating and drinking—after which Jesus again presents the opponents' ideological point of view, this time on himself: he is a glutton and a drunkard, a friend of tax collectors and sinners. The narratee knows from 9.9-13 that Jesus does eat and drink with people whom the Jewish leaders consider unacceptable dining companions. However, the narratee also knows from that passage that such is acceptable behaviour from Jesus'—and thus also the narrator's—ideological point of view. Therefore, to the narratee, the suggestion that Jesus is a glutton and a drunkard is ludicrous. As a result, the opponents are again held up to ridicule before the narratee for suggesting such a thing.

One issue remains to be determined in the analysis of this parable. While it is clear that the two groups of children represent Jesus and John on the one hand, and the Jewish leaders on the other hand, it is not clear which group of children represents John and Jesus, and which group represents the Jewish leaders. Craig L. Blomberg[61] sets out the two possible interpretations as follows:

> Does the group of children proposing the two games represent, alternatively, Jesus and John, so that it is the Jewish leaders who neither danced nor mourned? Or did the Jews try to temper John's stern message with greater levity and Jesus' 'permissiveness' with stricter legalism only to find both men uncooperative?[62]

Blomberg points out that the former interpretation finds support in the wording of Jesus' comments (vv. 18-19),[63] while the latter interpreta-

61. Craig L. Blomberg, *Interpreting the Parables* (Downers Grove, IL: InterVarsity Press, 1990), p. 209.

62. Blomberg cites Dieter Zeller ('Die Bildlogik') and Joseph A. Fitzmyer (*The Gospel According to Luke I–IX* [Garden City, NY: Doubleday, 1981], pp. 678-79) as proponents of the first option, and Olof Linton ('The Parable of the Children's Game, Baptist and Son of Man (Matt. XI.16-19 = Luke VIII.31-5): A Synoptic Text-Critical, Structural and Exegetical Investigation', *NTS* 22 [1976], pp. 159-79) and I. Howard Marshall (*The Gospel of Luke* [Exeter: Paternoster Press; Grand Rapids: Eerdmans, 1978], pp. 300-301) as proponents of the second option.

63. If the calling children represent Jesus and John, then Jesus' complaint that the opponents failed to dance represents a criticism of their rigidity as reflected in their accusation that Jesus is a glutton and a drunkard simply because he dines with tax collectors and sinners (cf. v. 19), while John's complaint that the opponents failed to mourn represents a criticism of their lack of true understanding of repentance as reflected in the fact that they take the absence of eating and drinking in John's life as evidence that he has a demon (cf. v. 18).

tion relies on the order of Jesus' comments.[64]

The RSV translates the parable's introduction: 'But to what shall I compare this generation? *It is like children* sitting in the marketplaces and calling to their playmates' (11.16; emphasis added).[65] This rendering of the parable's introduction suggests that the children who are calling represent 'this generation', thus constituting support for the second interpretation. Joachim Jeremias, however, cautions against putting too much weight on the wording of this type of introduction to a parable. He asserts that this formula reflects a Semitism, and should not be translated 'it is like...', but rather 'it is the case with...as with...'.[66] Therefore, the introductory clause should not be translated, '[this generation] is like children...calling to their playmates', but rather, 'it is the case with [this generation] as with children...calling to their playmates'. Rendering the introduction to the parable in this way, it is conceivable that 'this generation' could be represented by either the children who are calling or by the children who are being called.

Davies and Allison reject the view that identifies the children who are being called with 'this generation'. In dismissing this view, they argue:

> 'We piped to you and you did not dance' (usually taken to refer to Jesus) comes before 'We wailed and you did not mourn' (usually taken to refer to John). Yet John made his appeal before Jesus appeared on the scene...The parallelism between 11.17 and 18 naturally inclines one to associate John with the line, 'We piped to you and you did not dance', Jesus with the line 'We wailed and you did not mourn'...Those who speak (λέγουσιν) their complaint in v. 17 (the children) are like those who speak (λέγουσιν) their complaint in vv. 18 and 19 ('He has a demon', 'Behold, a glutton...').[67]

64. If the calling children represent the opponents of John and Jesus, then the sequence of the complaints regarding the failure to dance—John's sternness—and then the failure to mourn—Jesus' levity—parallels the sequence of the comments in the explanatory note on the response to John and then the response to Jesus (cf. vv. 18-19), and also parallels the sequence of John's and Jesus' respective ministries.

65. All major modern translations render ὁμοία ἐστίν in this, or an equivalent, manner.

66. Joachim Jeremias, *The Parables of Jesus* (New York: Charles Scribner's Sons, 2nd rev. edn, 1972), pp. 101-102; Jeremias lists several parables in Matthew using this formula (13.24, 31, 33, 45, 47; 18.23; 20.1; 22.2; 25.1) that prove his point.

67. Davies and Allison, *Saint Matthew*, II, p. 262. They also argue: '11.16

Together, these points build a strong case for concluding that 'this generation' is represented by the children who are calling, and so I adopt this interpretation. The parable depicts the Jewish leaders as levelling criticism at John and Jesus for their failure to meet the expectations of the Jewish leaders.

Note that this description of the Jewish leaders' attacks on John and Jesus (11.16-19) follows immediately after the description of the attacks on the Kingdom in the spiritual realm (11.12-15). Just as the Kingdom has been suffering from the violent assaults of evil spiritual beings, it has also been suffering from the verbal assaults of evil human beings.[68] By juxtaposing these two passages, the narrator highlights the motif of opposition against the Kingdom. Further, by drawing together these images of opposition from spiritual beings and from the Jewish leaders, the narrator produces the sense that the spiritual beings and the Jewish leaders are acting in concert in their opposition to the Kingdom. Therefore, Trilling's designation, 'die gottfeindliche Front', is appropriate, although with a wider sense than that understood by Trilling.[69]

At this point, Jesus has been speaking for 13 consecutive verses. This speech is a past event from the perspective of the narrator and the narratee;[70] however, in the absence of any indicator that it is being spoken in the past, the sheer volume of words causes the narratee to lose sight of the fact that the speech is a past event. Such a lengthy speech serves to synchronize the temporal positions of the speaker and the narratee, thus drawing the narratee into the scene.[71] Note also the lack of uptake by the characters in the story. This indicates that this material is addressed primarily to the narratee. With these features, the narrator prompts the narratee to take special note of this theme of opposition at this point in the narrative.

The content of the following pericope makes clear the reason for this emphasis. In 11.20-24, the narrator depicts Jesus as pronouncing woes

likens "this generation" to the children who reproach others for not joining their game'. Jeremias's observations noted above, however, negate this point.

68. For a discussion of the characterization of the Matthean religious leaders as 'evil', see Kingsbury, *Matthew as Story*, pp. 19-24.

69. See the discussion on Trilling on p. 31 above.

70. From the perspective of point of view on the temporal plane, the temporal positions of the narrator and the narratee are at a point subsequent to the resurrection, but prior to the Parousia; see Kingsbury, *Matthew as Story*, p. 28; Howell, *Matthew's Inclusive Story*, pp. 212-13.

71. Anderson, 'Point of View in Matthew', p. 13.

upon Chorazin, Bethsaida and Capernaum because of their lack of repentance. These are Jesus' harshest words up to this point in the narrative. Prior to ch. 11, Jesus has been shown announcing the Kingdom's coming and offering its blessings to the people of Israel. Then, in 11.11-19, he sets forth the results of his efforts: the Kingdom's coming has prompted eschatological warfare (v. 12) in which the Jewish leaders—and those aligned with their ideological point of view—side with the forces of evil (vv. 16-19). In short, Jesus' efforts have met with opposition and rejection, both in the spiritual realm and in the physical realm. This recognition by Jesus marks the turning point in his ministry. The picture of Jesus as offering the Kingdom's blessings now becomes a picture of Jesus as pronouncing woes upon those who have rejected his offer.

Although Jesus has expressed criticism of his opponents earlier in the narrative,[72] this is his first pronouncement of woes. Further, instead of calling for repentance as he did earlier in his ministry (4.17), Jesus clearly declares the fate of those who have opposed him and rejected him, a fate involving judgment (11.22, 24). Therefore, this pericope presents Jesus' first declaration of judgment up to this point in the narrative. Finally, Jesus begins to express his identity as judge, first introduced in 3.11-12 and kept alive in 9.14-15 and 11.2-6 by the questions posed to Jesus by John and John's disciples.

Although John is not mentioned again in the narrative until the account of his execution in ch. 14, the narrator evokes a memory of John in ch. 12. Here, the Pharisees charge that Jesus casts out demons by Beelzebul, the ruler of the demons (12.24). In response to this charge, Jesus responds:

> Either make the tree good and its fruit good, or make the tree rotten and its fruit rotten; for the tree is known from its fruit. Brood of vipers! How are you able to speak good things while you are evil? (12.33-34a).

In these verses, the stinging invective 'Brood of vipers!' appears in the context of the motif of trees bearing fruit. This same invective appeared in the context of this same motif in John's judgment speech against the Pharisees and Sadducees (3.7b-10). Here, the narrator manipulates diction to have Jesus' words match the earlier words used by John, thus prompting retrospection to ch. 3.

By casting the narratee's mind back to John's stance toward the

72. See, for example, 5.20, 8.12 and 10.14-15.

Pharisees and Sadducees, the narrator draws John's words of judgment into the present pericope as corroborative background for Jesus' words of judgment against the Pharisees. Indeed, John is the most appropriate witness to invoke for the purpose of underscoring Jesus' judgment of the Pharisees; it was John who was responsible for introducing the motif of Jesus as judge in the first place (3.11-12), and he is the only character in the narrative who recognizes Jesus in that role, albeit with a deficient understanding of the timing for its execution.[73]

In addition, retrospection to ch. 3 from here in ch. 12 effects the same two results as did retrospection from ch. 4 and ch. 7 earlier in the narrative.[74] First, because Jesus' words in the present passage echo words spoken earlier by John, the narrator continues to condition the narratee to expect elements of John's story to reappear later as part of Jesus' story. Secondly, because the movement in ch. 3 is oriented so strongly toward the pronouncement of Jesus as the Son of God in 3.17, retrospection to any point in ch. 3 draws the narratee's mind toward this climactic declaration.[75] As a result, the narratee views Jesus' words of 12.33-37 against the backdrop of the image of Jesus as the Son of God, and therefore sees Jesus' pronouncement of judgment against the Pharisees as a pronouncement made with the authority of the Son of God. In this way, the narrator continues to make use of John as a target for retrospection at the discourse level of the narrative without even mentioning him at the story level.

73. See the discussions on 3.14, 9.14 and 11.2-3 on pp. 96-97 and 104-107 above.

74. See the discussions on 4.17 and 7.15-20 on pp. 102-103 above.

75. See p. 103 above.

Chapter 7

JOHN: DEAD AND GONE

The Execution of John

The account of the execution of John (14.1-12) constitutes the third passage in the narrative in which major attention is paid to John.[1] An examination of this account, however, must begin with an analysis of 13.53-58, which serves to prepare the narratee to witness this execution. In this earlier pericope, the narrator states that Jesus comes to his home town and teaches in the synagogue there (v. 54a). This information is presented in summary narrative; therefore, it is evident that neither Jesus' homecoming nor his teaching is intended by the narrator to constitute the focus of this pericope. Instead, the focus is found in vv. 54b-57, material presented in scene narrative.[2]

In vv. 54b-56, the townspeople express incredulity over Jesus' wisdom and his ability to perform mighty deeds. The narrator concludes the account of their response to Jesus with the words, 'And they were offended by him' (v. 57a). Here, the narrator uses diction to prompt retrospection to the beatitude which concludes Jesus' list of messianic deeds reported in 11.5: 'blessed is the one who is not offended by me' (11.6). By doing so, the narrator leads the narratee to view the townspeople's offense at Jesus against the backdrop of his earlier challenge not to be offended at his display of messianic deeds. In this way, the townspeople's offense is depicted as a rejection of Jesus' messiahship.

The narrator then presents Jesus' reaction to the townspeople's rejection: 'A prophet is not without honour except in his country and in his house' (13.57b). This proverb operates in two ways. First, at the story

1. See the above discussions on 3.1-17 and 11.2-19 on pp. 81-99 and 106-26 for treatments of the other two.

2. For a discussion on summary narrative versus scene narrative, see n. 60 above.

level, it shows that Jesus is not surprised by the townspeople's response to him, since his ministry stands in line with the ministry of the prophets, who are rejected by their own people as a matter of course. Secondly, at the discourse level, this saying serves to encapsulate the theme of opposition and rejection that has been developing in the narrative. Since 11.12-19, where this theme is first highlighted,[3] Jesus has been shown repeatedly facing opposition and rejection.[4] Jesus now draws together all of this opposition and rejection into a proverb that could be summarized 'the fate of the prophets'.[5] It is with this image in mind that the narratee now encounters John's execution.

The first mention of John in this account occurs in a statement by Herod the Tetrarch, as he expresses his ideological point of view on the identity of Jesus. His statement begins, 'This is John the Baptist' (v. 2a). Because this statement by Herod identifies Jesus as John the Baptist, the narratee recognizes that it reflects an incorrect ideological point of view; the narratee knows from earlier in the narrative that Jesus and John are two co-existing characters. Nevertheless, in identifying Jesus as John, Herod's statement again raises the issue of the nature of the assimilation between Jesus and John that has been developing in the narrative. As the discussions on 4.17, 7.19 and 12.33-34a have shown, retrospection from these verses to ch. 3 has been conditioning the narratee to expect elements of John's story to reappear as part of Jesus' story. To this point, however, the assimilation between Jesus and John has been limited to phraseology; it has developed no further than the repetition by Jesus of words spoken by John.

Now the narrator further develops this assimilation by directing the narratee's attention beyond the level of phraseology to the level of experience. Up to this point in the narrative, each time John has appeared in the story-line, he has been depicted as one who acts: preaching and baptizing (3.1-15) and sending messages through his disciples (9.14; 11.2-3). John has never appeared in the story-line as one who is acted upon. This is true even of his arrest; the narrator does

3. See p. 126 above.

4. Cf. the Pharisees' opposition to Jesus on the issue of plucking grain on the Sabbath (12.1-8); the Pharisees' contention with him on the issue of healing on the Sabbath that culminates in their conspiring to destroy him (12.9-14); the Pharisees' accusation that he casts out demons by Beelzebul (12.22-32); the request of the scribes and Pharisees for him to provide a sign for them (12.38-42).

5. Cf. Trilling, 'Die Täufertradition', p. 274.

not include this event in the story-line as a narrated event, but merely mentions it at 4.12 in a participial phrase, with the event itself having occurred at some earlier time. Therefore, this account of John's execution represents the first time in the story-line that John is depicted as one being acted upon. As a result, the narratee—already conditioned to expect elements of John's story to reappear as part of Jesus' story—is now prompted to refine that understanding: not only will the words of John reappear later in the speech of Jesus, but also the things that happen to John will later happen to Jesus as well.

This pericope describes five things that happen to John: (1) he is arrested, bound and imprisoned (v. 3); (2) he is faced with the desire of his captor to have him executed, although that desire is tempered by fear of the crowds (v. 5); (3) he is ordered by his captor to be executed, although with reluctance on the part of his captor (v. 9); (4) he is put to death by a mode of execution appropriate for a criminal (v. 10);[6] (5) he has his corpse buried by his disciples (v. 12). After having witnessed these things in John's experience, the narratee now expects to see them in Jesus' experience as well.[7]

This description of John's fate is significant from the perspective of point of view on the spatial plane, because it constitutes one of only two passages of any significant length in which Jesus does not appear and is not even mentioned.[8] The presence or absence of this account makes no difference to the flow of this story about Jesus; therefore, its contribution to the narrative is not to be found at the story level.[9]

6. Davies and Allison, *Saint Matthew*, II, p. 474.

7. Cf. Davies and Allison, *Saint Matthew*, II, p. 476. This expectation by the narratee will be fulfilled in the account of Jesus' passion; see pp. 141-42 below.

8. The other passage is 3.1-10.

9. It could be argued that the execution of John is significant to the flow of the story-line in that the report of it prompts Jesus to withdraw to a desolate place (cf. v. 13). This argument is based on the assumption that the narrative of v. 13 acts as a continuation of the narrative of v. 12. This assumption, however, is not valid. It must be noted that v. 3 is introduced by an explanatory γάρ, thus indicating that vv. 3-12 constitute an explanatory note on a detail alluded to in v. 2, that is, that John is now dead. Therefore, v. 13 does not serve as a continuation of v. 12, but of v. 2. As a result, Jesus does not withdraw to a desolate place because he has heard of John's execution, but rather because he has heard that Herod thinks he is John who has risen from the dead. Cf. Lamar Cope, 'The Death of John the Baptist in the Gospel of Matthew; or, The Case of the Confusing Conjunction', *CBQ* 38 (1976), pp. 515-19.

Rather, the narrator's purpose in using this passage is to impact the narratee at the discourse level of the narrative. In this account of John's execution, the narratee is prompted to see this depiction of John's fate as a precursor of Jesus' fate. As a result, the narratee now anticipates Jesus' own arrest and execution. Therefore, everything that Jesus says and does from this point on in the narrative will be viewed in that light.

From the perspective of point of view on the temporal plane, this pericope is striking because it constitutes the most important divergence in the narrative between story time and discourse time;[10] the execution of John takes place at some point earlier in story time, but the narrator delays an account of it until this point in the narrative. This delay allows the narrator to use John's fate as an illustration of the motif 'the fate of the prophets' introduced at the end of ch. 13. Up to that point, Jesus had been shown as facing opposition and rejection from many sides.[11] Then the narrator drew together this growing theme of opposition and rejection into the motif of 'the fate of the prophets' (13.57). Only after the introduction of this motif does the narrator insert the account of John's execution. If the narrator had related John's execution in its appropriate spot in story time, it would have been too early to serve as an illustration for the fate of the prophets. Therefore, the narrator makes this divergence between story time and discourse time in order to have the account of John's execution follow the introduction of the motif of the fate of the prophets, thus presenting John's fate as an example.

With the account of his execution in 14.1-12, John is removed from the story-line in a conclusive manner. As a result, the narratee now really has no reason to expect to see him or hear of him again. Therefore, a reference to John two chapters later in the account of Peter's confession (16.13-20) serves to jolt the narratee.

Peter's Confession

This pericope begins with Jesus' questioning of his disciples on the popular opinion about his identity (v. 13), and with the disciples'

10. For a discussion on the distinction between story time and discourse time, see Powell, *What Is Narrative Criticism?*, pp. 36-37. See also Culpepper, *Anatomy of the Fourth Gospel*, pp. 53-54, who uses the term 'narrative time' instead of 'discourse time'.

11. See n. 4 above.

responding, 'Some say John the Baptist; others say Elijah; and others say Jeremiah or one of the prophets' (v. 14). An examination of this pericope as a whole reveals that this opening exchange regarding public opinion on Jesus' identity (vv. 13-14) is unnecessary at the story level of the narrative. The focus of this pericope is Peter's confession (v. 16), which constitutes a response to Jesus' second question, an inquiry as to the disciples' opinion on his identity (v. 15). The narrator could have omitted the first exchange and presented only the second exchange between Jesus and his disciples with no adverse effect on the flow of the story-line. Therefore, the significance of the first exchange, with its reference to John, must lie at the discourse level of the narrative.

The reference to the crowds' misunderstanding of Jesus as John the Baptist prompts retrospection to the account of John's execution (14.1-12) in which Herod the Tetrarch expressed the same misunderstanding. As a result, the dominant motif of that passage—the fate of the prophets—is drawn in as a backdrop against which the narratee views the disciples' report in 16.14 on popular opinion regarding Jesus' identity. In this report, Jesus is identified repeatedly and exclusively with prophets.[12] This identification of Jesus with prophets, viewed against a backdrop of the fate of the prophets, provides the narratee with another picture of what is in store for Jesus: he is about to suffer a fate that is in line with the fate of the prophets.

The narrator immediately follows this picture of Jesus' suffering the fate of the prophets with Peter's declaration that Jesus is the Messiah, the Son of the living God (16.16). By juxtaposing the idea of Jesus as Messiah with the idea of Jesus as suffering the fate of the prophets, the narrator prompts the narratee to see Jesus' messiahship in a new light. The narratee now sees that Jesus' messiahship involves his suffering the fate of the prophets.[13]

Descent from the Mount of Transfiguration

The next mention of John the Baptist occurs in ch. 17 in an interaction between Jesus and some of his disciples. After his transfiguration, Jesus

12. The references to 'Elijah', 'Jeremiah' and 'one of the prophets' each clearly identifies Jesus with a prophet. In like manner, the reference to 'John the Baptist' does the same; although John is labelled 'Baptist', the way in which he is presented in 3.7-12 clearly depicts him in a prophetic role, and he is expressly designated a prophet by Jesus in 11.9.

13. This idea is presented in explicit terms a few verses later in 16.21.

commands these disciples, 'Tell to no one the vision until the Son of Man has been raised from among the dead' (17.9). In response to Jesus' command for silence, the disciples ask, 'Then why do the scribes say that it is necessary for Elijah to come first?' (17.10). This question is connected syntactically to the preceding verse with the conjunction οὖν. Since the disciples' question of v. 10 does not logically follow Jesus' command in v. 9 to tell no one the vision, the conjunction οὖν must connect the question to the vision itself. Therefore, the disciples' response could be paraphrased, 'If you really are the Messiah as was suggested by the vision, where is Elijah who is supposed to precede you?'

The disciples' reference to the coming of Elijah prompts retrospection to the passage on John the Baptist in ch. 11, the one other place in the narrative that mentions the coming of Elijah. As a result, the description of the Kingdom's suffering violent attacks (11.12) with its identification of John as Elijah who is to come (11.14) is drawn in as a backdrop against which the narratee views the present pericope. Because of this, the narratee knows the answer to the disciples' dilemma: Elijah has indeed preceded Jesus in the person of John the Baptist. Therefore, the narratee is not surprised when he or she hears Jesus say: 'Elijah has already come' (17.12a). Further, against the backdrop of the image of the Kingdom's suffering violent attacks drawn in from 11.12-15, Jesus' assertion that 'they did to him whatever they wanted' (17.12c) depicts John as a casualty in the war raging between the Kingdom of Satan and the Kingdom of God.[14]

Jesus continues, 'In this way also the Son of Man is about to suffer by them' (v. 12d). Back in his command for silence, Jesus alluded to the fate of the Son of Man: 'Tell no one the vision *until the Son of Man has been raised from the dead*' (v. 9; emphasis added). However, the disciples' response focused exclusively on the vision, apparently ignoring this allusion to the suffering of the Son of Man. Now Jesus draws the disciples' attention back to this theme of suffering with his comment about the Son of Man at the end of v. 12: 'In this way also the Son of Man is about to suffer at their hands'. With the opening words 'In this way also', Jesus links his own fate to the fate of John; Jesus knows that, like John, he also will fall as a casualty of the war raging between the Kingdom of Satan and the Kingdom of God.

14. For a discussion on this war between the Kingdom of Satan and the Kingdom of God, see pp. 120-21 above.

This interpretation finds support in the wording of 17.12. Note that Jesus, in describing the fate of John, uses verbs in the third-person plural without specifying the subjects: '*they* did not recognize him, but *they* did to him whatever *they* wanted' (emphasis added). While the antecedent of these third-person plural subjects might appear to be the scribes mentioned in v. 10, the narratee knows from the account of John's execution that it was not the scribes who 'did to him whatever they wanted', but rather Herod the Tetrarch (14.1-12). Therefore, the third-person plural subjects implied by the verbs of v. 12 must be understood in some other way.

The backdrop of fierce opposition against the Kingdom drawn in from ch. 11 influences the narratee's understanding here. As noted above, the juxtaposition of the passage describing the attacks against the Kingdom by evil spiritual beings (11.12-15) with the 'Parable of the Children' and its rebuke against the Jewish leaders for their opposition against John and Jesus (11.16-19) creates the sense that the spiritual beings and the Jewish leaders act in concert in their opposition to the Kingdom, thus forming a common front of opposition spanning both the spiritual realm and the physical realm.[15] With the image of this common front of opposition drawn in as a backdrop against which the discussion on Elijah is viewed, the narratee sees the statement of v. 12—'they did to him whatever they wanted'—as referring to members of this common front. Therefore, the narratee understands that it is members of this common front of opposition, and not just the scribes, who collectively 'did not recognize [John]'. Likewise, the narratee understands that it is members of this common front of opposition, and not just Herod the Tetrarch, who collectively 'did to him whatever they wanted'. This understanding also influences the way in which the narratee views Jesus' concluding statement, 'In this way also the Son of Man is about to suffer by *them*' (v. 12d; emphasis added). The narratee understands this as another reference to members of the common front of opposition. As a result, Jesus' impending fate is characterized as the work of this common front of opposition that spans both spiritual realm and physical realm.

To close this pericope, the narrator states, 'Then the disciples understood that he spoke to them concerning John the Baptist' (17.13). With this assertion, the narrator informs the narratee that the disciples finally understand what the narratee already knew as early as 11.14, that John

15. See p. 126 above.

is Elijah who is to come. However, although this statement indicates that the disciples grasp Jesus' explanation on John as set out in vv. 11-12, it does not indicate that they grasp his concluding statement on the Son of Man. Therefore, just as the disciples' question of v. 10 suggests that they miss Jesus' allusion in v. 9 to his coming suffering, so also this statement by the narrator in v. 13 suggests that the disciples also miss Jesus' reference in v. 12 to his coming suffering.

Jesus' Confrontation with Jewish Leaders in Jerusalem

In 21.23-27, the narrator presents an interaction between Jesus and the Jewish leaders on the issue of authority. In this pericope, chief priests and elders of the people approach Jesus and ask, 'By what [ποίᾳ] authority do you do these things, and who gave to you this authority?' (v. 23). Douglas R.A. Hare asserts that the use of the interrogative pronoun ποίος assumes that there are different kinds of authority, and he suggests three possible kinds: from God, from Satan and from self.[16] However, this narrative exhibits a strong tendency toward simplifying issues down to only two possibilities; as Kingsbury puts it:

> Characteristic of a gospel story like Matthew is that the many conflicting evaluative points of view expressed by the various characters can fundamentally be reduced to two: the 'true' and the 'untrue'. No effort is made in Matthew to carve out room for grey areas. The measuring rod for distinguishing truth from untruth is, as the passage 16.23 indicates, 'thinking the things of God' (as opposed to 'thinking the things of men').[17]

Because of this tendency toward framing all issues in terms of the ideological point of view of God on the one hand and the ideological point of view of human beings on the other hand, I contend that the narratee would see only two kinds of authority as possible answers to the Jewish leaders' question regarding the source of Jesus' authority: divine authority or human authority.

Given the negative characterization of the Jewish leaders to this point in the narrative, the narratee knows that their question to Jesus does not represent a mere inquiry for information, but rather constitutes an attempt to entrap Jesus. In posing this question, the Jewish leaders try

16. Douglas R.A. Hare, *Matthew* (Louisville, KY: John Knox Press, 1993), p. 245.

17. Kingsbury, *Matthew as Story*, p. 34.

to create a dilemma for Jesus. They attempt to force him either to discredit himself in the eyes of the crowds by admitting that his authority does not come from God, or to make the blasphemous claim that he does indeed act with God's authority.[18]

Jesus responds by saying, 'I also will ask you a question, and if you answer me, I also will tell you by what authority I do these things. From where was the baptism of John, from heaven or from a human source?' (21.24-25a). At the story level of the narrative, this response creates a dilemma for the Jewish leaders, as demonstrated by their deliberations presented in vv. 25b-26. Jesus is thus released from the need to answer the dilemma that the Jewish leaders originally pose to him.

In addition, Jesus' response engages the narratee at the discourse level of the narrative. Note that Jesus does not ask the Jewish leaders about the source of John's authority; rather, he asks more specifically about the source of the authority behind John's baptism. With this reference to John's *baptism*, the narrator prompts retrospection to ch. 3. Because the movement in ch. 3 is oriented so strongly toward the pronouncement of Jesus as the Son of God in 3.17, the narratee's mind is drawn toward this climactic declaration.[19] As a result, the narratee views Jesus' response to the Jewish leaders in the present pericope against the backdrop of the image of Jesus as the Son of God. Therefore, at the story level the Jewish leaders are deprived of an answer from Jesus on the issue of the source of his authority, but at the discourse level the narratee is provided with the answer: Jesus acts with the authority of the Son of God.

The Jewish leaders' deliberations (vv. 25b-26) constitute another instalment in their negative characterization by the narrator. As the Jewish leaders deliberate on what answer to give to Jesus' question regarding the source of John's baptism, they first consider the possibility of responding, 'From heaven' (21.25b). The narratee knows that this response reflects a correct ideological point of view, for the account of John's ministry of baptism in 3.5-15 was prefaced by his legitimation for the task through the citation of his fulfilling a prophecy regarding the way-preparer of the Lord (3.3). Yet the narratee sees that the Jewish leaders are not willing to give this answer. Instead, they go on to

18. Cf. 9.2-8, where Jesus faces a charge of blasphemy when he claims authority to forgive sins.

19. See p. 102 above.

consider the possibility of responding, 'From a human source' (v. 26a). The narratee knows that this response reflects an incorrect ideological point of view, yet the narratee sees that it does reflect the ideological point of view of the Jewish leaders, for they would give this answer if not for fear of the crowd (v. 26b). Therefore, these deliberations depict the Jewish leaders as characters who reject a correct ideological point of view and adhere to an incorrect one.

Further, it should be noted that in the Jewish leaders' deliberations, they make no effort to ascertain the correct answer as they deliberate. Instead, they put all of their efforts into discerning the answer that will best suit their purposes.[20] As a result, they appear as characters whose words are nothing more than self-serving utterances. Because of this, the Jewish leaders' unreliability is accentuated.

In deciding against the answer 'From a human source', the Jewish leaders reason, '[W]e fear the crowd, for all hold John as a prophet' (v. 26). Here, the narrator crafts the Jewish leaders' words to match the description of Herod the Tetrarch's reluctance to kill John: 'he feared the crowd, because it held him as a prophet' (14.5). In this way, the narrator prompts retrospection to the account of John's execution, thus drawing in the dominant theme of that account—the fate of the prophets—as a backdrop against which the present confrontation between Jesus and the Jewish leaders is viewed. As a result, this confrontation is understood by the narratee as a step toward Jesus' meeting the fate of the prophets.

The narrator has Jesus continue his response to the Jewish leaders with a parable (21.28-32). In this parable, a father asks one of his sons to work in the vineyard (21.28). Although the son at first refuses, he later goes and thus does as his father asks (v. 29). The father also asks a second son to work in the vineyard (v. 30a). Although this son at first agrees, he later does not go and thus does not do as his father asks (v. 30b). When Jesus asks the Jewish leaders which of the two sons did the will of their father, they answer, 'The first' (v. 31a).[21] Jesus then interprets the parable for the Jewish leaders, by identifying tax collectors and prostitutes with the first son. Like the first son, the tax collectors and prostitutes move from disobedience to obedience, for they believed John when he 'came to [them] in the way of righteousness' (v. 32a),

20. Cf. Patte, *Matthew*, p. 294.

21. The manuscript evidence for vv. 29-31 exhibits significant textual problems. For a text-critical analysis of this material, see the Appendix.

that is, in obedience to the divine will.[22] Therefore, by recognizing obedience in the behavior of the first son, the Jewish leaders unwittingly endorse the stance of the tax collectors and prostitutes who understand John's ministry to be in accordance with the divine will. In this way, the Jewish leaders are tricked into admitting what they earlier refused to admit, that the authority behind John's baptism is indeed 'from heaven'.

The Jewish leaders' answer here is also pertinent to the question left unanswered in 21.23-27 regarding the source of Jesus' authority. Since the Jewish leaders are forced to admit that John's ministry of baptism was divinely ordained, they cannot avoid the conclusion that Jesus' messianic ministry is also divinely ordained. After all, it was through John's ministry of baptism that Jesus received his anointing as the Messiah.[23] As a result, the Jewish leaders are tricked into providing the answer to their original question regarding the source of Jesus' authority: Jesus' authority comes from God. In this way, the Jewish leaders themselves provide the answer that Jesus could not give without leaving himself open to a charge of blasphemy. Therefore, in this confrontation with the Jewish leaders, Jesus first avoids having to acknowledge that his authority is from heaven, and then tricks the Jewish leaders into making that acknowledgment for him.

It remains to consider the narrator's purpose in emphasizing Jesus' authority at this point in the narrative. This discussion on Jesus' authority is followed immediately by the 'Parable of the Wicked Tenants' (21.33-44). Kingsbury demonstrates that this parable constitutes the first public claim—albeit in allegory—that Jesus is the Son of God.[24] To prepare for this momentous pronouncement by Jesus, the narrator inserts the discussion on Jesus' authority for the purpose of emphasizing that it does indeed have its source in God. In this way, the narratee sees Jesus' claim to divine sonship in the 'Parable of the Wicked Tenants' as a claim made with divine authority.

As we have just seen, the narrator uses John in the material preparing for this first *public* pronouncement of Jesus as the Son of God.[25]

22. See pp. 97-98 above.
23. See p. 98 above.
24. Jack Dean Kingsbury, 'The Parable of the Wicked Husbandmen and the Secret of Jesus' Divine Sonship in Matthew: Some Literary-Critical Observations', *JBL* 105 (1986), pp. 643-55 (646-52).
25. See the discussion on 21.25-26 and 21.32, above on pp. 137-39.

Similarly, the narrator used John in the preparatory material for the first *private* pronouncement of Jesus as the Son of God: God's declaration at Jesus' baptism that 'This is my son'.[26] In both of these passages, the narrator uses John as a preparer of Jesus' way at the discourse level of the narrative to accompany his role in ch. 3 as the preparer of Jesus' way at the story level of the narrative.

The narrator describes the Jewish leaders' reaction to the 'Parable of the Wicked Tenants' by saying, 'And although they were seeking to seize him, *they feared the crowds, because they held him as a prophet*' (21.46; emphasis added). This statement is striking to the narratee, for the Jewish leaders said virtually the same thing only twenty verses earlier.[27] These two statements so close together impress on the narratee that the Jewish leaders are too weak to stand up for their convictions; in both episodes, the Jewish leaders wish to act, but decide not to act on their wishes for fear of the crowd. Therefore, these two statements contribute to the negative characterization of the Jewish leaders by showing these characters, who are supposed to be leaders for the crowd, being themselves led by the crowd.

The description in 21.46 of the Jewish leaders' reaction to the 'Parable of the Wicked Tenants' impacts the narratee in another way as well. It is evident that the narrator is here using diction to match the Jewish leaders' reaction with Herod the Tetrarch's reluctance to kill John for 'he feared the crowd, because it held him as a prophet' (14.5). This results in retrospection to the account of John's execution (14.1-12). In this way, the narrator brings to mind for the narratee the dominant theme of that account—the fate of the prophets—and draws it in as a backdrop against which the narratee views the Jewish leaders' murderous intentions. Thus the narratee sees the Jewish leaders' desire to seize Jesus as one more step toward Jesus' meeting the fate of the prophets.

As the story progresses, the Jewish leaders' opposition to Jesus mounts.[28] In the context of this growing opposition, Jesus unleashes a

26. See the discussion on 3.1-17 in Chapter 5.

27. Cf. '[W]e fear the crowd, for all hold John as a prophet' (21.26).

28. This growing opposition is evidenced by attempts in three consecutive pericopae to entrap him: in 22.15-22, Pharisees try to entrap Jesus with a question on whether or not it is lawful to pay taxes to Caesar; in 22.23-33, Sadducees attempt to trick him with a question on the resurrection of the dead; in 22.34-40, a Pharisee tests him by asking which is the greatest commandment in the law.

scathing diatribe against the Jewish leaders, a diatribe that increases in intensity as it progresses (23.1-36). As the diatribe reaches its climax in a pronouncement of judgment against the Jewish leaders, Jesus addresses them with the words, 'Brood of vipers!' (v. 33). This form of address prompts retrospection to ch. 3 by repeating John's stinging invective against the Jewish leaders who were coming out to witness his baptism (3.7). Because the movement in ch. 3 is oriented so strongly toward the pronouncement of Jesus as the Son of God at the end of the chapter (3.17), retrospection to any point in that chapter draws the narratee toward this climactic declaration.[29] As a result, the image of Jesus as the Son of God is drawn into ch. 23 as a backdrop against which Jesus' words of judgment are viewed. In this way, the narratee is shown that these words of judgment are spoken with the authority of the Son of God.

At the beginning of ch. 26, the narrator weaves into the narrative a sense of imminence regarding Jesus' fate, thus intensifying the theme of opposition against him. The narrator has Jesus say to his disciples, 'You know that after two days the Passover occurs, and the Son of Man will be handed over in order to be crucified' (26.2). To this point in the narrative, Jesus has already made three passion predictions,[30] but here for the first time, a passion prediction provides a specific time frame: in 'two days' Jesus will meet his fate.

Immediately following this passion prediction, the narrator describes a gathering of Jewish leaders planning to seize (κρατήσωσιν) and kill Jesus (vv. 3-4). To this point in the narrative, the verb κρατέω has been used only once, back in 14.3 to depict the seizure of John the Baptist by Herod the Tetrarch. In that context, the narratee was led to understand John's experience as prefiguring Jesus' experience: the things that happen to John will later happen to Jesus.[31] Now, in 26.4, the narratee sees this beginning to happen. Just as Herod seized John, so the Jewish leaders plan to seize Jesus.

The recurrence of the verb κρατέω operates in another way as well. Its use in 26.4 prompts retrospection to the earlier account of John's execution. As a result, the dominant motif of that account—the fate of the prophets—is drawn in as a backdrop to this passage in ch. 26; therefore, the narratee views this gathering of Jewish leaders as a further

29. See p. 102 above.
30. 16.21, 17.22-23 and 20.17-19.
31. See p. 131 above.

step toward Jesus' meeting the fate of the prophets.

The same dynamic operates later in ch. 26 as well. In the account of the circumstances surrounding, and following, Jesus' arrest (vv. 47-57), the verb κρατέω is used four times in the span of ten verses (vv. 48, 50, 55 and 57). As each of these usages of κρατέω also prompts retrospection to the account of John's execution, the narratee views the arrest of Jesus against the backdrop of the fate of the prophets, and thus as yet another step toward Jesus' meeting that fate.

As the story of Jesus' passion continues, the narratee recognizes additional details reminiscent of the earlier account of John's execution. In 27.15-26, Pilate reluctantly orders Jesus' execution, just as in 14.9 Herod the Tetrarch reluctantly ordered John's execution. In 27.32-50, Jesus is put to death by crucifixion, a mode of execution reserved for criminals, just as in 14.10 John was put to death by beheading, also a mode of execution reserved for criminals.[32] In 27.57-60, Joseph of Arimathea—specifically designated a disciple of Jesus (v. 57c)—carries out the burial of Jesus, just as in 14.12 the disciples of John carried out the burial of John. Throughout the account of Jesus' passion, the narratee is prompted to think back to the account of John's execution. In this way, the motif of the fate of the prophets is repeatedly drawn in as a backdrop against which the events of Jesus' passion are witnessed. In this way, the narrator induces the narratee to see Jesus' fate as an example of the fate of the prophets. Thus, the narrator continues to use John as a target of retrospection at the discourse level of the narrative long after John has been removed from the story-line as a character (14.1-12), and even long after the final reference to John in the narrative (21.32).

32. See n. 6 above.

CONCLUSIONS

This study demonstrates that the Matthean narrator utilizes John the Baptist to a great extent in his narrative. This is certainly true in ch. 3, a time in the story when John is free to move about as he pleases. However, even after John is arrested, imprisonment is not capable of thwarting John's usefulness to the narrator. In fact, even death cannot stop him. The narrator finds John useful for the execution of a variety of narrative moves whether he is free, bound, or even dead.

In his first appearance, John plays a significant role at the story level of the narrative, for he acts as the forerunner of Jesus. In this capacity, he administers the baptism that serves as Jesus' anointing as the Messiah, the 'Anointed One'. However, the narrator also includes many details in this introduction of John (3.1-15) that do not play a significant role at the story level of the narrative, for they have nothing to do with John's baptism of Jesus. For example, the description of John's food and clothing (v. 4) and the description of his rebuking the Pharisees and Sadducees (vv. 7-10) do not contribute to the development of the plot. Further, even after John fades from the story-line after his baptism of Jesus, the narrator continues to make mention of John throughout most of the rest of the narrative. These references, however, tend not to make a significant contribution at the story level. Rather, they find their significance in the contribution that they make at the discourse level. In other words, the narrator does not use these references to John to further the plot, but rather to make rhetorical moves in an effort to influence the way in which the narratee experiences the narrative.

At the story level, John's role as forerunner is exhausted after his baptism of Jesus, and so John fades from the story-line. At the discourse level, however, the narrator continues to present this theme of John as forerunner by casting him in the role of Elijah. The narrator begins this identification of John as Elijah with the description of John's clothing (3.4), crafted to match the description of Elijah's clothing in 2 Kgs 1.8. Later, the narrator makes this identification explicit by having Jesus—already established as a reliable source of the narrator's own ideological point of view—state that John is Elijah who is to come (11.14). However, the significance of this identification does not become clear until 17.9-13, where Jesus explains that Elijah had returned but was killed, and that he himself would meet the same fate. Here, the narratee finally understands that John is not only Jesus' forerunner in his preparing the way for Jesus' messianic ministry; in addition, through his death, John is Jesus' forerunner with regard to Jesus' fate.

At the discourse level of the narrative, the narrator enhances this theme of John as Jesus' forerunner to death by using John as the target of retrospection. In only two passages of any significant length does the narrator abandon a spatial position following Jesus or someone speaking about Jesus, and both of these passages pertain to John: the introduction of John into the narrative (3.1-10) and the account of John's execution (14.3-12a). An examination of these passages reveals that the narrator has established them as repositories of motifs that act as targets for retrospection from later points in the narrative. Therefore, these passages are not significant for the contribution they make at the story level of the narrative. Instead, they find their significance in the contribution that they can make to the process of retrospection operating at the discourse level of the narrative.

In John's introduction into the narrative (3.1-10), the narrator includes a number of motifs as part of John's phraseology. These include the summary of John's message: 'Repent, for the Kingdom of Heaven has drawn near' (v. 2); the stinging invective, 'Brood of vipers!' (v. 7); and the motif of trees bearing fruit (v. 10). Then, at various points later in the narrative, the narrator includes these same motifs as part of Jesus' phraseology: Jesus inaugurates his ministry with the words, 'Repent, for the Kingdom of Heaven has drawn near' (4.17); he addresses the Jewish leaders twice with the invective, 'Brood of vipers!' (12.34; 23.33); and he speaks of trees bearing fruit on two occasions (7.19; 12.33). This demonstrates the narrator's use of diction to have Jesus echo words spoken earlier by John. Each reiteration by Jesus of one of these motifs prompts retrospection to the initial presentation of that motif from the mouth of John in 3.1-10. In this way, the narrator conditions the narratee to expect to see an identification between John and Jesus according to which elements of John's story reappear later as part of Jesus' story. In this way, John acts as fore-runner for Jesus at the discourse level of the narrative.

In the account of John's execution (14.3-12a), the narrator again includes a number of motifs. However, these motifs do not occur as part of John's phraseology, but as part of John's experience: John is seized (κρατέω) by Herod (v. 3); John is threatened by Herod's desire to kill him, although this desire is tempered by fear of the crowd, which holds John to be a prophet (v. 5); John's execution is ordered by a reluctant Herod (v. 9); John is beheaded, a mode of execution reserved for criminals (v. 10); John is buried by his disciples (v. 12). Then, at various points later in the narrative, the narrator includes these same motifs as part of Jesus' experience (21.26, 46; 26.4, 43, 50, 55, 57; 27.15-26, 32-50). Each reiteration of one of these motifs again prompts retrospection to the initial presentation of that motif, this time from the experience of John in 14.3-12a. Thus, the narrator takes the identification between John and Jesus to a new level. Prior to ch. 14, this identification involves a general expectation for elements of John's story to reappear later as part of Jesus' story. With the new set of motifs in 14.3-12a, the identification between John and Jesus evolves into a more specific form: the events of John's experience will later recur as part of Jesus' experience as well. In this way, the narrator uses retro-spection at the discourse level of the narrative to enhance the theme of John's acting as Jesus' forerunner to death.

The dynamic of retrospection is used by the narrator for another pur-pose as well. An examination of the material in ch. 3 reveals that the movement of that chapter is oriented strongly toward the climactic pronouncement of Jesus as the Son of God which appears at the end of the chapter (v. 17). Because of this, when a later passage prompts retro-spection to any point in ch. 3, the narratee's mind is drawn toward this climactic pronouncement. As a result, the image of Jesus as the Son of God becomes established as a backdrop against which the narratee views the later passage that prompts retrospection to ch. 3. For exam-ple, the account of the inauguration of Jesus' ministry in 4.17 prompts retrospection to ch. 3, thus drawing in the image of Jesus as the Son of God as a backdrop. As a result, the narratee views Jesus as inaugurating his ministry with the authority of the Son of God. Likewise, the accounts of Jesus' debating with the Jewish leaders (21.24) and his pronouncing judgment upon them (12.33-34; 23.33) each contain details that prompt retrospection to ch. 3. By drawing in the image of

Jesus as the Son of God as a backdrop against which these passages are viewed, the narratee sees that Jesus debates and pronounces judgment with the authority of the Son of God.

The narrator's use of retrospection in this way is not confined to John the Baptist as he appears in ch. 3. The account of John's execution in 14.3-12a serves a similar function. Just as the motif of Jesus as the Son of God dominates ch. 3, this passage in ch. 14 is also dominated by a prominent theme: the fate of the prophets. As a result, when a later passage prompts retrospection to the account of John's execution in 14.3-12a, the theme of the fate of the prophets is drawn in as a backdrop against which the narratee views the later passage. Thus, when the narrator prompts retrospection to 14.3-12a from various points in the later account of Jesus' passion, the narratee is led to view the passion events against the backdrop of the fate of the prophets. The narratee sees the Jewish leaders' desire to arrest Jesus (21.46), their seizure of Jesus (26.50), Pilate's reluctant order for his execution (27.15-26), Jesus' crucifixion (27.32-50) and his burial by a disciple (27.57) all as steps in Jesus' suffering the fate of the prophets.

In addition to the narrator's use of John as a target of retrospection, the narrator also uses him to communicate the idea of Jesus as judge. Each time the narrator has John interact with Jesus, John expresses this ideological point of view. The narrator first prepares the narratee for this in ch. 3 where John describes the one coming after him as one who will baptize with the Holy Spirit and with fire (3.11), a clear reference to the bestowal of blessing and the execution of judgment. Immediately thereafter, Jesus appears, and John evidently expects Jesus to execute this ministry of baptism, for John says to Jesus: 'I have a need to be baptized by you' (3.14). Then, in ch. 9, John's disciples indicate their expectation that Jesus' disciples should be fasting in the face of the judgment that Jesus as judge brings (cf. 9.14). Finally, in ch. 11, John questions whether Jesus is indeed the one who is to come (11.2-3), for Jesus does not fulfil John's expectations regarding Jesus' role as judge.

Prior to ch. 11, Jesus is shown announcing the Kingdom's coming and offering its blessing to the people of Israel. During this part of his ministry, he has had no reason to execute his role as judge. However, in ch. 11, Jesus sets forth the results of his efforts: the Kingdom has suffered attacks by evil spiritual beings in the spiritual realm (11.12), and the Jewish leaders have added opposition against the Kingdom in the physical realm (11.16-19). In the face of this rejection of the

Kingdom, Jesus assumes his role as judge (11.20-24). In sum, the narrator first has John introduce Jesus as judge in ch. 3 prior to the start of his ministry; however, Jesus has no reason to execute that role until ch. 11. Therefore, the narrator uses John to keep alive the idea of Jesus as judge through the long portion of the narrative in which Jesus does not execute that role. This is the function of John's questions to Jesus in 3.14, 9.14 and 11.2-3—all of which relate to Jesus' role as judge.

To each of John's questions, the narrator has Jesus make a response, and each of Jesus' responses touches on his messiahship (3.15; 9.15; 11.4-5). In this way, the narrator uses John for a christological purpose; by having John ask these three questions, the narrator provides Jesus with three opportunities to elaborate on the nature of his messiahship. John also plays a significant role in the christological development of the narrative in another way. The first major expression of the theme of Jesus as the Son of God occurs at the end of ch. 3 with the pronouncement by the voice of God (3.17). This private proclamation does not make a significant impact on the characters at the story level, for Jesus is the only character privy to it. From the perspective of the narratee, however, this pronouncement constitutes a major event in the development of Jesus' character. To prepare for this momentous pronouncement, the narrator uses John in the preceding material. Later, the first public proclamation that Jesus is the Son of God occurs—albeit in allegory—in the 'Parable of the Wicked Tenants' (21.33-41), and again the narrator uses John in the preparatory material for that pronouncement. Therefore, the narrator uses John—the preparer of Jesus' way—at the discourse level of the narrative to prepare the narratee for both the first private and the first public proclamations of Jesus as the Son of God.

John not only plays a significant role in the characterization of Jesus; he also plays a significant role in the characterization of the Jewish leaders. His speech against the Pharisees and Sadducees (3.7-10) constitutes the narrator's first effort to characterize the Jewish leaders negatively, and the narrator continues this endeavour throughout the rest of the narrative. On two later occasions, John is used in this endeavour. The first of these instances occurs in the 'Parable of the Children' (11.16-19) in which the Jewish leaders are like children playing in the marketplace and John is like other children who do not respond with the expected dancing; here, John plays a part in a rebuke against the Jewish leaders for their opposition and rejection of the

Kingdom. John is used on a second occasion in Jesus' confrontation with the Jewish leaders over the source of his authority (21.23-27). Jesus draws John into the confrontation by asking the Jewish leaders about the source of John's baptism. Their deliberations over this question show how the Jewish leaders reject a correct ideological point of view in favour of an incorrect one. Further, the Jewish leaders choose their words not for how they reflect the truth, but for how they serve the Jewish leaders' purposes. All of this contributes to a negative characterization of them.

From this summary of the conclusions drawn by the present study, it is evident that John's primary role in the Gospel of Matthew is not at the story level of the narrative, but at the discourse level. With the exception of John's baptism of Jesus, the material on John in this narrative makes no significant contribution at the story level. In fact, most of the material on John could be excised from the narrative with little or no impact on the unfolding of the story. For example, the story-line of ch. 3 would remain intact without the citation of John as fulfilling prophecy (v. 3), the description of John's clothing and food (v. 4), his rebuke of the Pharisees and Sadducees (vv. 7-10), his words on the one coming after him (vv. 11-12) and the account of the exchange between John and Jesus (vv. 14-15). Further, the story-line of ch. 14 would not be adversely affected if all the details of John's execution were omitted. The narrator does not include these details for their contribution to the plot, but for their contribution at the discourse level of the narrative. Thus, the narrator uses John mainly to influence the way in which the narratee experiences the narrative; this is John's primary significance in the Gospel of Matthew.

Appendix

A TEXT-CRITICAL ANALYSIS OF MATTHEW 21.29-31

The manuscript evidence for Mt. 21.29-31 provides three different versions of the 'Parable of the Two Sons'. These three versions are summarized in the following table:

	Reading 1	*Reading 2*	*Reading 3*
Father	makes request	makes request	makes request
First Son	refuses, but later acts	agrees, but later does not act	refuses, but later acts
Second Son	agrees, but later does not act	refuses, but later acts	agrees, but later does not act
'Which did will of his father?'	the first son	the second son	the second son

Bruce M. Metzger points out that some scholars prefer the third reading because it is the most difficult, and thus best explains the rise of the other two.[1] However, Metzger goes on to assert that this reading is not only difficult, but nonsensical.[2] He does recognize Jerome's suggestion that the opponents intentionally give a perverse answer to spoil the point of the parable,[3] but in response, he asserts:

> But this explanation requires the further supposition that the Jews not only recognized that the parable was directed against themselves but chose to make a nonsensical reply rather than merely remain silent. Because such explanations attribute to the Jews, or to Matthew, far-fetched psychological or overly-subtle literary motives, the Committee judged that the origin of [this reading] is due to copyists who either committed a transcriptional blunder or who were motivated by anti-Pharisaic bias (i.e., since Jesus had characterized the Pharisees as those that say but do not practice (cf. Mt. 23.3), they must be represented as approving the son who said 'I go', and did not go).[4]

J. Ramsey Michaels's opinion on the third reading differs from both that of Jerome and that of Metzger. Michaels interprets the participle μεταμεληθείς in

1. Bruce M. Metzger, *A Textual Commentary on the Greek New Testament* (Stuttgart: Deutsche Bibelgesellschaft, 2nd edn, 1994), p. 45, cites Lachmann, Merx, Wellhausen and Hirsch as examples.
2. Metzger, *A Textual Commentary*, p. 45.
3. Metzger, *A Textual Commentary*, p. 45.
4. Metzger, *A Textual Commentary*, p. 45.

v. 29 to mean 'being regretful' and the finite verb ἀπῆλθεν in vv. 29 and 30 to mean 'went away'. On the basis of these understandings of these two key terms, Michaels reconstructs the parable as follows:

> What do you think of this; a certain man had two sons. Coming to the first he said, 'My boy, go today and work in the vineyard'. But he answered and said 'I will not'. Later he went away regretful. Coming to the second, the father said the same thing. He answered and said, 'Aye, sir' and did not go away.[5]

If μεταμεληθείς and ἀπῆλθεν are understood in this way, the Jewish leaders' answer—that it was the second son who did the will of his father—is no longer nonsensical nor perverse.

Michaels's understanding of the use of the verb ἀπῆλθεν in this parable requires some scrutiny. Although this verb can legitimately be rendered 'went away' in many contexts,[6] it appears that the narrator does not intend the narratee to understand it with this sense in the present context. In the preceding chapter, the narrator used the verb ἀπέρχομαι in the 'Parable of the Workers in the Vineyard' (20.1-16). In that parable, Jesus speaks of a householder who invites first one group of workers (v. 2), and then another group (v. 4), to work in his vineyard. The response of the second group of workers is described in v. 5 as οἱ δὲ ἀπῆλθον ('and they went'), clearly indicating movement into the vineyard. Now, here, in the 'Parable of the Two Sons', the verb ἀπέρχομαι is again used to describe the response to an invitation to work in a vineyard. Because this usage of the verb ἀπέρχομαι occurs so closely after its parallel usage in the 'Parable of the Workers in the Vineyard', I contend that the narratee would understand the two occurrences of this verb in the same way, that is, both usages of the verb ἀπέρχομαι describe movement into the vineyard. Therefore, Michaels's argument in support of the third reading is questionable.

The third reading also suffers from the lack of attestation by strong witnesses; it is supported by only one manuscript, Codex Bezae (D), with the only other attestation coming from several Old Latin versions and one Syriac text. It should be noted that all of these witnesses represent the Western text-type;[7] therefore, this reading suffers not only from a paucity of strong witnesses, but also from a lack of geographical distribution of the few witnesses that do support it. Further, Metzger suggests the inferiority of this reading because of the various forms in which the Jewish leaders' answer is found;[8] witnesses supporting this reading present the answer as either ὁ ὕστερος ('the latter'), ὁ ἔσχετος ('the last'), or ὁ δεύτερος ('the second'). On the basis of the foregoing, I conclude that the third reading should not be adopted.

An analysis of the external evidence pertaining to the first and second readings

5. J. Ramsey Michaels, 'The Parable of the Regretful Son', *HTR* 61 (1968), pp.15-26 (20-22).

6. For example, Mt. 13.25; 16.4; 19.22; 22.22; 27.60.

7. For the assignment of the witnesses cited in this discussion into text-types, see Bruce M. Metzger, *The Text of the New Testament: Its Transmission Corruption, and Restoration* (New York: Oxford University Press, 2nd edn, 1968), pp. 42-79.

8. Metzger, *A Textual Commentary*, p. 56.

does not conclusively favour one reading over the other, but it does indicate that the first enjoys slightly stronger support than the second. While both readings find attestation in strong Alexandrian[9] and Caesarean[10] witnesses, the first also has some Western[11] and early Byzantine[12] support. The breadth of the geographical distribution of witnesses to the first reading suggests that this reading should be preferred over the second reading.

Metzger's analysis of the internal evidence points to the same conclusion. Metzger provides two possible explanations for why a scribe, faced with the first reading, might have transposed the order of the two sons to yield the second reading. First, a scribe might have reasoned that if the first son had obeyed—as the first reading indicates—there would be no reason for the father to ask the second son.[13] An observation by J. Duncan M. Derrett, however, counters this explanation. Derrett asserts that, given the culture, all sons would have been expected to work in the family vineyard, and so the second son would have been asked regardless of what the first son had done.[14] Metzger's second possible explanation is more viable; he asserts:

> [I]t was natural to identify the disobedient son with either the Jews in general or with the chief priests and elders (verse 23) and the obedient son with either the Gentiles or the tax collectors and the harlots (verse 31)—and in accord with either line of interpretation, the obedient son should come last in chronological sequence.[15]

This provides a plausible explanation for why a scribe might have transformed the first reading into the second reading.

Based on this analysis of the internal and external evidence, I conclude that the first reading should be adopted.

9. The first reading is found in Codex Sinaiticus (א), while the second reading is found in Codex Vaticanus (B).

10. The first reading is supported by Family 1, while the second reading is supported by Family 13.

11. That is, the Vulgate and a few Old Latin texts.

12. That is, Codex Freerianus (W), dated from the late fourth or early fifth century.

13. Metzger, *A Textual Commentary*, p. 46.

14. J. Duncan M. Derrett, 'The Parable of the Two Sons', in *Studies in the New Testament* (Leiden: E.J. Brill, 1977), pp. 80-81.

15. Metzger, *A Textual Commentary*, p. 46.

BIBLIOGRAPHY

Abrahams, I., *Studies in Pharisaism and the Gospels* (1st series; New York: Ktav, 1917).

Abrams, M.H., *A Glossary of Literary Terms* (New York: Holt, Rinehart & Winston, 5th edn, 1988).

—*The Mirror and the Lamp: Romantic Theory and the Critical Tradition* (New York: W.W. Norton, 1953).

Achtemeier, Paul J., *Invitation to Mark: A Commentary on the Gospel of Mark* (Garden City, NY: Image, 1978).

—'*Omne verbum sonat*: The New Testament and the Oral Environment of Late Western Antiquity', *JBL* 109 (1990), pp. 3-27.

Agourides, Savas, ' "Little Ones" in Matthew', *BT* 35 (1984), pp. 329-34.

Albright, W.F., and C.S. Mann, *Matthew* (Garden City, NY: Doubleday, 1971).

Allen, Willoughby C., *A Critical and Exegetical Commentary on the Gospel According to St. Matthew* (Edinburgh: T. & T. Clark, 3rd edn, 1912).

Allison, Dale C., Jr, *The End of the Ages Has Come* (Philadelphia: Fortress Press, 1985).

—' "Elijah Must Come First" ', *JBL* 103 (1984), pp. 256-58.

Andersen, F.I. 'The Diet of John the Baptist', *AbrN* 3 (1961–62), pp. 60-74.

Anderson, Charles C., *Critical Quests of Jesus* (Grand Rapids: Eerdmans, 1969).

Anderson, Janice Capel, 'Double and Triple Stories, the Implied Reader, and Redundancy in Matthew', *Semeia* 31 (1985), pp. 71-89.

—'Matthew: Gender and Reading', *Semeia* 28 (1983), pp. 3-27.

—'Point of View in Matthew: Evidence' (paper presented at the Symposium on Literary Analysis of the Gospels and Acts; Society of Biblical Literature, 21 December 1981).

Asch, S.E., 'Forming Impressions of Personality', *Journal of Abnormal and Social Psychology* 41 (1946), pp. 258-90.

Augustine, *Confessions and Enchiridion* (trans. Albert C. Outler; London: SCM Press, 1955).

Aune, David E., 'The Apocalypse of John and the Problem of Genre', *Semeia* 36 (1986), pp. 65-96.

Aus, Roger, *Water into Wine and the Beheading of John the Baptist: Early Jewish-Christian Interpretation of Esther 1 in John 2.1-11 and Mark 6.17-29* (Atlanta: Scholars Press, 1988).

Bacon, Benjamin W., 'The "Five Books" of Matthew against the Jews', *Expositor* 15 (1918), pp. 56-66.

—'Jesus and the Law: A Study of the First "Book" of Matthew (MT. 3-7)', *JBL* 47 (1928), pp. 203-31.

—*Studies in Matthew* (New York: Henry Holt, 1930).

Badia, Leonard F., *The Qumran Baptism and John the Baptist's Baptism* (Lanham, MD: University Press of America, 1980).

Bammel, Ernst, 'The Baptist in Early Christian Tradition', *NTS* 18 (1971–72), pp. 95-128.

Barnard, L.W., 'Matt. III.11//Luke III.16', *JTS* 8 (1957), p. 107.

Barnett, P.W., 'Who Were the "Biastai" (Matthew 11.12-13)?', *RTR* 36 (1977), pp. 65-70.

Bartholomew, Gilbert L., 'Feed My Lambs: John 21.15-19 as Oral Gospel', *Semeia* 39 (1987), pp. 69-96.

Barr, David L., 'The Drama of Matthew's Gospel: A Reconsideration of its Structure and Purpose', *TD* 24 (1976), pp. 349-59.

Bassler, Jouette M., 'The Parable of the Loaves', *JR* 66 (1986), pp. 157-72.

Bauckham, Richard, 'The Martyrdom of Enoch and Elijah: Jewish or Christian?', *JBL* 95 (1976), pp. 447-58.

Bauer, David R., 'The Major Characters of Matthew's Story', *Int* 46 (1992), pp. 357-67.

—*The Structure of Matthew's Gospel: A Study in Literary Design* (Sheffield: Almond Press, 1988).

Beare, Francis W., *The Gospel According to Matthew* (Peabody, MA: Hendrickson, 1981).

Beavis, Mary Ann, 'The Trial before the Sanhedrin (Mark 14.53-65): Reader Response and Greco-Roman Readers', *CBQ* 49 (1987), pp. 581-96.

Beckwith, Roger T., 'The Feast of New Wine and the Question of Fasting', *ExpTim* 95 (1984), pp. 334-35.

Belsey, Catherine, *Critical Practice* (London: Routledge, 1980).

Benoit, Pierre, 'L'enfance de Jean-Baptiste selon Luc 1', *NTS* 3 (1956–57), pp. 169-94.

Berge, Paul S., 'Matthew 16.13-20', *Int* 29 (1975), pp. 283-88.

Berlin, Adele, 'Point of View in Biblical Narrative', in *A Sense of Text: The Art of Language in the Study of Biblical Literature* (Winona Lake, IN: Eisenbrauns, 1982), pp. 71-113.

Best, Ernest, 'Spirit Baptism', *NovT* 41 (1960), pp. 236-43.

Beyer, Hermann W., 'ἕτερος', *TDNT*, II, pp. 702-704.

Black, David Alan, 'Text of Mk 6.20', *NTS* 34 (1988), pp. 141-44.

Black, Matthew, *An Aramaic Approach to the Gospels and Acts* (Oxford: Clarendon Press, 3rd edn, 1967).

Böcher, Otto, 'Ass Johannes der Täufer kein Brot (Lk 7.33)', *NTS* (1971-72), pp. 90-92.

Blomberg, Craig L., *Interpreting the Parables* (Downers Grove, IL: InterVarsity Press, 1990).

Boismard, M.-É., 'Les traditions johanniques concernant le Baptiste', *RB* 70 (1963), pp. 5-42.

Boomershine, Thomas E., 'Biblical Megatrends: Towards a Paradigm for the Interpretation of the Bible in Electronic Media', in Kent Harold Richards (ed.), *Society of Biblical Literature 1987 Seminar Papers* (Atlanta: Scholars Press, 1987), pp. 144-57.

—'Mark, the Storyteller: A Rhetorical-Critical Investigation of Mark's Passion and Resurrection Narrative' (PhD dissertation; Union Theological Seminary, New York, 1974).

—'Peter's Denial as Polemic or Confession: The Implications of Media Criticism for Biblical Hermeneutics', *Semeia* 39 (1987), pp. 47-68.

Booth, Wayne C., 'Distance and Point-of-View', in Philip Stevick (ed.), *The Theory of the Novel* (New York: Free Press, 1967), pp. 87-107.

—*The Rhetoric of Fiction* (Chicago: University of Chicago Press, 2nd edn, 1983).

Borg, Marcus J., *Conflict, Holiness and Politics in the Teachings of Jesus* (Lewiston, NY: Edwin Mellen Press, 1984).

—*Jesus: A New Vision* (San Francisco: Harper & Row, 1987).

Botha, Pieter J.J., 'Mute Manuscripts: Analyzing a Neglected Aspect of Ancient Communication', *Theologia Evangelica* 23 (1990), pp. 35-47.
Bowen, Clayton Raymond, 'John the Baptist in the New Testament', in Robert Hutcheon (ed.), *Studies in the New Testament* (Chicago: University of Chicago Press, 1936), pp. 49-76.
—'Prolegomena to a New Study of John the Baptist', in Robert Hutcheon (ed.), *Studies in the New Testament* (Chicago: University of Chicago Press, 1936), pp. 30-48.
Braumann, Georg, 'Dem Himmelreich wird Gewalt angetan (Mt 11 12 par.)', *ZNW* 52 (1961), pp. 104-109.
Bretscher, Paul, ' "Whose Sandals?" (Matt 3.11)', *JBL* 86 (1967), pp. 81-87.
Brock, Sebastian, 'The Baptist's Diet in Syriac Sources', *OrChr* 54 (1970), pp. 113-24.
Brooke, George, 'The Feast of New Wine and the Question of Fasting', *ExpTim* 95 (1984), pp. 175-76.
Brooks, James A., and Carlton L. Winbery, *Syntax of New Testament Greek* (Lanham, MD: University Press of America, 1979).
Brower, Kent, 'Elijah in the Markan Passion Narrative', *JSNT* 18 (1983), pp. 85-101.
Brown, Raymond, *The Birth of the Messiah* (Garden City, NY: Doubleday, 1977).
—'Jesus and Elisha', *Perspective* 12 (1971), pp. 85-99.
—'Three Quotations from John the Baptist in the Gospel of John', *CBQ* 22 (1960), pp. 292-98.
Brownlee, William, 'A Comparison of the Covenanters of the Dead Sea Scrolls with Pre-Christian Jewish Sects', *BA* 13 (1950), pp. 49-72.
—'John the Baptist in the New Light of Ancient Scrolls', in Krister Stendahl (ed.), *The Scrolls and the New Testament* (New York: Harper & Brothers, 1957), pp. 33-53.
Bruce, F.F., *Second Thoughts on the Dead Sea Scrolls* (Grand Rapids: Eerdmans, 1961).
Bruner, Frederick Dale, *Matthew: A Commentary* (2 vols.; Dallas: Word Books, 1990 [1987]).
Büchsel, Friedrich, 'γεννητός', *TDNT*, I, p. 672.
—'ἐπίκειμαι', *TDNT*, III, p. 655.
Bultmann, Rudolf, *The History of the Synoptic Tradition* (trans. John Marsh; Oxford: Basil Blackwell, rev. edn, 1972).
—'ἀφίημι κτλ.', *TDNT*, I, pp. 509-12.
Burkill, T.A., 'Should Wedding Guests Fast? A Consideration of Mark 2.18-20', in *New Light on the Earliest Gospel: Seven Markan Studies* (Ithaca, NY: Cornell University Press, 1972).
Burkitt, F.C., 'PHARES, PEREZ, and Matthew xi 12', *JTS* 30 (1929), pp. 254-58.
Burnett, Fred W., 'Prolegomenon to Reading Matthew's Eschatological Discourse: Redundancy and the Education of the Reader in Matthew', *Semeia* 31 (1985), pp. 91-109.
Cameron, Peter Scott, *Violence and the Kingdom: The Interpretation of Matthew 11.12* (Frankfurt: Peter Lang, 2nd edn, 1988).
Catchpole, David, 'On Doing Violence to the Kingdom', *Journal of Theology for Southern Africa* 25 (1978), pp. 50-61.
Charlesworth, James H., *Jesus within Judaism* (New York: Doubleday, 1988).
Chatman, Seymour, *Story and Discourse: Narrative Structure in Fiction and Film* (Ithaca, NY: Cornell University Press, 1978).
Coggan, F.D., 'Note on St. Matthew iii.15: Ἄφες ἄρτι οὕτω γὰρ πρέπον ἐστὶν ἡμῖν πληρῶσαι πᾶσαν δικαιοσύνην', *ExpTim* 60 (1949), p. 258.

Combrink, H.J. Bernard, 'The Structure of the Gospel of Matthew as Narrative', *TynBul* 34 (1983), pp. 61-90.
Conroy, Charles, *Absalom Absalom! Narrative and Language in 2 Sam. 13-20* (Rome: Biblical Institute Press, 1978).
Cope, Lamar, 'The Argument Revolves: The Pivotal Evidence for Marcan Priority is Reversing itself', in William R. Farmer (ed.), *New Synoptic Studies* (Macon, GA: Mercer University Press, 1983), pp. 143-59.
—'The Death of John the Baptist in the Gospel of Matthew; or, The Case of the Confusing Conjunction', *CBQ* 38 (1976), pp. 515-19.
Conzelmann, Hans, *The Theology of St. Luke* (trans. Geoffrey Buswell; New York: Harper & Row, 1961).
Cothenet, É., 'Les prophètes chrétiens dans l'évangile selon saint Matthieu', in M. Didier (ed.), *L'évangile selon Matthieu: Rédaction et théologie* (Gembloux: Duculot, 1972), pp. 281-308.
Cotter, Wendy J., 'The Parable of the Children in the Market-Place, Q (Lk) 7.31-35: An Examination of the Parable's Image and Significance', *NovT* 29 (1987), pp. 289-304.
Culler, Jonathan, *On Deconstruction: Theory and Criticism after Structuralism* (Ithaca, NY: Cornell University Press, 1982).
Cullmann, Oscar, 'ὁ ὀπίσω μου ἐρχόμενος', in A.J.B. Higgins (ed.), *The Early Church* (trans. A.J.B. Higgins; London: SCM Press, 1956), pp. 177-82.
Culpepper, R. Alan, *Anatomy of the Fourth Gospel* (Philadelphia: Fortress Press, 1983).
Dalman, Gustaf, *Arbeit und Sitte in Palästina*, III (Hildesheim: Georg Olms, 1964).
Dana, H.E., and Julius R. Mantey, *A Manual Grammar of the Greek New Testament* (New York: Macmillan, 1941).
Daniélou, J., 'Les manuscrits de la Mer Morte et les origines du christianisme', *Flambeau* 55 (1979), pp. 249-53.
Danker, Frederick W., 'Luke 16.16: An Opposition Logion', *JBL* 77 (1958), pp. 231-43.
Darr, John A., *On Character Building: The Reader and the Rhetoric of Characterization in Luke–Acts* (Louisville, KY: Westminster/John Knox Press, 1992).
Davies, Margaret, *Matthew* (Sheffield: JSOT Press, 1993).
Davies, Stevan L., 'John the Baptist and Essene Kashruth', *NTS* 29 (1983), pp. 569-71.
Davies, W.D., *Jewish and Pauline Studies* (Philadelphia: Fortress Press, 1984).
Davies, W.D., and Dale C. Allison, Jr, *A Critical and Exegetical Commentary on the Gospel According to Saint Matthew* (3 vols.; Edinburgh: T. & T. Clark, 1997 [1988]).
Dawsey, James M., *The Lukan Voice: Confusion and Irony in the Gospel of Luke* (Macon, GA: Mercer University Press, 1986).
De la Potterie, Ignare, 'Jean-Baptiste et Jésus: Témoins de la vérité d'après le IVe Evangile', in E. Castelli (ed.), *Le témoignage* (Paris: Aubier, 1972), pp. 317-29.
Derrett, J. Duncan M., 'Herod's Oath and the Baptist's Head', *BZ* 9 (1965), pp. 49-59, 233-46.
—'The Parable of the Two Sons', in *Studies in the New Testament* (Leiden: E.J. Brill, 1977).
Descamp, Albert, and André de Halleux (eds.), *Mélanges bibliques* (Gembloux: Ducolot, 1970).
Dewey, Joanna, 'Mark as Interwoven Tapestry: Forecasts and Echoes for a Listening Audience', *CBQ* 53 (1991), pp. 221-36.

—'Point of View and the Disciples in Mark', in Kent Harold Richards (ed.), *Society of Biblical Literature 1982 Seminar Papers* (Chico, CA: Scholars Press, 1982), pp. 97-106.

Dibelius, Franz, 'Der Kleinere ist im Himmelreich größer als Johannes (Mt 11,11)', *ZNW* 11 (1910), pp. 190-92.

Dibelius, Martin, *Die urchristliche Überlieferung von Johannes dem Täufer* (Göttingen: Vandenhoeck & Ruprecht, 1911).

Dobbeler, Stephanie von, *Das Gericht und das Erbarmen Gottes: Die Botschaft Johannes des Täufers und ihre Rezeption bei den Johannesjüngen im Rahmen der Theologiegeschichte des Frühjudentums* (Frankfurt: Athenäum, 1988).

Dodd, C.H., *The Parables of the Kingdom* (London: Collins, rev. edn, 1961).

Donahue, John R., *The Gospel in Parable* (Philadelphia: Fortress Press, 1988).

Doyle, Rod, 'Mt 11.12: A Challenge to the Evangelist's Community', *Colloquium* 18 (1985), pp. 20-30.

Droosten, P.H., 'Proems of Liturgical Lections and Gospels', *JTS* 6 (1905), pp. 99-106.

Dubois, Jean-Daniel, 'La figure d'Elie dans la perspective Lucanienne', *RHPR* 53 (1973), pp. 155-76.

Dunkerley, Roderic, 'The Bridegroom Passage', *ExpTim* 64 (1953), pp. 303-304.

Dunn, James D.G., 'Spirit-and-Fire Baptism', *NovT* 14 (1972), pp. 81-92.

Edwards, Richard A., *Matthew's Story of Jesus* (Philadelphia: Fortress Press, 1985).

—'Matthew's Use of Q in Chapter Eleven', in Joël Delobel (ed.), *Logia: Les paroles de Jésus—The Sayings of Jesus* (Leuven: Leuven University Press, 1982), pp. 257-75.

—'Uncertain Faith: Matthew's Portrait of the Disciples', in Fernando F. Segovia (ed.), *Discipleship in the New Testament* (Philadelphia: Fortress Press, 1985), pp. 47-61.

Eisler, Robert, *The Messiah Jesus and John the Baptist According to Flavius Josephus' Recently Rediscovered 'Capture of Jerusalem' and the Other Jewish and Christian Sources* (trans. Alexander Haggerty Krappe; New York: Dial Press, 1931).

Eissfeldt, Otto, 'Πληρῶσαι πᾶσαν δικαιοσύνην in Matthäus 3 15', *ZNW* 61 (1970), pp. 209-15.

Ellis, Peter F., *Matthew: his Mind and his Message* (Collegeville, MN: Liturgical Press, 1974).

Enslin, Morton, 'John and Jesus', *ZNW* 66 (1975), pp. 1-18.

Ernst, Josef, *Johannes der Täufer* (Berlin: W. de Gruyter, 1989).

Eslinger, Lyle, 'The Wooing of the Woman at the Well: Jesus, the Reader and Reader-Response Criticism', *Journal of Literature & Theology* 1 (1987), pp. 167-83.

Faierstein, Morris M., 'Why Do the Scribes Say that Elijah Must Come First?', *JBL* 100 (1981), pp. 75-86.

Farmer, W.R., 'John the Baptist', *IDB*, II, pp. 955-62.

Feather, J., *The Last of the Prophets: A Study of the Life, Teaching, and Character of John the Baptist* (Edinburgh: T. & T. Clark, 1894).

Filson, F.V., 'John the Baptist', *ISBE*, II, pp. 1108-11.

Fish, Stanley E., *Is there a Text in this Class? The Authority of Interpretive Communities* (Cambridge, MA: Harvard University Press, 1980).

—'Literature in the Reader: Affective Stylistics', in Tompkins (ed.), *Reader-Response Criticism*, pp. 70-100.

—*Self-Consuming Artifacts: The Experience of Seventeenth-Century Literature* (Berkeley: University of California Press, 1972).

Fitzer, Gottfried, 'φθάνω, προφθάνω', *TDNT*, IX, pp. 88-92.

Fitzmyer, Joseph A., More about Elijah Coming First', *JBL* 104 (1985), pp. 295-96.
—*The Gospel According to Luke I–IX* (Garden City, NY: Doubleday, 1981).
Fleddermann, Harry, 'John and the Coming One (Matt 3.11-12//Luke 3.16-17)', in Richards (ed.), *Society of Biblical Literature 1984 Seminar Papers*, pp. 377-84.
Flusser, David, *Die rabbinischen Gleichnisse und der Gleichniserzähler Jesus* (Bern: Peter Lang, 1981).
Foerster, Werner, 'ἁρπάζω', *TDNT*, I, pp. 472-73.
—'ἐξουσία', *TDNT*, II, pp. 562-74.
—'ἔχιδνα', *TDNT*, II, pp. 815-16.
Forster, E.M., *Aspects of the Novel* (New York: Harcourt Brace Jovanovich, 1927).
Fowler, Robert M., *Let the Reader Understand: Reader-Response Criticism and the Gospel of Mark* (Minneapolis: Fortress Press, 1991).
—*Loaves and Fishes: The Function of the Feeding Stories in the Gospel of Mark* (Chico, CA: Scholars Press, 1981).
—'The Rhetoric of Direction and Indirection in the Gospel of Mark', *Semeia* 48 (1989), pp. 115-34.
—'Who is "the Reader" of Mark's Gospel?', in Kent Harold Richards (ed.), *Society of Biblical Literature 1983 Seminar Papers* (Chico, CA: Scholars Press, 1983), pp. 31-53.
Frankemölle, Hubert, *Jahwebund und Kirche Christi: Studien zur Form- und Traditiongeschichte des 'Evangeliums' nach Matthäus* (Münster: Aschendorff, 1973).
Freeman, Curtis W., 'Matthew 3.13-17', *Int* 47 (1993), pp. 285-89.
Freund, Elizabeth, *The Return of the Reader* (London: Methuen, 1987).
Friedman, Norman, 'Point of View in Fiction: The Development of a Critical Concept', in Robert Scholes (ed.), *Approaches to the Novel: Materials for a Poetic* (San Francisco: Chandler Publishing, 1961), pp. 113-42.
Fuchs, Albert, 'Intention und Adressaten der Busspredigt des Täufers bei Mt 3,7-10', in Fuchs (ed.), *Jesus in der Verkündigung der Kirche* (Freistadt: Plöchl, 1976), pp. 62-75.
Funk, Robert W., *The Poetics of Biblical Narrative* (Sonoma, CA: Poleridge Press, 1988).
Gardner, Richard B., *Matthew* (Scottdale: Herald Press, 1991).
Garland, David E., *Reading Matthew: A Literary and Theological Commentary on the First Gospel* (New York: Crossroad, 1993).
Genette, Gérard, *Narrative Discourse: An Essay in Method* (trans. Jane E. Lewin; Ithaca, NY: Cornell University Press, 1980).
George, Augustin, 'Le parallèle entre Jean-Baptiste et Jésus en Lc 1–2', in Descamp and Halleux (eds.), *Mélanges bibliques*, pp. 147-71.
Geyser, A.S., 'Semeion at Cana of the Galilee', in W.C. Unnik (ed.), *Studies in John* (Leiden: E.J. Brill, 1970), pp. 12-21.
—'The Youth of John the Baptist: A Deduction from the Break in the Parallel Account of the Lucan Infancy Story', *NovT* 1 (1956), pp. 70-75.
Gibson, J., 'HOI TELONAI KAI HAI PORNAI', *JTS* 32 (1981), pp. 429-33.
Glasson, T. Francis, 'John the Baptist in the 4th Gospel', *ExpTim* 67 (1955–56), pp. 245-46.
Gnilka, Joachim, ' "Das Martyrium Johannes" des Täufers (Mk 6,17-29)', in P. Hoffmann (ed.), *Orientierung an Jesus: Zur Theologie der Synoptiker für Josef Schmid* (Freiburg: Herder, 1973), pp. 78-92.

Goguel, Maurice, *The Life of Jesus* (trans. Olive Wyon; New York: Macmillan, 1933).

—*Au seuil de l'évangile: Jean-Baptiste* (Paris: Payot, 1928).

Goody, Jack, *The Domestication of the Savage Mind* (Cambridge: Cambridge University Press, 1977).

Goppelt, Leonard, *Theology of the New Testament* (trans. John E. Alsup; Grand Rapids: Eerdmans, 1981).

Goulder, M.D., *Midrash and Lection in Matthew* (London: SPCK, 1974).

Gowler, D.B., 'A Socio-Narratological Character Analysis of the Pharisees in Luke–Acts' (PhD dissertation; Southern Baptist Theological Seminary, 1989).

Graham, Helen, 'A Passion Prediction for Mark's Community: Mk 13.9-13', *BTB* 16 (1986), pp. 18-22.

Graham, William A., *Beyond the Written Word: Oral Aspects of Scripture in the History of Religion* (Cambridge: Cambridge University Press, 1987).

Green, H. Benedict, *The Gospel According to Matthew* (Oxford: Oxford University Press, 1975).

—'The Structure of St. Matthew's Gospel', in Frank L. Cross (ed.), *Studia Evangelica IV: Papers Presented to the Third International Congress on New Testament Studies.* I. *The New Testament Scriptures* (Berlin: Akademie Verlag, 1968), pp. 47-59.

Griffiths, D.R., 'St. Matthew iii.15', *ExpTim* 62 (1950), pp. 155-57.

Grundmann, Walter, *Das Evangelium nach Matthäus* (Berlin: Evangelische Verlagsanstalt, 6th edn, 1986).

—'μέγας', *TDNT*, IV, pp. 529-41.

Güttgemanns, Erhardt, *Candid Questions Concerning Gospel Form Criticism* (trans. William G. Doty; Pittsburgh: Pickwick Press, 1979).

Gundry, Robert H., *Matthew: A Commentary on his Literary and Theological Art* (Grand Rapids: Eerdmans, 1982).

Hahn, Ferdinand, 'Die Bildworte vom neuen Flicken und vom jungen Wein', *EvT* 31 (1971), pp. 357-75.

—*The Titles of Jesus in Christology: Their History in Early Christology* (trans. Harold Knight and Georg Ogg; London: Lutterworth, 1969).

Hare, Douglas R.A., *Matthew* (Louisville, KY: John Knox Press, 1993).

Harnack, Adolf von, *What Is Christianity?* (trans. Thomas Bailey Saunders; Introduction by Rudolf Bultmann; Philadelphia: Fortress Press, 1986).

Harrington, Daniel J., *The Gospel of Matthew* (Collegeville, MN: Liturgical Press, 1991).

Harvey, A.E., *Jesus and the Contraints of History* (Philadelphia: Westminster Press, 1982).

Hasler, Victor, 'φθάνω', *EDNT*, III, pp. 421-22.

Hauck, Friedrich, 'ἐπιβάλλω', *TDNT*, I, pp. 528-29.

Hawkins, John C., *Horae Synopticae: Contributions to the Study of the Synoptic Problem* (Grand Rapids: Baker Book House, 2nd edn, 1968).

Hayward, Robert, 'Phineas—The Same as Elijah: The Origin of a Rabbinic Tradition', *JJS* 29 (1979), pp. 22-34.

Hill, David, 'ΔΙΚΑΙΟΙ as a Quasi-Technical Term', *NTS* 11 (1964–65), pp. 296-302.

—*The Gospel of Matthew* (Grand Rapids: Eerdmans, 1972).

—*New Testament Prophecy* (Atlanta: John Knox Press, 1979).

Hollenbach, Paul, 'The Conversion of Jesus: From Jesus the Baptizer to Jesus the Healer', *ANRW*, II.25.1, pp. 196-219.

—'Social Aspects of John the Baptizer's Preaching Mission in the Context of Palestinian Judaism', *ANRW*, II.19.1, pp. 850-75.

—'John the Baptist', *ABD*, III, pp. 867-99.
Hooker, Morna, *Jesus and the Servant* (London: SPCK, 1959).
—'John the Baptist and the Johanine Prologue', *NTS* 16 (1969–70), pp. 354-58.
—' "What Does Thou Here, Elijah?" A Look at St Mark's Account of the Transfiguration', in L.D. Hurst and N.T. Wright (eds.), *The Glory of Christ in the New Testament* (Oxford: Clarendon Press, 1987), pp. 59-70.
Horsley, Richard A., *Jesus and the Spiral of Violence* (San Francisco: Harper & Row, 1987).
—' "Like One of the Prophets of Old": Two Types of Popular Prophets at the Time of Jesus', *CBQ* 47 (1985), pp. 435-63.
Houghton, Ross C., *John the Baptist, the Forerunner of our Lord: His Life and Work* (New York: Hunt & Eaton, 1889).
Howell, David B., *Matthew's Inclusive Story: A Study on the Narrative Rhetoric of the First Gospel* (Sheffield: Sheffield Academic Press, 1990).
Hughes, John, 'John the Baptist: The Forerunner of God Himself', *NovT* 14 (1972), pp. 191-218.
Hutton, W.R., 'The Kingdom of God has Come', *ExpTim* 64 (1952), pp. 89-91.
Iser, Wolfgang, *The Act of Reading: A Theory of Aesthetic Response* (Baltimore: The Johns Hopkins University Press, 1978).
—*The Implied Reader: Patterns of Communication in Prose Fiction from Bunyan to Beckett* (Baltimore: The Johns Hopkins University Press, 1974).
—'The Reading Process: A Phenomenological Approach', in *idem*, *The Implied Reader*.
Jeremias, Joachim, *The Parables of Jesus* (New York: Charles Scribner's Sons, 2nd rev. edn, 1972).
—*The Problem of the Historical Jesus* (trans. Norman Perrin; Philadelphia: Fortress Press, 1964).
—'Ἠλ(ε)ίας', *TDNT*, II, pp. 928-41.
—'λίθος, λίθινος', *TDNT*, IV, pp. 268-80.
—'νύμφη, νυμφίος', *TDNT*, IV, pp. 1099-1106.
Jones, Gwilyn H., *1 and 2 Kings* (2 vols.; Grand Rapids: Eerdmans, 1984).
Jones, James L., 'References to John the Baptist in the Gospel According to St. Matthew', *ATR* 41 (1959), pp. 298-302.
Kähler, Martin, *The So-Called Historical Jesus and the Historic Biblical Christ* (trans. Carl E. Braaten; Philadelphia: Fortress Press, 1964).
Kaiser, Walter C., Jr, 'The Promise of the Arrival of Elijah in Malachi and the Gospels', *GTJ* 3 (1982), p. 221-33.
Käsemann, Ernst, 'The Problem of the Historical Jesus', in *Essays on New Testament Themes* (trans. W.J. Montague; Naperville:, IL Allenson, 1964).
Kazmierski, Carl R., *John the Baptist: Prophet and Evangelist* (Collegeville, MN: Liturgical Press, 1996).
—'The Stones of Abraham: John the Baptist and the End of Torah (Matt 3,7-10 par. Luke 3,7-9)', *Bib* 68 (1987), pp. 22-39.
Keck, Leander E., 'The Spirit and the Dove', *NTS* 17 (1970), pp. 41-67.
Kee, Alistair, 'The Old Coat and the New Wine', *NovT* 12 (1970), pp. 13-21.
—'The Question about Fasting', *NovT* 11 (1969), pp. 161-73.
Keegan, Terence J., *Interpreting the Bible: A Popular Introduction to Biblical Hermeneutics* (New York: Paulist Press, 1985).

Kelber, Werner H., 'Biblical Hermeneutics and the Ancient Art of Communication: A Response', *Semeia* 39 (1987), pp. 97-105.

—*The Oral and the Written Gospel: The Hermeneutics of Speaking and Writing in the Synoptic Tradition, Mark, Paul, and Q* (Philadelphia: Fortress Press, 1983).

Kelly, Joseph G., 'Lucan Christology and the Jewish-Christian Dialogue', *JES* 21 (1984), pp. 688-708.

Kennedy, George A., *New Testament Interpretation through Rhetorical Criticism* (Chapel Hill: University of North Carolina Press, 1984).

Kermode, Frank, *The Genesis of Secrecy: On the Interpretation of Narrative* (Cambridge, MA: Harvard University Press, 1979).

Kilpatrick, G.D., 'The Order of Some Noun and Adjective Phrases in the New Testament', *NovT* 5 (1962), pp. 111-14.

—*The Origins of the Gospel According to St. Matthew* (Oxford: Clarendon Press, 1946).

Kingsbury, Jack Dean, 'The Developing Conflict between Jesus and the Jewish Leaders in Matthew's Gospel: A Literary-Critical Study', *CBQ* 49 (1987), pp. 57-73.

—'The Figure of Jesus in Matthew's Story: A Literary-Critical Probe', *JSNT* 21 (1984), pp. 3-36.

—*Matthew* (Philadelphia: Fortress Press, 2nd edn, 1986).

—*Matthew as Story* (Philadelphia: Fortress Press, 2nd edn, 1988).

—*Matthew: Structure, Christology, Kingdom* (Philadelphia: Fortress Press, 1975).

—'Observations on the "Miracle Chapters" of Matthew 8–9', *CBQ* 40 (1978), pp. 559-73.

—'The Parable of the Wicked Husbandmen and the Secret of Jesus' Divine Sonship in Matthew: Some Literary-Critical Observations', *JBL* 105 (1986), pp. 643-55.

—'The Plot of Matthew's Story', *Int* 46 (1992), pp. 347-56.

—'Reflections on "The Reader" of Matthew's Gospel', *NTS* 34 (1988), pp. 442-60.

Kissinger, Warren S., *The Lives of Jesus: A History and Bibliography* (New York: Garland Publishing, 1985).

Kistemaker, Simon J., *The Parables of Jesus* (Grand Rapids: Baker Book House, 1980).

Kittel, Ronald Alan, 'John the Baptist in the Gospel According to Mark' (unpublished Doctor of Theology dissertation, Graduate Theological Union, 1976).

Knox, John, 'The "Prophet" in New Testament Christology', in R.A. Norris (ed.), *Lux in Lumine: Essays to Honor W. Norman Pittenger* (New York: Seabury, 1966), pp. 23-34, 171-74.

Kraeling, Carl H., *John the Baptist* (New York: Charles Scribner's Sons, 1951).

—'Was Jesus Accused of Necromancy?', *JBL* 59 (1940), pp. 147-57.

Kratz, Reinhard, 'λίθος', *EDNT*, II, pp. 352-53.

Krentz, Edgar, 'None Greater among those Born from Women: John the Baptist in the Gospel of Matthew', *CurTM* 10 (1983), pp. 333-38.

Krieger, Norbert, 'Barfuss Busse tun', *NovT* 1 (1956), pp. 227-28.

Kümmel, Werner Georg, *The New Testament: The History of the Investigation of its Problems* (trans. S. McLean Gilmour and Howard Clark Kee; Nashville: Abingdon Press, 1972).

—*Promise and Fulfilment: The Eschatological Message of Jesus* (London: SCM Press, 2nd edn, 1961).

Lagrange, M.-J., *Evangile selon Saint Matthieu* (Paris: Librairie Lecoffre, 1923).

Lang, F., 'Erwägungen zur eschatologischen Verkündigung Johannes des Täufers', in G. Strecker (ed.), *Jesus Christus in Historie und Theologie: Neutestamentliche*

Festschrift für Hans Conzelmann zum 60. Geburtstag (Tübingen: J.C.B. Mohr, 1975), pp. 459-73.
LaSor, William Sanford, *The Dead Sea Scrolls and the New Testament* (Grand Rapids: Eerdmans, 1972).
Lategan, Bernard C., 'Coming to Grips with the Reader', *Semeia* 48 (1989), pp. 3-17.
—'Current Issues in the Hermeneutical Debate', *Neot* 18 (1984), pp. 1-17.
—'Reference: Reception, Redescription and Reality', in Bernard C. Lategan and Willem S. Vorster (eds.), *Text and Reality: Aspects of Reference in Biblical Texts* (Atlanta: Scholars Press, 1985), pp. 67-93.
—'Structural Interrelations in Matthew 11–12', *Neot* 11 (1977), pp. 115-29.
Légasse, Simon, 'εὐδοκέω', *EDNT*, II, p. 75.
Leivestad, Ragnar, 'An Interpretation of Matt 11 19', *JBL* 71 (1952), pp. 179-81.
Lewis, F. Warburton, 'Who were the Sons of the Bride-Chamber? (Mark ii.18-22)', *ExpTim* 24 (1913), p. 285.
Lewis, R.R., 'ἐπίβλημα ῥάκους ἀγνάφου (Mk.ii.21)', *ExpTim* 45 (1934), p. 185.
Licht, Jacob, *Storytelling in the Bible* (Jerusalem: Magnes Press, 1978).
Lincoln, Andrew, 'Matthew: A Story for Teachers?', in David J.A. Clines, Stephen E. Fowl and Stanley E. Porter (eds.), *The Bible in Three Dimensions: Essays in Celebration of Forty Years of Biblical Studies in the University of Sheffield* (Sheffield: JSOT Press, 1990), pp. 103-25.
Linton, Olof, 'The Parable of the Children's Game, Baptist and Son of Man (Matt. XI. 16-19 = Luke VII. 31-5): A Synoptic Text-Critical, Structural and Exegetical Investigation', *NTS* 22 (1976), pp. 159-79.
Lohmeyer, Ernst, *Das Urchristentum. 1. Buch: Johannes der Täufer* (Göttingen: Vandenhoeck & Ruprecht, 1932).
Lohr, Charles H., 'Oral Techniques in the Gospel of Matthew', *CBQ* 23 (1963), pp. 403-35.
Longman, Tremper, III, *Literary Approaches to Biblical Interpretation* (Grand Rapids: Zondervan, 1987).
Lord, Albert B., 'The Gospels as Oral Traditional Literature', in Walker (ed.), *The Relationship among the Gospels*, pp. 33-91.
Lotman, J.M., 'Point of View in a Text' (trans. L.M. O'Toole) *New Literary History* 6 (1975), pp. 339-52.
Louw, Johannes P., and Eugene A. Nida, *Greek–English Lexicon of the New Testament Based on Semantic Domains* (2 vols.; New York: United Bible Societies, 2nd edn, 1989).
Lowe, Malcolm, 'From the Parable of the Vineyard to a Pre-Synoptic Source', *NTS* 28 (1982), pp. 257-63.
Lubbock, Percy, 'Point of View', in James E. Miller Jr (ed.), *Myth and Method: Modern Theories of Fiction* (Lincoln: University of Nebraska Press, 1960), pp. 53-62.
Luchins, Abraham, 'Primacy-Recency in Impression Formation', in Carl I. Hovland (ed.), *The Order of Presentation in Persuasion* (New Haven: Yale University Press, 1957).
Luz, Ulrich, *Matthew 1–7: A Commentary* (trans. Wilhelm C. Linss; Minneapolis: Augsburg, 1989).
McCullagh, Archibald, *The Peerless Prophet; or, The Life and Times of John the Baptist* (New York: Anson D.F. Randolph, 1888).

McKenzie, John L., 'The Gospel According to Matthew', in Raymond E. Brown, Joseph A. Fitzmyer and Roland E. Murphy (eds.), *Jerome Biblical Commentary* (Englewood Cliffs, NJ: Prentice–Hall, 1968), II, pp. 62-114.

McKnight, Edgar V., *The Bible and the Reader: An Introduction to Literary Criticism* (Philadelphia: Fortress Press, 1985).

McNeile, Alan Hugh, *The Gospel According to St. Matthew* (Grand Rapids: Baker Book House, 1915).

—'Τότε in St. Matthew', *JTS* 12 (1911), pp. 127-28.

Magness, J. Lee, *Sense and Absence: Structure and Suspension in the Ending of Mark's Gospel* (Atlanta: Scholars Press, 1986).

Mailloux, Steven, *Interpretive Conventions: The Reader in the Study of American Fiction* (Ithaca, NY: Cornell University Press, 1982).

Malbon, Elizabeth Struthers, 'The Jewish Leaders in the Gospel of Mark: A Literary Study of Marcan Characterization', *JBL* 108 (1989), pp. 259-81.

—'Narrative Criticism: How does the Story Mean?', in Janice Capel Anderson and Stephen D. Moore (eds.), *Mark and Method: New Approaches in Biblical Studies* (Minneapolis: Fortress Press, 1992), pp. 23-49.

Malherbe, Abraham J., *Social Aspects of Early Christianity* (Baton Rouge: Louisiana State University Press, 1977).

Malina, Bruce J., and Jerome H. Neyrey, *Calling Jesus Names: The Social Value of Labels in Matthew* (Sonoma, CA: Poleridge, 1988).

Manson, T.W., *The Teaching of Jesus: Studies of its Form and Content* (Cambridge: Cambridge University Press, 1951).

Marshall, I. Howard, *The Gospel of Luke: A Commentary on the Greek Text* (Exeter: Paternoster Press; Grand Rapids: Eerdmans, 1978).

Marxen, Willi, *Mark the Evangelist: Studies on the Redaction History of the Gospel* (trans. James Boyce, Donald Juel, William Poehlmann and Roy A. Harrisville; Nashville: Abingdon Press, 1969).

Matera, Frank J., 'The Plot of Matthew's Gospel', *CBQ* 49 (1987), pp. 233-53.

Maurer, Christian, 'ῥίζα', *TDNT*, VI, pp. 985-90.

Meeks, Wayne A., *The First Urban Christians: The Social World of the Apostle Paul* (New Haven: Yale University Press, 1983).

Meier, John P., 'John the Baptist in Josephus: Philology and Exegesis', *JBL* 111 (1992), pp. 225-37.

—'John the Baptist in Matthew's Gospel', *JBL* 99 (1980), pp. 383-405.

—*Law and History in Matthew's Gospel: A Redactional Study of Mt. 5.17-48* (Rome: Biblical Institute Press, 1976).

—*Matthew* (Collegeville, MN: Liturgical Press, 1990).

—'Salvation History in Matthew: In Search of a Starting Point', *CBQ* 37 (1975), pp. 203-13.

Menahem, R., 'A Jewish Commentary on the New Testament: A Sample Verse', *Immanuel* 21 (1987), pp. 43-54.

Menken, M.J.J., 'The Quotation from Isa 40.3 in Jn 1.23', *Bib* 66 (1985), pp. 190-205.

Menoud, Philippe, 'Le sens du verbe BIAZETAI dans Lc 16.16', in Descamp and de Halleux (eds.), *Mélanges bibliques*, pp. 207-12.

Merkel, Helmut, 'Das Gleichnis von den "ungleichen Söhnen" (Matth. XXI. 28-32)', *NTS* 20 (1974), pp. 254-61.

Metzger, Bruce M., *The Text of the New Testament: Its Transmission, Corruption, and Restoration* (New York: Oxford University Press, 2nd edn, 1968).
—*A Textual Commentary on the Greek New Testament* (Stuttgart: Deutsche Bibelgesellschaft, 2nd edn, 1994).
Meyer, Ben F., *The Aims of Jesus* (London: SCM Press, 1979).
Meyer, F.B., *John the Baptist* (New York: Revell, 1900).
Michaels, J. Ramsey, 'The Parable of the Regretful Son', *HTR* 61 (1968), pp. 15-26.
Michel, O., 'μικρός', *TDNT*, IV, pp. 648-59.
Miller, Robert J., 'Elijah, John and Jesus in the Gospel of Luke', *NTS* 34 (1988), pp. 611-22.
Mitton, C. Leslie, 'Uncomfortable Words: IX. Stumbling-Block Characteristics in Jesus', *ExpTim* 82 (1971), pp. 168-72.
Moore, Ernest, 'ΒΙΑΖΩ, ΑΡΠΑΖΩ and Cognates in Josephus', *NTS* 21 (1975), pp. 519-43.
—'Violence to the Kingdom: Josephus and the Syrian Churches', *ExpTim* 100 (1989), pp. 174-77.
Moore, Stephen D., *Literary Criticism and the Gospels: The Theoretical Challenge* (New Haven: Yale University Press, 1989).
Moiser, Jeremy, 'Moses and Elijah', *ExpTim* (1985), pp. 216-17.
Morosco, Robert E., 'Matthew's Formation of a Commissioning Type-Scene out of the Story of Jesus' Commissioning of the Twelve', *JBL* 103 (1984), pp. 539-56.
Morris, Leon, *The Gospel According to Matthew* (Grand Rapids: Eerdmans, 1992).
Moule, C.F.D., *The Epistles of Paul the Apostle to the Colossians and to Philemon* (Cambridge: Cambridge University Press, 1958).
—*An Idiom Book of New Testament Greek* (Cambridge: Cambridge University Press, 2nd edn, 1959).
Moulton, James Hope, and George Milligan, *The Vocabulary of the Greek Testament Illustrated from the Papyri and Other Non-Literary Sources* (Grand Rapids: Eerdmans, 1930).
Murphy-O'Connor, Jerome, 'The Structure of Matthew XIV–XVII', *RB* 82 (1975), pp. 360-84.
Mussner, Franz, 'Der nicht erkannte Kairos', *Bib* 40 (1959), pp. 599-612.
Nagel, W., 'Neuer Wein in alten Schläuchen (Mt 9,17)', *VC* 14 (1960), pp. 1-8.
Neill, Stephen, and Tom Wright, *Interpretation of the New Testament: 1861–1985* (Oxford: Oxford University Press, 2nd edn, 1988).
Nepper-Christensen, Poul, 'Die Taufe im Matthäusevangelium: Im Lichte der Traditionen über Johannes den Täufer' (trans. Dietrich Harbsmeier), *NTS* 31 (1985), pp. 189-207.
Nestle, Eberhard, 'Zur Taube als Symbol des Geistes', *ZNW* 7 (1906), pp. 358-59.
Nodet, Étienne, 'Jésus et Jean-Baptiste selon Josephe', *RB* 92 (1985), pp. 321-48, 497-524.
O'Neill, J.C., 'The Source of the Parables of the Bridegroom and the Wicked Husbandmen', *NTS* 39 (1988), pp. 485-89.
—*Jesus the Messiah: Six Lectures on the Ministry of Jesus* (Cambridge: Cochrane, 1980).
Ong, Walter J., 'Maranatha: Death and Life in the Text of the Book', in *Interfaces of the Word: Studies in the Evolution of Consciousness and Culture* (Ithaca, NY: Cornell University Press, 1977).
—*Orality and Literacy: The Technologizing of the Word* (London: Methuen, 1982).
—'The Psychodynamics of Oral Memory and Narrative: Some Implications for Biblical Studies', in Robert Masson (ed.), *The Pedagogy of God's Image: Essays on Symbol and the Religious Imagination* (Chico, CA: Scholars Press, 1982), pp. 55-73.

—*Rhetoric, Romance and Technology: Studies in the Interaction of Expression and Culture* (Ithaca, NY: Cornell University Press, 1971).

Osten-Sacken, Peter von der, 'ἐλάχιστος', *EDNT*, I, pp. 426-27.

Pamment, Margaret, 'Moses and Elijah in the Story of the Transfiguration', *ExpTim* 92 (1981), pp. 338-39.

Patte, Daniel, *The Gospel According to Matthew: A Structural Commentary on Matthew's Faith* (Philadelphia: Fortress Press, 1987).

Patzia, Arthur Gerald, 'Did John the Baptist Preach a Baptism of Fire and the Holy Spirit?', *EvQ* 40 (1968), pp. 21-27.

Payot, Christian, 'L'interprétation johannique du ministère de Jean-Baptiste (Jn 1)', *Foi Vie* 68.3 (1969), pp. 21-37.

—'Jean-Baptiste censuré', *ETR* 45 (1970), pp. 273-83.

Pedersen, Sigfred, 'Die Proklamation Jesu als des eschatologischen Offenbarungsträgers (Mt. xvii 1-13)', *NovT* 17 (1975), pp. 241-64.

Perkins, Pheme, *Hearing the Parables of Jesus* (New York: Paulist Press, 1981).

Perrin, Norman, *Jesus and the Language of the Kingdom: Symbol and Metaphor in New Testament Interpretation* (London: SCM Press, 1976).

—*The Kingdom of God in the Teaching of Jesus* (London: SCM Press, 1963).

—*Rediscovering the Teaching of Jesus* (London: SCM Press, 1967).

Perry, Menakhem, 'Literary Dynamics: How the Order of a Text Creates its Meanings', *Poetics Today* 1 (1979), pp. 35-64, 311-61.

Petersen, Norman R., '"Point of View" in Mark's Narrative', *Semeia* 12 (1978), pp. 97-121.

—'The Reader in the Gospel', *Neot* 18 (1984), pp. 38-51.

Plummer, Alfred, *A Critical and Exegetical Commentary on the Gospel According to S. Luke* (Edinburgh: T. & T. Clark, 5th edn, 1922).

—*An Exegetical Commentary on the Gospel According to S. Matthew* (London: Elliot Stock, 1910).

Porter, Stanley E., 'Why Hasn't Reader-Response Criticism Caught on in New Testament Studies?', *Journal of Literature and Theology* 4 (1990), pp. 278-92.

Powell, Mark Allan, 'Direct and Indirect Phraseology in the Gospel of Matthew', in Eugene H. Lovering, Jr (ed.), *Society of Biblical Literature 1991 Seminar Papers* (Atlanta: Scholars Press, 1991), pp. 405-17.

—'The Religious Leaders in Matthew: A Literary-Critical Approach' (unpublished Doctor of Philosophy Dissertation Union, Theological Seminary of Virginia, 1988).

—'Toward a Narrative-Critical Understanding of Matthew', *Int* 46 (1992), pp. 341-46.

—*What is Narrative Criticism?* (Minneapolis: Fortress Press, 1990).

Pratt, Elizabeth Ellen, 'Jewelry of Bible Times and the Catalog of Isa 3.18-23', *AUSS* 17 (1979), pp. 71-84, 189-201.

Pryke, J., 'John the Baptist and the Qumran Community', *RevQ* 4 (1963–64), pp. 483-96.

Przybylski, Benno, 'The Role of Mt 3.13-4.11 in the Structure and Theology of the Gospel of Matthew', *BTB* 4 (1974), pp. 222-35.

Radl, Walter, 'μέλλω', *EDNT*, II, pp. 403-404.

Rawlinson, A.E.J., *St. Mark* (London: Methuen, 7th edn, 1949).

Reicke, Bo, 'The Historical Setting of John's Baptism', in E.P. Sanders (ed.), *Jesus, the Gospels and the Church* (Macon, GA: Mercer University Press, 1985), pp. 209-24.

—'Die Verkündigung des Täufers nach Lukas', in Fuchs (ed.), *Jesus in der Verkündigung der Kirche*, pp. 50-61.

Reimarus, Hermann Samuel, 'Concerning the Intention of Jesus and his Teaching', in Charles H. Talbert (ed.), *Reimarus: Fragments* (trans. Ralph S. Fraser; Philadelphia: Fortress Press, 1970), pp. 59-269.

Reumann, John, 'The Quest for the Historical Baptist', in John Reumann (ed.), *Understanding the Sacred Text: Essays in Honor of Morton S. Enslin on the Hebrew Bible and Christian Beginnings* (Valley Forge, PA: Judson Press, 1972), pp. 181-99.

Resseguie, James L., 'Point of View in the Central Section of Luke (9.51–19.44)', *JETS* 25 (1982), pp. 41-47.

—'Reader-Response Criticism and the Synoptic Gospels', *JAAR* 52 (1984), pp. 307-24.

Rhoads, David, 'Narrative Criticism and the Gospel of Mark', *JAAR* 50 (1982), pp. 411-34.

Rhoads, David, and Donald Michie, *Mark as Story: An Introduction to the Narrative of a Gospel* (Philadelphia: Fortress Press, 1982).

Richards, Kent Harold (ed.), *Society of Biblical Literature 1983 Seminar Papers* (Chico, CA: Scholars Press, 1983).

Richards, W.L., 'Another Look at the Parable of the Two Sons', *BibRes* 23 (1978), pp. 5-14.

Richardson, Peter, 'Gospel Traditions in the Church in Corinth (with Apologies to B.H. Streeter)', in Gerald F. Hawthorne and O. Betz (eds.), *Tradition and Interpretation in the New Testament* (Grand Rapids: Eerdmans, 1987), pp. 301-18.

Rife, J.M., 'The Standing of John the Baptist', in E.H. Barth and R.E. Cocroft (eds.), *Festschrift to Honor F. Wilbur Gingrich* (Leiden: E.J. Brill, 1972), pp. 205-208.

Rivkin, Ellis, 'Locating John the Baptist in Palestinian Judaism: The Political Dimension', in Richards (ed.), *Society of Biblical Literature 1983 Seminar Papers*, pp. 79-85.

Robertson, A.T., *A Grammar of the Greek New Testament in the Light of Historical Research* (New York: Harper & Brothers, 5th edn, 1931).

Robinson, James M., *A New Quest of the Historical Jesus* (London: SCM Press, 1959).

Robinson, John A.T., 'The Baptism of John and the Qumran Community', in *Twelve New Testament Studies* (London: SCM Press, 1962), pp. 11-27.

—'Elijah, John and Jesus', in *Twelve New Testment Studies* (London: SCM Press, 1962), pp. 28-52.

Robinson, J. Armitage, *St Paul's Epistle to the Ephesians* (London: Macmillan, 2nd edn, 1904).

Rolland, Philippe, 'From the Genesis to the End of the World: The Plan of Matthew's Gospel', *BTB* 2 (1972), pp. 155-76.

Running, Leona Glidden, 'Garments', *ISBE*, II, pp. 401-407.

Salvatorelli, Luigi, 'From Locke to Reitzenstein: The Historical Investigation of the Origins of Christianity', *HTR* 22 (1929), pp. 263-369.

Saenger, Paul, 'Silent Reading: Its Impact on Late Medieval Script and Society', *Viator* 13 (1982), pp. 367-414.

Saldarini, Anthony J., 'Delegitimation of Leaders in Matthew 23', *CBQ* 54 (1992), pp. 659-80.

Sanders, E.P., *Jesus and Judaism* (Philadelphia: Fortress Press, 1985).

Saulnier, Christiane, 'Hérode Antipas et Jean le Baptiste: Quelque remarques sur les confusions chronologiques de Flavius Josèphe', *RB* 91 (1984), pp. 362-76.

Schechter, Solomon, *Aspects of Rabbinic Theology* (New York: Schocken Books, 1909).

Schlatter, Adolf, *Der Evangelist Matthäus: Sein Zeil, Sein Selbständigkeit* (Stuttgart: Calwer Verlag, 1957).

—*Johannes der Täufer* (ed. D. Wilhelm Michaelis; Basel: Friedrich Reinhardt, 1956).

Schleiermacher, Friedrich, *The Life of Jesus* (trans. S. MacLean Gilman; Introduction by Jack C. Verheyden; Philadelphia: Fortress Press, 1975).
Schmitt, J., 'Le milieu baptiste de Jean le Précurseur', *RevScRel* 47 (1973), pp. 391-407.
Schnackenburg, Rudolf, 'Tradition und Interpretation im Spruchgut des Johannesevangeliums', in Josef Zmijewski and Ernst Nellessen (eds.), *Begegnung mit dem Wort* (Bonn: Peter Hanstein, 1980), pp. 141-59.
Scholes, Robert, and Robert Kellogg, *The Nature of Narrative* (New York: Oxford University Press, 1966).
Schönle, Volker, *Johannes, Jesus und die Juden* (Frankfurt am Main: Peter Lang, 1982).
Schrenk, Gottlob, 'βιάζομαι, βιαστής', *TDNT*, I, pp. 609-14.
—'εὐδοκέω', *TDNT*, II, pp. 738-42.
Schütz, Roland, *Johannes der Täufer* (Zürich: Zwingli-Verlag, 1967).
Schwarz, Günther, 'τὸ δὲ ἄχυρον κατακαύσει', *ZNW* 72 (1981), pp. 264-71.
Schweitzer, Albert, *The Quest of the Historical Jesus: A Critical Study of its Progress from Reimarus to Wrede* (trans. W. Montgomery; New York: Macmillan, 1948).
Schweizer, Eduard, *The Good News According to Mark* (trans. Donald H. Madvig; Richmond, VA: John Knox Press, 1970).
—*The Good News According to Matthew* (trans. David E. Green; Atlanta: John Knox Press, 1975).
—'Matthew's Church', in Graham Stanton (ed.), *The Interpretation of Matthew* (trans. Robert Morgan; Philadelphia: Fortress Press, 1983), pp. 129-55.
Scobie, Charles H.H., *John the Baptist* (London: SCM Press, 1964).
Scott, Bernard Brandon, 'The Birth of the Reader: Matthew 1.1–4.16', in John T. Carroll, Charles H. Cosgrove and E. Elizabeth Johnson (eds.), *Faith and History: Essays in Honor of Paul W. Meyer* (Atlanta: Scholars Press, 1990), pp. 35-54.
—*Hear Then the Parable: A Commentary on the Parables of Jesus* (Minneapolis: Fortress Press, 1989).
—'How to Mismanage a Miracle: Reader-Response Criticism', in Richards (ed.), *Society of Biblical Literature 1983 Seminar Papers*, pp. 439-49.
Seesemann, Heinrich, 'παλαιός', *TDNT*, V, pp. 717-20.
Seitz, Oscar J.F., 'What do these Stones Mean?', *JBL* 79 (1960), pp. 247-54.
Selden, Raman, and Peter Widdowson, *A Reader's Guide to Contemporary Literary Theory* (Lexington: The University Press of Kentucky, 3rd edn, 1993).
Silva, Moises, 'New Lexical Semitisms?', *ZNW* 69 (1978), pp. 253-57.
Slatoff, Walter J., *In Defense of Readers: Dimensions of Literary Response* (Ithaca, NY: Cornell University Press, 1970).
Smith, Derwood, 'Jewish Proselyte Baptism and the Baptism of John', *ResQ* 25 (1982), pp. 13-32.
Smith, John Merlin Powis, *A Critical and Exegetical Commentary on the Book of Malachi* (Edinburgh: T. & T. Clark, 1912).
Snyman, A.H., 'Analysis of Mt 3.1-4.22', *Neot* 11 (1977), pp. 19-31.
Stählin, Gustav, 'σκάνδαλον, σκανδαλίζω', *TDNT*, VII, pp. 339-78.
Staley, Jeffrey Lloyd, *The Print's First Kiss: A Rhetorical Investigation of the Implied Reader in the Fourth Gospel* (Atlanta: Scholars Press, 1988).
Stanley, David Michael, 'John the Witness', *Worship* 32 (1958), pp. 409-16.
Steinhauser, Michael, 'The Patch of Unshrunk Cloth (Mt 9,16)', *ExpTim* 87 (1976), pp. 312-13.

Steinmann, Jean, *Saint John the Baptist and the Desert Tradition* (trans. Michael Boyer; New York: Harper & Brothers, 1958).
Stenger, Werner, 'βιάζομαι', *EDNT*, I, pp. 216-17.
Stock, Augustine, *The Method and Message of Mark* (Wilmington, DE: Michael Glazier, 1989).
Stratton, Charles, 'Pressure for the Kingdom', *Int* 8 (1954), pp. 414-21.
Strauss, David Friedrich, *The Life of Jesus Critically Examined* (ed. Peter C. Hodgson; trans. George Eliot; Philadelphia: Fortress Press, 1972).
Strecker, Georg, *Der Weg der Gerechtigkeit: Untersuchung zur Theologie des Matthäus* (Göttingen: Vandenhoeck & Ruprecht, 3rd edn, 1971).
Streeter, Burnett Hillman, *The Four Gospels: A Study of Origins* (London: Macmillan, rev. edn, 1930).
Suggs, M. Jack, 'Matthew 16.13-20', *Int* 39 (1985), pp. 291-95.
Synge, F.C., 'Mark ii.21 = Matthew ix.16 = Luke v.36: The Parable of the Patch', *ExpTim* 56 (1944), pp. 26-27.
Talbert, Charles H., 'Oral and Independent or Literary and Interdependent? A Response to Albert B. Lord', in Walker (ed.), *The Relationship among the Gospels*, pp. 93-102.
Tannehill, Robert C., 'The Disciples in Mark: The Function of a Narrative Role', *JR* 57 (1977), pp. 386-405.
—'The Gospel of Mark as Narrative Christology', *Semeia* 16 (1980), pp. 57-89.
—*The Narrative Unity of Luke–Acts: A Literary Interpretation*. I. *The Gospel According to Luke* (Philadelphia: Fortress Press, 1986).
—*The Sword of his Mouth: Forceful and Imaginative Language in Synoptic Sayings* (Philadelphia: Fortress Press, 1975).
Tatum, W. Barnes, *In Quest of Jesus: A Guidebook* (Atlanta: John Knox Press, 1982).
—*John the Baptist and Jesus: A Report of the Jesus Seminar* (Sonoma, CA: Polebridge, 1994).
Taylor, Joan E., *The Immerser: John the Baptist within Second Temple Judaism* (Grand Rapids: Eerdmans, 1997).
Telfer, W., 'The Form of a Dove', *JTS* 29 (1928), pp. 238-42.
Thiering, B.E., 'Are the "Violent Men" False Teachers?', *NovT* 21 (1979), pp. 291-97.
Thiselton, Anthony C., 'Reader-Response Hermeneutics, Action Models, and the Parables of Jesus', in Roger Lundin, Anthony C. Thiselton and Clarence Walhout (eds.), *The Responsibility of Hermeneutics* (Grand Rapids: Eerdmans, 1985), pp. 79-113.
Thompson, G.H.P., 'Called–Proved–Obedient: A Study in the Baptism and Temptation Narratives of Matthew and Luke', *JTS* 11 (1960), pp. 1-12.
Thompson, William G., 'An Historical Perspective in the Gospel of Matthew', *JBL* 93 (1974), pp. 243-62.
—'Reflections on the Composition of Mt 8.1-9.34', *CBQ* 33 (1971), pp. 365-88.
Thyen, H. 'ΒΑΠΤΙΣΜΑ ΜΕΤΑΝΟΙΑΣ ΕΙΣ ΑΦΕΣΙΝ ΑΜΑΡΤΙΩΝ', in J.M. Robinson (ed.), *The Future of Our Relgious Past: Essays in Honour of Rudolf Bultmann* (trans. C.E. Carlston and R.P. Scharlemann; London: SCM Press, 1971), pp. 131-68.
Tolbert, Mary Ann, *Perspectives on the Parables: An Approach to Multiple Interpretations* (Philadelphia: Fortress Press, 1979).
Tompkins, Jane P., 'An Introduction to Reader-Response Criticism', in Tompkins (ed.), *Reader-Response Criticism*, pp. ix-xxvi.
—'The Reader in History: The Changing Shape of Literary Response', in Tompkins (ed.), *Reader-Response Criticism*, pp. 201-32.

—*Reader-Response Criticism: From Formalism to Post-Structuralism* (Baltimore: The Johns Hopkins University Press, 1980).

Torrence, T.F., 'Proselyte Baptism', *NTS* 1 (1954-55), pp. 150-54.

Thrall, Margaret E., 'Elijah and Moses in Mark's Account of the Transfiguration', *NTS* 16 (1969–70), pp. 305-17.

Trilling, Wolfgang, *The Gospel According to St. Matthew* (New York: Crossroads, 1991).

—'Die Täufertradition bei Matthäus', *BZ* 3 (1959), pp. 271-89.

—*Das Wahre Israel: Studien zur Theologie des Matthäus-Evangeliums* (Munich: Kösel, 1968).

Turner, C.H., 'Ο ΥΙΟΣ ΜΟΥ Ο ΑΓΑΠΗΤΟΣ', *JTS* 27 (1926), pp. 113-29.

Turner, Nigel, *A Grammar of New Testament Greek*. III. *Syntax* (ed. James Hope Moulton; Edinburgh: T. & T. Clark, 1963).

Tyson, Joseph B., 'The Birth Narratives and the Beginning of Luke's Gospel', *Semeia* 52 (1991), pp. 103-20.

Uspensky, Boris, *A Poetics of Composition: The Structure of the Artistic Text and Typology of a Compositional Form* (trans. Valentina Zavarin and Susan Wittig; Berkeley: University of California Press, 1973).

Viviano, Benedict T., 'Social World and Community Leadership: The Case of Matthew 23.1–12, 34', *JSNT* 39 (1990), pp. 3-21.

Vorster, Willem S., 'Characterization of Peter in the Gospel of Mark', *Neot* 21 (1987), pp. 57-76.

—'The Reader in the Text: Narrative Material', *Semeia* 48 (1989), pp. 21-39.

Walker, Rolf, *Die Heilsgeschichte im ersten Evangelium* (Göttingen: Vandenhoeck & Ruprecht, 1967).

Walker, William O. (ed.), *The Relationship among the Gospels: An Interdisciplinary Dialogue* (San Antonio, TX: Trinity University Press, 1978).

Wardhaugh, Ronald, *Reading: A Linguistic Perspective* (New York: Harcourt, Brace and World, 1969).

Weaver, Dorothy Jean, *Matthew's Missionary Discourse: A Literary Critical Analysis* (Sheffield: JSOT Press, 1990).

Webb, Robert L., 'The Activity of John the Baptist's Expected Figure at the Threshing Floor (Matthew 3.12 = Luke 3.17)', *JSNT* 43 (1991), pp. 103-11.

—*John the Baptizer and Prophet* (Sheffield: JSOT Press, 1991).

Weimann, Robert, 'Structure and History in Narrative Perspective: The Problem of Point of View Reconsidered', in *Structure and Society in Literary History: Studies in the History and Theory of Historical Criticism* (Charlottesville: University Press of Virginia, 1976).

Wentling, Judith L., 'A Comparison of the Elijah Motifs in the Gospels of Matthew and Mark', in Philip Sigal (ed.), *Proceedings: Eastern Great Lakes Biblical Society, 1982* (Grand Rapids: Eastern Great Lakes Biblical Society, 1982), pp. 104-22.

Westermann, Claus, *Isaiah 40–66: A Commentary* (trans. David M.G. Stalker; Philadelphia: Westminster Press, 1969).

Wharton, J.A., 'Root', *IDB*, IV, p. 128.

Wilder, Amos N., *Eschatology and Ethics in the Teachings of Jesus* (New York: Harper & Brothers, rev. edn, 1950).

Wilson, Jeffrey, 'The Integrity of Jn 3.22-36', *JSNT* 10 (1981), pp. 34-41.

Wink, Walter Philip, 'Jesus' Reply to John: Matt 11.2-6//Luke 7.18-23', *Forum* 5 (1989), pp. 121-28.

—'John the Baptist', *IDBSup*, pp. 487-88.

—'John the Baptist and the Gospel' (unpublished Doctor of Theology dissertation; Union Theological Seminary, New York, 1963).

—*John the Baptist in the Gospel Tradition* (Cambridge: Cambridge University Press, 1968).

Wolf, Peter, 'Gericht und Reich Gottes bei Johannes und Jesu', in Peter Fiedler and Dieter Zeller (eds.), *Gegenwart und kommender Reich* (Stuttgart: Katholisches Bibelwerk, 1975), pp. 43-49.

Wrede, William, *The Messianic Secret* (trans. J.C.G. Greig; Cambridge: James Clarke, 1971).

Wright, Benjamin G., III, 'A Previously Unnoticed Greek Variant of Matt 16.14: "Some Say John the Baptist..." ', *JBL* 105 (1986), pp. 694-97.

Wright, N.T., *Jesus and the Victory of God* (Minneapolis: Fortress Press, 1996).

Young, Brad H., *Jesus and his Jewish Parables: Rediscovering the Roots of Jesus' Teachings* (New York: Paulist Press, 1989).

Young, Edward J., *The Book of Isaiah* (3 vols.; Grand Rapids: Eerdmans, 1972).

Zeller, Dieter, 'Die Bildlogik des Gleichnisses Mt 11 16-17/Lk 7 31-32', *ZNW* 68 (1977), pp. 252-57.

Ziesler, J.A., 'The Removal of the Bridegroom: A Note on Mark II.18-22 and Parallels', *NTS* 19 (1972–73), pp. 190-94.

INDEXES

INDEX OF REFERENCES

INDEX OF AUTHORS